Library of Old English and Medieval Literature

SKELTON

SKELTON

The Life and Times of an Early Tudor Poet

by

H. L. R. EDWARDS

*This is the legeand of my lif,
thought Latyne it be nane.*

DUNBAR

 BOOKS FOR LIBRARIES PRESS
FREEPORT, NEW YORK

First Published in 1949 by Jonathan Cape Limited

Reprinted 1971 by arrangement with the
Administrators of the Estate of H. L. R. Edwards
and Jonathan Cape Limited

INTERNATIONAL STANDARD BOOK NUMBER:
0-8369-5673-7

LIBRARY OF CONGRESS CATALOG CARD NUMBER:
77-148879

PRINTED IN THE UNITED STATES OF AMERICA

TO

Ε Π Η

IN HOMAGE

CONTENTS

CONTENTS

CONTENTS

Book Five: COURTIER

PREFACE

THIS BOOK attempts, perhaps, the impossible. It is an effort to present an unduly neglected figure to the general reader as well as to the scholar. This has meant, for the first, the clearing away of much scaffolding which is normally left standing by the exhausted builder; and, for the second, the stacking of it in some order at the back of the book. In other ways, too, I have kept my joint audience in mind. Latin references have been translated, and English ones presented in modern spelling. (Quotations from Skelton himself are taken from my projected edition of his works, and their spelling is a compromise.*) The problem of an unfamiliar background I have tried to solve by means of a long and – inevitably – dullish Introduction. Those who prefer their biography pure are advised to skip hastily over to Chapter One. Thereafter they will, I trust, find interest and excitement in plenty.

It should be stressed, however, that my picture is of a man rather than a poet. Any attempt at literary criticism would have doubled the book in size and ruined whatever proportion it may now possess. But here, at least, is all the biographical material the critic should require.

Since 1938 no less than three books on Skelton have seen the light. The first of them, Mr. J. L. Lloyd's, was avowedly an introduction to the poet and contained little that was new. That of Professor Gordon, though not published till 1944, seems to have been written mainly before 1937 and in consequence largely ignores more recent material. Much the most significant of the three is Dr. William Nelson's *John Skelton, Laureate*, which appeared in New York in 1939. Rather (as the author admits) a collection of papers than a biography, it is nevertheless a most impressive feat of scholarship: incisively written, original and provocative. Beyond question, this work forms the greatest single advance in a century of research.

It was the publication of this which decided the shape of my own

* My numbering also differs from that of the standard Dyce, but is near enough to make reference easy.

book. Having trodden amiably on Dr. Nelson's heels through a
great deal of his investigation, and produced a couple of theses
on the poet, it seemed to me that the time had come for a full-dress
biography of Skelton. Much laborious argument was no longer
necessary, and it might be possible to make a fresh start from this
firmer level. Of my success the reader must judge for himself.
But the work does contain a quantity of new material, and has
entailed a thorough examination of the old. It has indeed occupied
me fairly constantly since 1932.

The Skelton that emerges is, at any rate, refreshingly different
from the figure in the textbooks. Less heroic, perhaps, but definitely more human. I have tried not to go beyond the facts; they
are picturesque enough to need no trimming. But the facts are
only a selection, and selection itself distorts. It is some consolation
to think that, were we to surmount this difficulty, we should still
be faced with another and ultimate problem. Skelton himself
has posed it for us, in his own inimitable fashion:

> Though Galien and Diascorides
> With Ipocras and maister Avicen
> By ther phesik doth many a man ease,
> And though Albumasar can thé enform and ken
> What constellacions ar good or bad for men,
> Yet whan the rain raineth, and the gose winketh,
> Litel woteth the gosling what the gose thinketh.

It must be confessed that I have aspired to the modest role of
Galen, not the gosling.

A few minor details may be dealt with here. The question of
money values is a vexed one. The estimates usually given rarely
allow for the steep rise in the cost of living during our own century.
I follow the lower of the figures given by Dr. H. E. Salter in 1936:
between thirty and thirty-five times.* This, considering that a
major war has since intervened, is manifestly erring on the safe
side.

In reading the quotations, it is important to remember that
Skelton's English was still pronounced very much like modern

* G. Baskerville, *English Monks and the Suppression of the Monasteries*, Bedford Hist.
Ser., 1940, pp. 296-7.

PREFACE

French, with open vowels. It had, however, a strong stress, tend-
ing to fall on the last syllable of longer words.

I have not included a bibliography. The notes supply full references, and it seemed superfluous to add another to the book-lists
already available in Messrs. Nelson and Gordon, and in the
Cambridge Bibliography.

The acknowledgments I owe are many. First and foremost to
Mr. Robert Graves, whose enthusiasm it was that (all unknown to
him) turned my attention to the poems of Skelton. To the late
Professor Cyril Brett of Cardiff, who guided my early steps in
research, and to the University of Wales for the fellowship which
made possible so much of this work. To Miss Enid Welsford, of
Newnham, and Miss Edith Batho of University College, London,
for untiring assistance and encouragement. To Professor Bryn
Davies, Fuad I University, Cairo, for the material on Elis
Gruffydd. To Dr. William Nelson for a regular interchange of
ideas and discoveries which has proved as valuable as it was
stimulating. And not least, to the officials of our great libraries
and national collections, for their invariably ready help.

My special thanks, however, are due to Professor F. M. Salter
of the University of Alberta, Canada. The months I spent working
with him on the *Diodorus* were all too brief; but they provided me
with a model of how research should be pursued. Far more of
this book is due to his friendly inspiration than I can hope to
acknowledge.

H. L. R. E.

LISBON

INTRODUCTION

The dissolving warrior in his iron hat.
LAWRENCE DURRELL: *Five Soliloquies.*

§ I. SKELTON'S ENGLAND

MOST MODERN historians begin with the state of of affairs when Skelton died, in 1529. Newness is its keynote. A New World, fabulously rich, unrolling before the astonished eyes of Europe; a New Europe of rival nations, no longer bound by a common loyalty; a New Religion, in which the individual took the place of the group; a New Morality, which accepted a dual standard for public and private life; and a New Learning, spread by the new art of printing, which found a sanction for all these changes in the authors of Greece and Rome. It is easy to pick holes in this jigsaw of impossible novelties; it is even fashionable, to-day, to do so; all the same, it appears to me in its main essentials a just picture. But we are not nearly so well acquainted with the age, in England, that heralded all this newness – the age in which Skelton spent his days. And to Skelton above all, who cut his poems straight from the living rock, it is impossible to render justice without knowing something of the climate and countryside he worked in.

The date of his birth, as we might expect, is uncertain. There are reasons for putting it about 1460. The year of grace fourteen hundred and sixty. It was just seven years since the Turks had stormed Constantinople, suddenly increasing the drift of Greek scholars to the hungry West. In Italy Botticelli was thirteen, Leonardo a boy of eight; Machiavelli was not to be born for nine years. The German Luther had to wait another twenty-three; the Dutch Erasmus at least six or seven. Our earth was still the centre of the universe, and Rome of Christendom – western Christendom, that is. The first book had only just been set up in print. America and the Cape were still wrapped in their local mists, unknown to Europe. Western civilisation remained small, compact, stable, and sure of its facts. Slowly, very slowly, France was recovering from the devastation of the Hundred Years' War.

In a sadly reduced Paris, another year would see Louis XI ascend the throne, thereby assuring (among other things) the release of a lean and swarthy clerk named Villon from the prison of Meun.

And England? A quarter of a century had still to elapse before the arrival of her New Monarch. A bloody civil war was to intervene. But simultaneously a great new social group was preparing to take over from the baronial magnates who were so intent on self-destruction. It was in the fifteenth century that the Business Man laid the foundations of his power.

Even in Chaucer's day his beaver hat, his self-centred politics and his poor opinion of that uneconomic creature woman had been quietly noted by the poet. But the next century saw him really come into his own.

Land – a good, broad estate – was the usual medium. And how they struggled for this land of theirs! Margaret Paston summed it up with proverbial succinctness. 'Men cut large thongs here of other men's leather,' she observes in 1465.[1] The habit was not easy to cure: half a century later we shall meet it again. Meanwhile, Sir John Felbrigg dragged out neighbour Wyndham's wife by the hair of her head to get possession of a desirable property. In this he was, it is true, only imitating his betters, like the Duke of Norfolk with his three thousand men at Caister, or the grand dispute between the Shrewsburies and the Marquess Berkeley which culminated in the 'battle' of Nibley Green.[2]

The real hero of Skelton's age, however, was no duke or marquess. Rather, he was Jack of Newbury: John Winchcomb, the great clothier, whose legend reached print only in Elizabeth's time, but who lived and died a contemporary of Skelton's.[3] The hundred prentices he brought to Flodden and his noble entertainment of the King and Queen – these were merely exaggerations of a fact. Chivalry had gone, though its afterglow still lingered in Malory and Bayard and the joust. Now, in place of the Knight we have the Burgess, sober, thrifty, pious, but always successful, with both feet planted firmly on the soil that had made him.

Social theory, it must be admitted, shows little recognition of the fact. For this we must go to the less official literature of the time – to Boccaccio's story of the poor squire Guiscardo and his noble mistress, translated no less than three times during our period; to Medwall's *Fulgens*, where the heroine breaks away from her source and bravely announces that she will marry the low-born Gaius; or the Epilogue to *Gentleness and Nobility*, which declares dogmatically that the ruling class

Should *come thereto* because of their virtue. [4]

Merit is the only nobility. The statement is as old as Seneca, at least; [5] but its force was now being felt with quite a new keen-ness. True, there was some tendency for 'virtue' to be confused with the crude energy that went to produce wealth, or worldly success. But if the new bourgeoisie had its own weaknesses, it had also a profound strength. As well as a Wolsey it produced a Colet and a More; and from its widening ranks were to spring nine-tenths of the national genius. The barriers were going down before other and finer things than greed. Nevertheless – as More saw – the price was a high one, and we have still not paid it in full.

But no sketch of England between 1460 and 1530 can afford to neglect religion. In our secular age it needs a pretty vigorous leap of the imagination to picture the role played by the Church in medieval society. It was all-pervasive – and precisely for that reason we find it hard to visualise.

Cowls and rope-girdles in the street were the least of the changes one would observe. The monks, friars and nuns scattered through Skelton's England totalled only about nine thousand. [6] But Holy Church was obtrusive in so many ways. She was by far the greatest landowner in the country; and as such she found herself involved in countless other activities. As the master-builder alone, her grand erections had come to serve such diverse functions as schools, hotels, museums and hospitals for the poor. And in its more modest sphere the parish church was similarly inclusive. Whatever a man did, be it selling dear or sitting on the ale-bench or merely sleeping with his wife, Sir John the parson had his recognised say in the matter.

From top to bottom, in fact, social life was inextricably tangled up with religion. No doubt in theory all this was excellent. Religion can only be effective in so far as it penetrates the everyday world. But, unfortunately, it had not worked out quite like this. In penetrating the world for the laudable purpose of its reclama-tion, Holy Church had, imperceptibly, grown rather worldly herself. Long before the decisive tour of Cromwell, visitations had

INTRODUCTION

shown that the great experiment in asceticism was not shaping well in England. The Church of the fifteenth century, in fact, had subsided into the comfort of a huge vested interest. As such it was a target too big to be missed.

Set against this languid leviathan a new dynasty, impatient of spiritual interference, and a new commercial class, eager for material independence, and you have the religious history of Skelton's age. The doctrinal quarrel came later. What appeared first was a series of attacks on clerical privilege, including property.

It was the New King who led the attack. At first it was against sanctuary – the criminal's right, once on holy ground, to laugh at the law. Henry VII persuaded the Pope to exclude the traitor from this protection. It was not much, but it was a beginning. What worried his subjects more than sanctuary, however, was the riotous clerk. He too was the Church's care; but the ecclesiastical courts were notoriously tenderer than the State towards their straying sheep. So in 1512 Parliament passed an Act declaring that all clerks below the rank of sub-deacon who committed murder or felony should lose their benefit of clergy. Another check to the Church.

The appetite grows by feeding. Skelton himself did not live to see the culmination of these inroads – the suppression of every monastery in the land, and the Church's subjection to the King. He sensed the danger, as we see from *Colin Clout*. But the main process was as unmoral as it was irresistible. No age can serve God and Mammon, and the Early Tudor age was committed to the latter. It was in vain that, as the Church's doom approached, the noble figures of More, Fisher and Reynolds rose in protest. The State-within-the-State had had its day; the morrow was with Skelton's burly pupil.

Social change, however, has a genius for disguising itself. In appearance – even, to a great extent, in thought – Early Tudor England remained as devout as ever it had been in the Age of Faith. New noble and new bourgeois continued to attend church, and when they died, left ample provision for it in their pious wills. At every society dinner-table the next Crusade was a staple topic of conversation. Somehow it never came; but it was always in people's thoughts – even the King's. And, from the King to the Prior of Walsingham's mistress, men and women still went on pilgrimage, if they no longer indulged (like Margery Kempe) in visions or boisterous sobbings at mass. Certainly no one thought it at all strange that a man should be burnt on a cartful of thorns for objecting to such forms of devotion.

We shall never understand Skelton, in short, until we realise that, in his lifetime, it was still possible for the mother of one king and the chancellor of another to pierce their flesh with hair shirts. Only, perhaps, with the latter do we glimpse the birth of a new and significant feeling – the feeling that such behaviour was *eccentric*. The Lady Margaret's asceticism was avowed and public: she had openly separated from her last husband in order to devote herself to a life of holy chastity. More's behaviour was different. For his own part he never questioned the virtue of his self-castigation – but he carefully hid the habit from his wife. By this time, though, we have reached the New Generation.

§ 2. DUNCE OR HUMANIST?

Before turning to Skelton's life, there is another question we cannot help asking. Which side did he take in the great intellectual controversy of the age? Was he a humanist, or did he line up with the forces of conservatism – with the dunsical scholastics that were the butt of the new movement? The answer, we shall find, is not a simple one. And, as so often, it resolves itself into a question of semantics. Where one critic will deny Skelton any shred of the new learning, another claims that, on the contrary, he can only be understood in the context of Early Tudor humanism.[7] Obviously, everything hinges upon what is meant by humanism, new learning or Renaissance.

This is no place for argument. Briefly, the trouble lies in a confusion between the terms *humanism* and *Renaissance*. The humanist was first and foremost a scholar: one who devoted himself to the *litterae humaniores* of the ancient world – Latin and, above all, Greek. Greek, and exact scholarship: these are the humanist touch-stones. The latter, indeed, necessarily implied the former. The deeper a man's knowledge of Latin, now, the more he realised how it stemmed from Greek and how vital it was to learn as much as he could of the parent tongue. This applied to literature, science, medicine, even religion. How could one study the New Testament or the early Fathers without a competent knowledge of Greek? The very idea suddenly became preposterous.

But what we call the Renaissance is by no means to be equated with a new trend in scholarship. It was vastly wider and less conscious; but if one has to define it in a word, that word must be *secular*. Even Colet's use of the historical method for Biblical study was the application of a secular science to religion. And in Italy, where the movement began, the appeal of antique Rome was irresistible. The fervour of religion was reversed and devoted to the new cult of paganism. Niccolò Niccoli went about Florence like a missionary, urging its young bloods to 'devote themselves to virtue, i.e. to Greek and Latin literature.'

What emerged was a new type of personality, in some ways akin to the humanist, in others notably different. The Renaissance Man. His view of life has a robust *this-worldly* stress. In behaviour he is governed less by the Church than by the classics. One recognises him at once by his optimistic faith in the virtues of the flesh, by the new zest he brings to the art of living, and above all by his overweening vanity.

But where does Skelton stand in all this? His Greek may be dismissed very briefly: he had practically none. Sprinkled over his works one can find several dozen words and one or two phrases of Greek; but without exception they can all be traced to a Latin source. Yet his ignorance has been overrated. If he sinned, he sinned in what appears to be good company. Rather naturally, he relied on his dictionary; and his dictionary – the *Breuiloquus* – was technically humanist, even if Reuchlin produced it when he was barely twenty. Several of his errors derive from this compendium. Another, the mis-scansion of *Socrates*, is carefully backed by no less an authority than Gaguin, doyen of the French humanists. Elsewhere, he quotes Petrarch, Boccaccio, Mantuan; even Erasmus is laid under contribution. [8]

The rollcall of humanist names in Skelton, in fact, is rather impressive – until one comes to look it over. And then the impression dwindles considerably. In no case is the work quoted of a genuinely humanist or 'advanced' nature. It is always a lexicon, a grammar or a book of proverbs that he plunders. And this remains true to the end. In his very last poem he goes out of his way to defend a false spelling. Dyce obscured this by his habit of regularising Skelton's Latin; but line 101 of the *Replication* originally read:

Necque negatiuis,

and a gloss underlined the fact: '*Necque non neque legas.*' In other words, Skelton believed that *neque* should be spelt with a *c*, as if it were *nec* plus *-que*. Reasonable as this may sound, he was doomed to be wrong again. [9]

These may seem trifles; but one has to remember that, at the time we are speaking of, a slip in quantity or spelling was enough to mark a man for life. Nevertheless, as a Latinist of the older school, Skelton cuts no ill figure. Even Warton, who breathed Augustan air, had to admit that 'Skelton, notwithstanding his scurrility, was a classical scholar.' By the time he left the university, he not only had a comprehensive knowledge of the Latin classics, but he could turn a pretty set of verses himself. In his work he manages to quote from Vergil, Ovid, Juvenal, Horace, Persius, Martial, Seneca, Claudian, and in prose, Cicero, Livy, Sallust, Valerius Maximus and Justin – I give the list roughly in order of frequency. Like every other poet he makes mistakes; but the general tone of his references (and this is the only point of importance) is that of a man who was both at home with, and genuinely fond of, the great writers of ancient Rome.

Where he differed sharply from the humanist was in his stout approval of the schoolmen and all they stood for. This is clearest, perhaps, in his championship of medieval logic. For reasons which need not detain us, *dialectica* had gradually risen, by the fifteenth century, to the position of 'the art of arts and science of sciences,' as one textbook put it. And it was exactly here that the humanist launched his attack. More, Erasmus and Rabelais never tire of jeering at the pedantry of the logician, with his 'good defending argument . . . in *tertii primae*, in *Darii*, or elsewhere.'

To the average humanist, in a word, logic immediately argued a dunce. But for Skelton the position is exactly reversed. One cannot open his works without coming across some evidence of his sturdy and lifelong devotion to *dialectica*. It is indeed the main source of that 'obscurity' so often charged against him by the modern reader. His hawking parson is a *simplex syllogista* and therefore, by definition, a fool. And so with the ignorant priests of *Colin Clout*, or the young heretics of the *Replication*. They know nothing of enthymemes or elenchi, and that, in Skelton's eyes, is sufficient for their damnation.

His quarrel with Lily the grammarian can be traced to the same weakness. In education too Skelton was all for 'the modes of signifying' – grammar with a solid logical foundation. But the humanists preferred reading to rules; and Lily's gibe may be taken as typical of their verdict on this outmoded conservatism:

> Whilst thou to get the more esteem
> A learned Poet fain would seem,
> Skelton, thou art, let all men know it,
> Neither learned, nor a Poet.*°

Intellectually, it should now be obvious, Skelton was the very antithesis of the humanist proper. So far as Greek was concerned he took his place, contentedly, well to the rear of the Hellenistic front in England. In Latin literature his knowledge was of the poetic type, wide rather than exact, and he felt far too kindly towards the medieval with his barbarous neologisms. As for the New World, the Discoveries are not so much as mentioned in his work.[10] To the last, Skelton remained a devout scholastic, convinced that logic was the keystone of the intellect and deeply suspicious of the new enthusiasms he saw everywhere around him.

Nevertheless, the Renaissance had not passed him by. There is a vigour, an ebullience in his writing which is not the medieval vigour. We shall have ample evidence of this when we come to *Philip Sparrow*. But the simplest and most obvious proof lies in Skelton's attitude to himself. For the first time in English literature we come upon a poet who rejects the medieval convention of modesty and claims outright that he is a genius. 'Written by me, Skelton, laurelled bard of the Britons'° is his proud signature to *Philip Sparrow*. The cipher in *Ware the Hawk!* resolves itself into a boast that he is unique: the phoenix of England. The only change in *Colin Clout* is that of emphasis. His manner in this poem is rustic, he admits; all the same, 'they will sing me and praise me everywhere, so long as the English race retains its fame.' *Why Come Ye Not* is curt in its decisiveness:

> This the bard wrote
> Whom thousands quote.

And surely nowhere else in the world has a poet devoted a work as long as the *Garland*, sixteen hundred lines of it, to pure self-praise,

---

* Fuller's trans. Quotations so marked (°) will be found, in the original Latin, in Appendix III.

winding up with the assertion that he is his country's Catullus, her Adonis, her Homer!

Once Skelton had broken the ice, other poets were not slow to follow: Elizabethan literature is full of the new literary egotism. And its source too is clear: it is the Horatian *aere perennius*, which became the creed of the Italian Renaissance. When Skelton adopted it, however, in his faraway island, he was flying dead in the face of medieval ethics, which demanded first a lowly apology for writing at all, and second a humble confession of one's lack of skill in the art.

But Skelton's was not just idle vanity. There was very real ground for his lofty boast that he stood alone in Early Tudor literature. His lifework was to be, not scholarship – however much he flattered himself on that – but the enriching and polishing of his mother-tongue. (A curious polish, some may think, as they read *Elinor Rumming*; but as to the enrichment there can be no question.) Where the humanist like Budé – or even, at first, Sir Thomas More, whose *Utopia* was written in Latin – felt that his native tongue was unequal to the requirements of learning, Skelton deliberately set out to convert some of those riches into good current English coin. And in this he lines up with the great vernacular writers of the Renaissance – Folengo, Pulci, Ariosto, Rabelais.

To sum up. Skelton was neither a humanist nor a dunce – though most humanists, I fear, would have dubbed him the latter; he was a man of the Renaissance. In type, he stands beside the Renaissance lords of the vernacular. His sense of kinship with the Roman poets gives him the same Cellinesque swagger. He has the same devotion to his mother-tongue. Even his feuds are an Italian fashion. In all his work he reveals the budding national pride from which Christendom was to blossom violently into a new Europe. And in his devotion to the things of this world, in his healthy robustness of perception, in his independence, in his satirist's clearsightedness – in his very vulgarity, he expresses the English counterpart of the earthy, Catholic paganism of the High Renaissance.

§ 3. 'SWEET SMOKE OF RHETORIC!'

But, once again, we are dealing with a poet. And fifteenth-century literary theory was very different from our own.[11] Poetry was not an art, but a science; an affair of style. Its rules were the concern of *rhetorica*. This had little resemblance to the classical rhetoric. By the time the medieval textbooks came to be written, it had sunk to a mere process of decoration. The most popular of these later manuals was the *New Poetics* of an Englishman, Geoffrey de Vinsauf, written in Latin verse about 1210.

Although Geoffrey does mention the other aspects of writing, his only real interest is in expansion. No less than 469 lines of the treatise are devoted to *amplificatio*. Ornament, in Geoffrey's eyes, is the poet's first concern. He gives the student eight distinct methods of 'lingering.' The first of them, *interpretatio*, is nothing more than the reduplication of terms which flourishes everywhere in fifteenth-century literature. Then there is periphrasis and comparison, followed by apostrophe or *exclamatio*, and four others. All these, with their subdivisions, are illustrated by lengthy examples of his own invention.

Geoffrey's influence was, bluntly, as pernicious as it was pervasive. He and his fellow rhetoricians lent all their authority to the 'aureate school' of poets, who regarded it as their prime duty to adopt every kind of tawdry gilding, as opposed to the plain statement. It is hard to imagine a more deplorable approach to good writing.

Nevertheless, Skelton stands apart from his contemporaries not only in genius, but in his devotion to rhetoric. In a poet laureate (as we shall see) this is at least understandable: it was a product of his special training in the art. But so completely have we lost the tradition that it only becomes apparent on a close scrutiny.

The earliest work of his that survives is in prose – the translation, from Poggio's Latin, of Diodorus Siculus.[12] Why he picked on Diodorus we shall discuss later. Here, it is only necessary to remark that, stylistically, it is the most extravagant specimen of aureation in our language. Usk, or the early Hall, pale to nothing beside it.

In one of his rare asides Skelton makes it quite clear what he conceives a translator's duty to be:

> Sith it is standing with our literature of interpretation, afforcing th' office by translation our matter to dilate, so to proceed by suspensive continuance that nothing unto our process be left unremembered. . . .[13]

"Our matter to dilate:" that is the key. Where Poggio sought to compress, Skelton expanded. It was, in a sense, missionary work. Obsessed by the feeling that English lacked the mighty resources of *lingua latina*, he set out to supply some of its deficiencies. The *Diodorus* must have been his first large-scale attempt; for there is a noticeable change as the work proceeds.

The early pages are still fairly straightforward prose. But this was not Skelton's aim. What he wanted was orotundity – *florida verborum venustas*; and as he wrote on, all else – accuracy, form, discrimination – was sacrificed to this one end. Every notion is repeated, if possible three or four times – 'overpassed superficially without regard'; 'very great and huge mighty wells. . . .' Steadily the inflation increases, until by the time Book Five is reached it has soared to the stylistic stratosphere of:

> Jupiter, so as he was much amorous, surprised inwardly with the passing beauty of dame Semeles, whose goodly eye, as a smaragdine stone radiant, enpierced through the starry heaven the inward aspect of Jupiter's heartly mind or thought, that he, of his godly consideration provoked, deigned himself to associate with humility, from his high celestial throne to make his progress down into this vale of middle earth, such miracles to show by the power of his magnificence, transforming himself in figure of our nature human, of purpose to be familiarly conversing and friendly acquainted with this said lady Semele; whose features, so lustily by dame Nature's curious operation ennewed, incited the great god Jupiter to resort down from his celestine court of heavenly glory, with her to keep company in her earthly coverture of this world transitory: between whom the fiery brand of charity unfeigned so fervently was kindled, that each of them to other shewed their hearts covertly wounded; and shortly to conclude, for the sanative relievement of their privy hurts either to other was conformable, that kindness for kindness between them was enured.[14]

It is not easy to believe that Skelton has swelled eight brief words of Poggio into nearly two hundred – and has added practically nothing to the sense! Yet that the ornament is purely formal a single glance will show. Not a word of it is intended to render more precise the meaning. So the *Diodorus* survives, in its one incomplete manuscript, as the *reductio ad absurdum* of the theory that a thing should be said not as accurately, but in as many different ways, as possible.

With this clue in our hands, we shall find Skelton's verse much more comprehensible. The Skeltonic, of course, is based solidly upon amplification. But it is the same with the formal verse. Look at the decoration of the early *Northumberland Elegy* or the late *Garland of Laurel*: in both it is the purest tautology. When Skelton writes—

> Thus stode I in the frithy forest of Galtres,
> Ensowked with silt of the miry wose,[15]

it is important to realise that *frithy* means no more than 'woody'; just as *silt of the miry ooze* (a favourite locution in the *Diodorus*) is only a rhetorical triplication of the single notion 'mud.' This will save us many a hunt after subtle distinctions that simply do not exist. Such, whether we like it or not, was the Early Tudor conception of style.

To follow out in detail the rhetorical element in Skelton's verse would be tedious. That he knew his Geoffrey is obvious: he actually quotes him on two occasions.[16] And part of the *Northumberland Elegy* follows, almost word for word, the famous lament for Richard I that Chaucer had made such ironical use of in the *Nun's Priest's Tale*.[17]

Geoffrey's crowning achievement, however, was his *descriptio* of a fair lady. It is the thirteenth-century recipe for Perfect Girlhood:

> Nature's compasses form the round of the head; the hue of gold gleams in the tresses; lilies bloom in the forehead's mirror; the brows are black as whortleberries, and a Milky Way divides their twin bows; a ruler guides the shape of the nose, lest it fall to one or other side of the mean; the two eyes shine like guardians of the forehead, with the light of an emerald or a star; her face rivals Aurora's, not ruddy nor yet pale, but at once both and neither; her mouth is brief in its loveliness, and like the half of a circle; the lips pout, swelling as if pregnant – but moderately red, and warm indeed, yet with a chastened warmth; her snowy teeth are linked in seemly array, all of a size; the scent of incense and of her breath are as one; and Nature, greater than Art, has made her

chin gleam above the gleaming of marble. A milk-white column is the precious support of this head, bearing the face aloft like a mirror. From the crystal throat such brightness comes as will dazzle the beholder's eye and rouse his heart to frenzy. The shoulders are set by fixed law, neither drooping as if to fall nor jutting as if to rise, but exactly level; and the arms please as much by their elegant shape as by their alluring length. Into the slim fingers go a soft and slender substance, a smooth and silky appearance, a long straight form; the grace of the hands displays itself here above all. The bosom, a thing of snow, reveals on either side breasts like virgin jewels that match one another. The girdle's place is slight, and embraceable within the fist's small span. Of the parts beneath I am silent; here the mind speaks more fitly than the tongue. But the leg extends gracefully; and a foot supremely tiny wantons in that tininess.[18]

From this pattern almost every poet in Europe was to shape his lady's likeness. In England alone we can spy her beneath Chaucer's Duchess, Hawes' La Belle Pucelle and the heroine of the *Court of Love*, to mention but three. There are modifications, of course. The English beauty has generally grey eyes rather than green; her hair is like gold wire, and the blue of her veins receives honourable mention. But the form persists: a complete catalogue of charms, working down, in the phrase of Hawes, 'from toppe to too' – with a modest hiatus.

By the time Skelton came to write *Philip Sparrow* he was master of his medium. There is no rigid itemising about his 'commenda-tion' of Jane Scrope.[19] All is spontaneity and artlessness. And yet, when we come to examine this charming informal portrait, traces of the old Geoffrey formula still remain. Face, eyes, brows, it goes – though cleverly broken up by the refrain; then veins, complexion, cheeks, lips and mouth. So far it is almost wholly in the convention. Then Skelton breaks into the famous description of the 'wart upon her cheek' – a blemish which, so far as I know, no previous panegyrist would have dared to mention.[20] Hereafter, it is another story: the Elizabethan beauty, like the one celebrated by Gascoigne, might decently be set off by a scar.

With another digression upon Jane's manners, we return to the pattern: her 'handes soft as silk,' with their little fingers; her tiny waist, her 'sides long and streit,' and pretty foot. Then, after a word about her golden tresses (forgotten earlier), we move on to her costume; and it is here that Skelton introduces – as only he could do – the traditional appeal to modesty:

> Her kirtel so goodly laced,
> And under that is braced
> Such plasures that I may
> Neither write nor say;
> Yet though I write not with ink,
> No man can let me think,
> For thought hath liberté,
> Thought is frank and fre;
> To think a mery thought
> It cost me litel nor nought.[21]
>
> let=prevent, hinder.

With this sublimely innocent, impudent comment Skelton proves himself not only a rhetorician but a poet. For while it is in one sense nothing but a translation of Geoffrey's

> Taceo de partibus infra:
> Aptius hic loquitur animus quam lingua . . .[22]

– at the same time its lilt and poise stamp it indelibly as Skelton's own. Like Chaucer, he had learnt to advance through, and eventually far beyond, his dreary poet's handbook.

Book One

TUTOR

CHAPTER ONE

PRENTICE POET

And thus this sweete clerk his tyme spente
After his freends fyndyng and his rente.
                    CHAUCER: *Miller's Tale.*

§ 1. EARLY DAYS

THIS, THEN, was the bluff, devout but changing
England that Skelton was born into. It is time we turned
to the poet who was to reflect it so admirably in his
'mirror encleared.'

We set off in the mists of conjecture. No one has yet discovered
where Skelton was born.[1] The evidence (such as it is) balances
nicely between north and south. It is true that *Skelton* is a northern
name, not to be confused with the East Anglian *Shelton*. Unhappily, this does not take us very far. By the fifteenth century
members of the clan had infiltrated through the entire country.
A number of possible parents have been picked out of them,
but they remain, alas! conjectural. All we can say is that in
origin, at least, John Skelton sprang from the 'blustering bold
people' of the north.[2]

The date of his birth too is obscure. The Rev. Dyce was inspired
as much by the Biblical span as anything else when he suggested
1460. In default of a better this may still serve; but let us remember
that it is possibly out by even a whole decade.

Who his parents were is, we have said, a mystery; but one casual
hint suggests that, whatever else they may have been, they did not
rank as 'gentle.' In his flyting with Sir Christopher Garnish
Skelton cries indignantly: 'Disparage ye mine ancestry?'[3] – but
the only claims to gentility that he puts forward are his University
laurel and his royal tutorship. Decisive? – no; but if Skelton *had*
claims to family he was not the man to conceal them. The point

is not without its relevance when we come to consider his attitude
to Early Tudor society.

We know nothing of his education until, at the age of fourteen
or so, he made his way – escorted, if he could afford it, by the
University 'fetcher' – along one of the grassy, level roads that
penetrated the Cambridgeshire fens. For, as he tells us at the end
of his days, 'it was Cambridge that first lovingly suckled me with
her pap of wisdom.'[4]

His choice of a foster-mother was significant. Until the very end
of the fourteenth century, Cambridge had given no hint of a
serious rivalry with Oxford: considerably younger than her sister,
she had remained, in Rashdall's phrase, a third-rate university.
Then came the Lollard scare. The heresy-hunt followed; and
Oxford, nursery

> Of that heresiark
> Called *Witclyftista*,
> The devilish *dogmatista*,[5]

promptly fell under a cloud. Her prestige and numbers diminished
steadily while those of Cambridge mounted, until in the days of
Henry VII the latter was able to claim nine out of the twenty
bishops of the realm. Her claim to its first poet was perhaps not
so immediately obvious.

At the moment he arrived, however, Cambridge could hardly
be described as flourishing. Nothing could flourish in the pestil-
ential atmosphere of civil war. Looking back on this period in
his royal address of 1506, Chancellor Fisher was to recall it with
small affection. 'Somehow,' he said, '. . . whether it were the
continual strifes with the townsmen, and the wrongs they did us,
– or the long abiding of the fever, that tried us with a cruelty
above the ordinary, carrying off many of our learned men, – or
that there were few or no helpers and patrons of letters, – whatever were the cause, doubtless there had stolen over well nigh
all of us a weariness of learning and study.'[6] Skelton's freshman
enthusiasm must have found it hard to keep going in these
academic doldrums.

Distraction was another matter. The Skelton of the *Merry Tales*
could be relied on to find some means of entertainment. When an

inter-student quarrel broke out, it would be interesting to know which side he took – north or south of Trent? Or there was the milder pleasure of roaming, on fine afternoons, to 'Trumpington, not far fro Cantëbridge,' with its brook, its bridge and its mill. Later on, like Chaucer, he too would write a tale about a Cambridgeshire miller and his wife –

> A wanton wench, and wele coud bake a cake;
> The millar was loth to be out of the way;
> But yet for all that, be as be may,
> Whether he rode to Swaffham or to Some,
> The millar durst not leave his wife at home[7]
>
> Some=Soham, Cambs.

Let us hope Skelton did not follow Chaucer in making her the Vicar's daughter; since it was the Vicar of Trumpington who copied out his poems for him when he was Parson of Diss.

Or, for a change, he might take the easterly road that runs by Stow-cum-Quy. The manor house there was owned by the Ansteys, who were prominent among the local gentry. A noble building it sounds, in the long Latin will of John Anstey the Elder (who died in 1460), with its richly-furnished hall and chapel, great chamber and painted chamber, its spacious privy (large enough to hold the spare furniture), and roomy garret containing the best bed. John's grandson Anthony was now living here, with his sister Gertrude.

When Anthony died in 1482 he left the considerable Anstey estate to his sister – who was married to a Roger Stathum. Years later, when Skelton was spending Christmas with the Countess of Surrey, was he referring to a long-past student's rebuff when he began his song to Mistress Gertrude Statham:

> Though ye wer hard-herted
> And I with you thwarted
> With wordes that smarted . . . ?[8]

Surely it is more than coincidence that the same poem contains an unkind Latin satire upon a certain Roger Statham. Is it *very* rash to conclude from all this that, to the end of his days, the poet nourished a grudge against the 'gnatsnapper' who had carried off Gertrude Anstey from under his boyish nose?[9]

§ 2. ACQUAINTANCES AT CAMBRIDGE

It is possible that Skelton was attached to Peterhouse. When, in 1489, he wrote his lament on the Earl of Northumberland, he went on to dedicate the poem to 'that excellent doctor of theology, master Ruckshaw.'

Dr. William Ruckshaw[10] could hardly have been a 'friend' of Skelton's, as is sometimes stated. The brilliant son of a York apothecary, he was already a master of arts when the poet was a baby, in 1460-1. From then until 1474 he was fellow of Peterhouse. After this date he must have spent some of his time in Yorkshire, where he held various livings; but he continued his Cambridge career, obtaining his D.D. in 1480. Indeed, nine years later he was still owing commons at Peterhouse. He must have been a man of parts, this apothecary's son. Several of the great northern families made him their confidant: the Plumptons, the Cliftons – whose trustee he was – and, feudal head of them all, the great house of Percy. It was the Earl of Northumberland who presented him to his two main benefices.

One thing we may be sure of: Ruckshaw had a deep and genuine love of books. A third of his will, in 1504, is devoted to ensuring that his precious library falls into the right hands. His church of Lowthorpe gets a dictionary and a Summa. The master of his favourite Sempringham order is to dispose of his manuscripts, while *dominus* Marmaduke Constable receives all his printed books (*in paupiro impressos*). Ruckshaw, at any rate, did not despise this new-fangled invention, which had sprung into being during his own lifetime and was to revolutionise the mind of Europe.

Was this capable doctor of divinity the first of Skelton's tutors? It seems very likely. Skelton was also a Peterhouse name at this time. We hear of a William Skelton of Peterhouse, who in 1500 became Vicar of the near-by Cherry Hinton.[11] A relation of the poet's? Again we cannot be sure. But everything goes to suggest that, in his verses to Dr. Ruckshaw, Skelton was addressing an old and still respected mentor.

There were other men he must have known during these years. John Blythe, for instance.[12] A nephew of the Archbishop of York, Blythe went up to Cambridge and ended as its Chancellor. But his talents were not confined to the academic world. In the Church he rose to be Bishop of Salisbury; at Court he started as one of the

King's chaplains and became Master of the Rolls. Blythe, in fact, was one of Henry VII's most trusted councillors. In the year 1480, however, he had just been created master of arts. So that when we find Skelton in the Bishop's company fifteen years later, he was possibly cementing an acquaintance first formed during the lectures given, as was customary, by the newly-fledged M.A.

But what of his actual contemporaries? Two at least deserve our attention. The energetic and charming John Suckling[13] was later to become 'simultaneously fellow, president and bursar of Corpus Christi College, fellow, president and later Proctor [Master] of Godshouse, proctor of the university, rector of Fendrayton' – a sufficient testimonial to his qualities. But at the time we are speaking of, he was still a clever young arts student. In 1482 he combined the degrees of B.A. and master of grammar; and we have good reason to believe, not only that Skelton was following the same courses, but that he struck up an acquaintance with Suckling in doing so.

Eminent as they were in their age, both Blythe and Suckling are forgotten to-day. That is far from being the case with yet a third John – John Fisher.[14] The scholar whose mild and haggard features gaze past us out of Holbein's drawing is known to everyone. Erasmus called him a saint; and St. John of Rochester he has since in fact become. But the youthful Fisher is less familiar. Born not in 1459, as commonly thought, but ten years later,[15] this son of a Yorkshire mercer showed himself, even in that age of rapid maturity, something of a prodigy. Before going on to arts and theology, he decided to sit for his grammar degree; and he took it the year after Suckling – at the age of fourteen! Only Oxford's 'boy bachelor' Wolsey, with his B.A. at fifteen, can compete with this record.

Fisher too, then, was engrossed in Vergil and Ovid at a time when Skelton was pretty certainly engaged in the same studies. Of course, they may never have met; and if they did, difference of age and temperament is likely to have prevented any close friendship. But in view of later events the possibility is an intriguing one.

It was a pleasant custom of the time – as it still is on the Continent – for the student to sample a number of universities in the course of his education. At Cambridge certain provisions were made to this end: Peterhouse, for instance, was authorised by

PRENTICE POET

statute to send one or two students to Oxford. Perhaps the 'egregious' Dr. Ruckshaw put in a word for his star pupil. Possibly Skelton was just smitten by restlessness, or the rumour of an inspiring teacher. Or he may simply have wanted to put as many miles as possible between himself and the heartless Gertrude. Whatever the cause, Skelton left Cambridge – so far as we know without taking any degree – and made his way, at some unascertained date, to Oxford.

§ 3. LAURELS AT OXFORD

Soon after the end of June 1490 the press of William Caxton – that tireless purveyor of Gallic culture to the more serious gentlemen of England – turned out an English version of the *Eneydos*, a French romance based (at some distance) on the *Aeneid*. The good Caxton had few illusions about his quality as a translator, and he makes this clear from the start:

> But I pray master John Skelton, late created poet laureate in the university of Oxenford, to oversee and correct this said book, and t'address and expoun' whereas shall be found fault to them that shall require it. For him I know for sufficient to expoun' and english every difficulty that is therein; for he hath late translated the epistles of Tully, and the book of Diodorus Siculus, and divers other works out of Latin into English – not in rude and old language but in polished and ornate terms, craftily, as he that hath read Vergil, Ovid, Tully, and all the other noble poets and orators, to me unknown. And also he hath read the nine Muses, and understand their musical sciences, and to whom of them each science is appropred: I suppose he hath drunken of Helicon's well. Then I pray him and such other to correct, add or 'minish whereas he or they shall find fault.[16]

Our view of Skelton clarifies suddenly. At the age of thirty or so he is, in Caxton's eyes, the finished scholar. Already he has translated a number of the classics into English, and the university of Oxford has crowned him poet laureate.

The latter dignity calls for some explanation.[17] To begin with, the name of *poet* had nothing to do, necessarily, with verse; it was used freely of any man of learning or letters. *Laureate* too might have a purely figurative sense. Thus Skelton, in his *Garland*,

34

lumps together a miscellaneous group of writers as 'poets laureate' – and then goes on to say of the English trio, Chaucer, Gower and Lydgate, that 'they wanted nothing but the laurel.'[18] Here, two meanings appear side by side. For, though it could be treated metaphorically, the term *poet laureate* had developed a definite technical usage. In Skelton's day it was the name given to a graduate in the faculty of rhetoric.

In the fragmentary registers of Oxford for the period, only two cases of the degree are specifically mentioned. The first is in 1511. William Bulman, scholar of the art of rhetoric, supplicates that 'the study he has made in the art may suffice for his admission to read any book in the same art, and that after his admission he may be laureated. This is granted on condition that he read the first book of Tully's *Offices* and the first book of his *Letters* publicly and gratis.' The other is the well-known schoolmaster, Whittinton, here described as chaplain and scholar of the rhetorical art. On 13 April 1513 he supplicates that 'his fourteen years' study of the art, with twelve years' teaching, may suffice for his laureation here. This is granted on condition that he compose a hundred verses and take the degree at the next commencement.' On 3 July he is permitted to wear silk in his hood, and on the 4th he is simultaneously crowned with the laurel and admitted B.A.[19]

So far all seems clear. Unfortunately, the registers contain four more supplicats which sound very similar, except that they do not mention the laurel – and of the persons concerned one is a student of rhetoric, two of grammar, and one of both grammar and rhetoric. This has caused great confusion. Most recent scholars end by following Warton: taking it for granted that all these candidates were actually laureated, and that the poet laureate was therefore a graduate in 'grammar, which included rhetoric and versification.'[20]

This seems to me a reversal of the truth. However closely interwoven in practice, grammar and rhetoric were at least as distinct as history and economics in a modern university. Moreover, of the traditional *trivium* (grammar, rhetoric and logic) grammar ranked officially as the lowest. But in any case a separate degree in grammar had long existed, both at Oxford and Cambridge. (We have seen Suckling and Fisher both sitting for it.) Candidates were examined 'in the making of Latin verses and composition, and in their knowledge of Latin authors and the

parts of speech.' If successful they were dubbed master (sometimes bachelor) of grammar, and at their inception solemnly
presented with the schoolmaster's insignia – the rod and birch.[21]

It is evident, then, that the grammar degree was something
like the diploma of an elementary schoolteacher. A certain amount
of rhetoric would naturally enter into the course, as did grammar
into laureation: for the two subjects went hand in hand. This
accounts for the anomalies in the register.[22]

In general, though, rhetoric stood for the more advanced
study of Latin literature. And as the Renaissance increased the
prestige of 'eloquence,' some attempt was made, at Oxford, to
recognise this by admitting a new distinction, borrowed from
the Continent: that of Poet Laureate. The qualifications were in
many ways similar to those for the grammar degree; but, one
imagines, a higher standard altogether would be demanded of the
laureate. And instead of the rod and birch, successful candidates
were publicly crowned with a laurel wreath. That they belonged
to the faculty of rhetoric is certain: Bulman and Whittinton
both claim it, and the poet Hawes, in his *Pastime of Pleasure*,
introduces Lady Rhetoric alone of the arts as wearing 'a garland
of the laurel green.'[23]

So, when Caxton described Skelton as 'late created poet
laureate,' he was referring to a degree in rhetoric granted him
by the University of Oxford. No doubt it was for this that he wrote
the lost comedy *Achademios* and the translation of Cicero's *Letters*,
which are mentioned together in the *Garland*.[24]

§ 4. ENTER THE KING

But we have not yet solved all the problems connected with this
elusive laureateship. When Skelton refers to it himself, later on,
he does so in a curious way:

> A king to me myn habit gave:
> At Oxforth the université
> Avanced I was to that degré;
> By hole consent of their senate
> I was made poet laureate.[25]

What possible connexion can there be between a robe presented
by the King and a degree of the university? We are suddenly

confronted with what looks very like the modern meaning of the term 'laureate.'

The 'habit' itself offers no difficulty: Skelton has described it for us, proudly, in more than one of his poems.[26] It was a royal livery of green and white – the Tudor colours – with CALLIOPE inscribed across it in letters of gold attached with silk thread. But how did this official dress get involved with an academic distinction?

The answer takes us into the earlier history of laureation. Its origins matter little; but it first comes into prominence with the Renaissance – as the public recognition of a distinguished author. Most famous of all these ceremonies was the garlanding of the great poet Petrarch on the Roman Capitol. From now on, with the spread of the new learning, the right to laureate became a privilege that was jealously sought, on the one hand by emperors, popes and princes, and on the other by university authorities.

Throughout the fifteenth century prince after prince is found claiming this odd form of reflected glory. Meanwhile, the universities were busy turning out poets laureate from their faculties of rhetoric; and the Early Tudor court was soon crowded with them – the French André, the Italian Carmeliano, the English Kay, Skelton and (later) Whittinton. There were other 'orators' too. Henry VII, who held his throne by conquest rather than strict right, encouraged these rhetoricians for the same reason as the average Italian despot – to gloss over the chinks in his dynastic armour. And there is reason to believe that, if he did not laureate Skelton with his own hands, at any rate he graced the ceremony with his presence.

Caxton does not give us the actual date of laureation. But Skelton himself provides a clue. He was in the habit of dating his poems by a private calendar, which began some time between 29 October and 17 November 1488.[27] It has been suggested that the important event thus signalled was his laureation. I do not think so. Whittinton – the only person whose laureation is actually recorded – received his garland on 4 July. And in the year 1488 King Henry was in the neighbourhood of Oxford during that month. For the early part of it he was at Kenilworth, some distance away; but on 16 July he was lodging at the Abbey of Abingdon, just outside the city, and after moving to Woodstock he returned to Abingdon on the 26th. Is it unreasonable to suppose that he paid one of his not infrequent visits to the University during this period? And if he did, may he not have placed the laurel crown on the head of his future panegyrist? That he more than once presented degrees at Cambridge we know: why not at Oxford likewise?[28] At any rate the dates fit; and that is all we can say with certainty.

Remains the link between habit and laurel. And this is where the private calendar comes in. For the event that Skelton commemorated later in the year must have been *his entry, as a rhetorician, into the royal service*. All record of it has been lost; but that is hardly a matter for surprise. No other incident in his career suggests itself as being of such importance.

In November 1488, then, John Skelton, Poet Laureate, began a new life – as one of the throng of literary men that clustered hopefully about the Red Dragon's throne at Westminster.

CHAPTER TWO

KING'S MAN

Wher was a gretter maister eek than y,
Or bet aqweyntid at Westmynstre yate?
HOCCLEVE: *La Male Regle.*

§ 1. FIRST OF THE TUDORS[1]

ON SUNDAY, 21 August 1485, Henry Tudor, Earl of Richmond, lay outside Bosworth with a small army. In the opposing camp were the forces of Richard III, King of England; among them the Earl of Northumberland and the Duke of Norfolk (whose Reigate levy included one John Skelton). Between the two armies lay Thomas, Lord Stanley. He had been prominent in Richard's council, but he was also third husband to the mother of Henry Tudor. Which side would he support? Till the battle had actually begun no one could be sure. Henry's men, says a chronicler, were almost in despair 'whenas lo! William Stanley with three thousand men came to the rescue....'[2] It was the sign that everyone demanded. Fighting vigorously, Richard was cut down, and it was a Stanley who picked the gold circlet out of the hawthorn bush and set it on the head of Harry Richmond. A sanguinary tyrant had been replaced by – what?

A shrewd mind, at least. Of them all, probably, Henry had the clearest picture of the situation. Under those drooping lids the grey eyes looked out with alert scepticism in the lean triangular face; and what they saw called supremely for tact.

There is no need to pursue him in the cautious sequence, so exactly right, of his early steps. If he was to keep his crown, however, Henry needed all the help he could get. His chief problem was to avoid the terrorism of Richard III and yet increase his personal majesty to a degree that would render him safe from attack. Physically, nothing was easier. He had only to provide himself with a bodyguard, like Louis XI. This he did, promptly. But assassination was not the real danger. Rather, it was loss of prestige – the awe and sympathy of his own people, the awe

39

and respect of the courts of Europe. This was an altogether
subtler affair, and it called for a new weapon – propaganda.

With his Continental training, Henry turned naturally to the
foreigner – and especially the Italian. He was the acknowledged
well of Latin undefiled. A group of them were already installed
at Richard's court, but they were perfectly ready to use tongue
and pen in the service of the 'usurper.' Some were members of
Italian business-houses; others were papal officials; one or two
were just prowling scholars, on the lookout for a profitable niche
at court. Soon Henry's household was alive with them – Carmeliano, Opiciis, Vitelli, the Giglis, Polydore Vergil among the
Italians; André, Quentin Poulet, Giles d'Ewes among the French
and Flemings. Their airs and gesticulations made them unpopular,
no doubt, with the native courtier; but they were too useful to
neglect. Besides representing England abroad – where the standard of an envoy's Latin was becoming more and more important
– they did secretarial work, and wrote poems in praise of Henry
and his family. The royal manuscripts are full of their opuscula.
Nor was Henry mean in his rewards. Gifts and payments to them
swarm in the accounts of the privy purse.

But Henry was acute enough to see that he could not retain
his popularity on imported talent alone. He was always sensitive
to the English point of view. And from time to time he must have
looked around for an Englishman who would build up the Tudor
Legend in a form understanded of the people.

Was it his chaplain, John Blythe,[4] that he discussed the matter
with one day? And did Blythe remember a quick, confident
youngster at Cambridge who had shown a singular knack at
englishing his Tully? Did he remind Henry of this talented youth,
who had been laureated at Oxford that very year – perhaps by
the King in person? However it happened, in November 1488
Skelton made his début at the palace in Tudor white and green,
an avowed servant of the epic Muse Calliope.

His official patent has disappeared. It is possible that he was
merely recognised as a royal official without fee – like Shakespeare
under Elizabeth. This would at once explain the absence of his
name from the royal account-books. But these are far from
complete; and it may be that Skelton was actually given a grant
like the one made to Bernard André two years earlier. In November 1486 André had received a pension of ten marks (now

about £200) a year until he obtained preferment. Officially this was a reward for his teaching. But in fact it was a retainer for his facile and prolific pen. André was the ideal court panegyrist. Whenever an event took place that might reflect glory on the King, he was ready with a Latin or French poem on it. And this is exactly what Skelton was expected to do – in Latin if he cared to, but preferably in English. Or so at least (as we shall see) he interpreted his duties. [5]

It was not long before he was called upon to justify his epic robe. In January 1489 King Henry had persuaded Parliament to make him a special subsidy for the protection of Brittany against France. Coming on the heels of the tax levied during the Simnel rebellion, it aroused a storm of opposition – especially in the north. The royal commissioners there, faced with something like open revolt, handed over their responsibility to Henry Percy, fourth Earl of Northumberland. Percy knew the temper of his people; and he at once wrote to Henry explaining that the new levy was regarded as unjust. But when it came to money Henry was adamant. Not one penny should be abated: if necessary, the tax was to be collected by force.

The Earl did his best. On 28 April he invited the leader of the dissidents, John a' Chambre, to meet him at a hunting-lodge on his Topcliffe estate and discuss the matter peaceably. Chambre – 'a very *boutefeu*, who bare much sway amongst the vulgar' – brought along with him a mob of supporters that far outnumbered the Earl's retinue. There, before them all, Percy read out the King's letter. But his haughty delivery – he was not a man to truckle, Percy – made them believe that these were his own recommendations. Stirred up by the firebrand Chambre, they fell upon the Earl's little company. Percy himself, some say, was killed in the hall of Cocklodge; others maintain that he was dragged off to Thirsk, and there beheaded under an elm-tree. The rebels then proceeded to raise the countryside in defence of their liberties.

Henry was getting used to his annual rebellion by this time. Prompt steps were taken to deal with this new outbreak. England's finest soldier, the Earl of Surrey, was released from the Tower and sent posting north to crush the rebels. Henry himself prepared to follow with reinforcements. By 30 May it was all over. Surrey was left in Percy's place as sub-warden of the marches, with headquarters at Sheriff Hutton. And the fateful subsidy was exacted to the last penny.[6]

It was now the turn of the poets. André obliged with his usual Latin lament; and Skelton capped it in English. As the first of his court poems, the *Northumberland Elegy* is of particular interest. We have already seen how its technique followed the approved pattern. Skelton was obviously anxious to conform in every way to the tradition. There is no hint of Renaissance vanity here. Humbly, as a man 'both halt and lame,' he appeals to Clio to banish his 'homely rudeness and dryness'; and the apology is repeated throughout the poem. Whereas, of course, it is as 'fresh' and aureate as he can well make it.[7]

But already the man was asserting himself under the poetic mask. From some source or other – none of the surviving records even hints at it – Skelton had learnt that the Earl's followers deserted him as soon as the trouble started. And the stiff framework of the Galfridian elegy is shaken by a sudden fury. To insult the 'rude villains' who had committed the massacre was quite in order – though the pleasure with which he sets about it is noticeable. But Skelton goes on to make the grave charge of treachery against the Earl's household:

> But had his nobil men done wel that day,
> Ye had not ben hable to have said him nay.

> Bot ther was fals packing, or els I am begyl'd:
>   Howbeit the mater was evident and plain,
> For if they had occupied ther spere and ther shelde,
>   This noble man doutless had not be slain.
>   But men say they were linked with a double chain
> And held with the commons under a cloke;
> Which kindel'd the wild fire that made all this smoke.[8]

hable=able.   packing=collusion.   occupied=used.

This wholesale accusation of cowardice and, what was more, double-dealing cannot have been very palatable to the survivors. For the traitor to his benefactor Dante had reserved the very lowest circle in Hell: it was the great unpardonable crime of the period. And that Skelton put forward the charge at all shows, not only that he was convinced of its truth, but that there was small likelihood, henceforth, of his spending much time in the north of England. Whatever his past, he was a royal retainer now. The Latin dedication does indeed talk of the Percy heir – then a boy of eleven – as 'my' lord, and it ends with a promise of service. But this might, perfectly well, be nothing more than convention. Certainly there is no sign in Skelton's later work of any Percy allegiance. His solitary reference to the new Earl is the taunt, in 1522, that—

> The erle of Northumberland
> Dare take nothing on hand[9]

through fear of Wolsey. From this time on Skelton was, proudly and exclusively, a Tudor official.

§ 2. A HUMANIST LOSES HIS TEMPER

He was soon to have further calls upon his 'homely Muse.' The peace of Europe, always rather precarious, was now in danger again.[10] This time the immediate cause was Brittany and its young Duchess Anne. Charles VIII of France and Maximilian, King of the Romans, were angling for her hand in marriage. Maximilian seemed to have won; but with his usual fecklessness he had married Anne by proxy instead of coming in person to the ceremony. This was Charles's loophole. He set his agents secretly to persuade the Duchess of his own superior attractions – no easy matter if one may judge by his portrait. At the same time he continued to talk as though his promised union with Maximilian's daughter would go through.

It was important, in the meantime, to keep England neutral. Of the two rivals she naturally tended to favour Maximilian; but all that Charles wanted was delay. So, on 21 August 1489, a solemn embassy left for England, ostensibly to discuss a treaty of alliance, but in fact to keep Henry in suspense until it was too late for action. As their official spokesman the French had chosen Robert Gaguin, General of the Maturins and the most distinguished humanist they possessed. If he couldn't pull the wool over an Englishman's eyes, no one could.

Bacon has translated for us the first oration he made before the council, and a very fine one it is. But the English were strangely unimpressed. After consulting with the King, Chancellor

Morton replied 'in a brief and plain manner.' It was only reasonable that in the treaty they sought, 'the king our master's title to France . . . be handled'; otherwise there could be no treaty. Somewhat damped, the French ambassadors retired to Paris for further instructions. Another meeting at Calais produced no better results, even though they now had the help of a papal nuncio. Charles's little game was by this time too obvious, and after a second abortive visit to London, early in 1490, they were asked to leave the country.

Gaguin's feelings may be imagined. And as he packed his bags he relieved them by 'dashing off,' in André's phrase, 'some insolent lines against the king' of this perfidious Albion. English and French would agree, he wrote, when the she-wolf offered her teats to the little lamb; when the hind and the wolf drank from the same spring. . . . And he rounded off with a final fling at Henry in person.

A direct insult to the King's majesty! It was the signal for every writer in Henry's court to rush to his defence. Giovanni Gigli, Carmeliano, Vitelli, André each produced a retort in kind. André, he tells us, replied 'not (as they) in a few lines but in almost two hundred: truly, there is nothing bolder than a bad poet!' But even the best of them, the King's secretary, Carmeliano, merely blustered:

> Peace, Englishmen, is vain; now try the arts of war,
> And let a prostrate France give peace, refused before!°

It was hardly an occasion for subtlety, perhaps.

In the only detailed account of the squabble that has come down to us, we are forcibly struck by the entire absence of an English name among the English King's defenders. Apart from himself (a Frenchman) André mentions three others – all of them Italians. Evidently Henry had little faith in his countrymen's command of Latin.

But, though his effort has been lost, one Englishman did join in the chorus of hate – John Skelton. The *Garland* mentions his

Recule ageinst Gaguine of the French nacion.

(This is why, when Gaguin appears among the orators who welcomed Skelton into the Court of Fame, he 'frowned . . . full angerly and pale.') That Skelton's poem was written in English is almost certain. That would be one reason why it has disappeared. None of the three MSS. which preserve pieces of the contest include it; and the fragment Brie thought he had discovered turns out to be part of a religious poem. It is a comment on changing values that, to-day, we would gladly give the entire works of all the Latinists in return for the missing *Recule*.

§ 3. FURTHER LAURELS

Fairly obviously, war was now only a matter of time. Realising this, in December 1491 Charles forced the issue. He invaded Brittany and compelled the orphan Duchess to marry him; thus overreaching Maximilian and absorbing the last great independent area of modern France. Henry had half-expected it; but he made good use of the occasion. Funds were enthusiastically voted; and by November 1492 Henry set sail for Calais with an army of nearly 27,000 men. Probably he was the only man among them who did not take his French claim seriously.

An English fleet had already been busy off the Netherlands. These had come into Maximilian's hands by marriage; but title and possession were two different things, and he had found his Flemings a doubtful acquisition. It was 13 October before his troops, with the help of the English Navy, reduced the last rebel outpost. Meanwhile, in France Henry laid siege to Boulogne and waited for Maximilian's promised support. Of course it never came: Maximilian had rarely been known to keep a promise. So, while the King of the Romans 'lay still like a dormouse, nothing doing,' his ally discovered that France was willing to negotiate. By 3 November the Treaty of Etaples was ready for signing. In it Henry promised Charles – for a large annual pension – to withdraw his men from the Continent and not to support Maximilian further.

The King of the Romans was furious. **Dilatory** as he seemed, he really had been meaning business this time; and Henry's retirement appeared to him the blackest treachery. Maximilian never forgave the English for thus adopting his own favourite habit of the *volte-face*.

But where, we ask, does Skelton come in in all this? In 1493 he is said to have been laureated overseas; and Whittinton informs us that the university was Louvain.[11] But when was

45

he thus honoured? There are only two possibilities – before 1482, and in 1492-3; for between the former year, when Bruyn ceased to read, and 1492, when Francesco de Crema took over, there had been no professor of 'the science of poetry' at Louvain.[12] The former seems too early; and no mention of a Louvain laurel is made by Caxton in 1490. So Skelton has been pictured as studying quietly at Louvain during the unsettled period we have been describing.

But was he? His name is not mentioned in the list of foreign students at the University after 1485.[13] On the other hand, he was now a servitor of royalty, with a robe to prove it. It was natural that he should have accompanied the King on this first and only foreign war of the reign. But the war soon dwindled into the routine investment of Boulogne. Sieges are not very exciting events for the layman. Apart from the death of Sir John Savage, captured and killed as he rode 'about the walls to view and see their strength,' there was nothing for Skelton to celebrate. So no doubt he decided to ride over and visit the famous Flemish university. This new rhetorician Francesco was said to be a good man. (Erasmus, who stayed with him five years later, found him *egregie litteratus* – of quite outstanding culture.)[14]

Universities are notoriously respectful of authority. Henry was now an ally of Maximilian's. What could be more graceful a compliment than to honour this Oxford laureate of his who had just turned up? It was thus, I imagine, that Skelton received the laurel from this Continental seat of learning. What is more, it must have happened within a remarkably brief space of time; for on 3 November Henry's truce with Charles had reduced Maximilian to spluttering fury. But by that time Skelton was back at Calais, flaunting his garland and, it may be, a pair of new Louvain gloves.

Once he returned to England, his *alma mater* was not slow to follow suit. Among the Cambridge graces for 1492-3 occurs the entry:

> Granted to John Skelton, poet, crowned with laurel at Oxford and overseas, that he be decorated by us with the same.[15]

Had this anything to do with the fact that John Blythe, king's chaplain, was now Chancellor of his old university? Perhaps; but at any rate Skelton must have felt that his stock was rising appreciably.

§ 4. CHAPEL ROYAL

One of Skelton's duties, beyond a doubt, was to help with the various and elaborate court entertainments. In the next reign an autograph poem of his got mixed up with the revels accounts – to which fact, indeed, we owe its preservation.[16] While Henry VII was by no means as lavish as his son in providing amusement for his court, he did recognise its necessity for impressing the world at large; and it was under him that the Chapel Royal, apart from its ordinary functions, expanded into a full-scale dramatic company.[17]

William Cornish may not have been the 'Octavian Shakespeare' imagined by Professor Wallace, but he was certainly the Noel Coward of his day. As an impresario for the court's festivities, he was unrivalled. Back in 1480 he had been a modest teacher of the children in the Westminster Abbey choir.[18] But his peculiar gifts soon made themselves apparent. At Michaelmas 1493 the King had paid him £5 for unnamed services, and in November he received 13s. 4d. for a 'prophecy' – that strangely popular art-form of the age. It is obvious that Cornish was already the moving spirit behind the royal revels. He did not become Master of the Chapel Children until 1509; but all through the career of Henry VII, and still more in the following reign, it was Cornish who organised the elaborate pageants, masks and dances that delighted the Early Tudor court.

Like so many of his kind, Cornish was not an easy man to get on with. To his children he was an absolute Herod: when Wolsey offered one of his singing-boys to the King, Pace begged Cornish to treat him decently – 'otherwise,' he adds grimly, 'than he doth his own.' But much could be forgiven a man of his ready wit. During a shortage of fodder at Abingdon, Cornish was ready with 'a merry supplication unto the king's grace for a bottle of hay and an horse-loaf.'[19] Such a temperament, at once lively and irascible, had much in common with that of Skelton Laureate. And in fact we know that Cornish set at least one of Skelton's songs to music. Roared out by the lusty throats of the Chapel gentlemen, *Mannerly Margery* must have gone down well. Its cynicism was of the healthy, open kind congenial to that realistic age.

Skelton's other contributions to the amusement of his sovereign have been lost, probably for good. But one other sign remains of his association with the Chapel Royal. The single MS. of his *Diodorus* was written out for Robert Pen. And Pen, like Cornish, was a gentleman of the Chapel. In that capacity he attended the funeral of Henry VII and the coronation of Henry VIII; in 1520 his voice was among those raised at the famous Field of Cloth of Gold; and he received the usual pension and gifts of cloth from both monarchs. In his will, written with his own hand on 26 September 1538, Pen decreed 'that Mr Subdean of the king's chapel, with all my fellows, have every man a penny that is at my *dirige* or my mass, to drink and to say God have mercy on my soul.'

Surely, as one of the first admirers of our poet, Pen deserves a similar tribute from ourselves.[20]

§ 5. TOWN *VERSUS* GOWN

The double jurisdiction of Town and University was the cause of endless friction all over Christendom. Everyone will remember the picturesque affair of the *Pet-au-Deable* in the Paris of Villon, when the Sorbonne held over the city the threat of suspending all sermons until satisfaction was given by the Provost. Cambridge too had its feud, which went back to the middle of the thirteenth century. Rights granted by the Crown, now to the city fathers, now to the University, seem to have overlapped; and as each of the parties clung jealously to the letter of their privilege, trouble was bound to ensue – fostered as it was, with sedulous care, by the joyous undergraduates.

In 1494 the University determined to get the matter cleared up at the source.[21] Dr. Rudd, the Vice-Chancellor, was chosen, together with John Suckling of Godshouse, to procure a definite decision from the London courts, both ecclesiastical and secular.

Two days' travelling, with a halt at Barkway, brought the little party to Fleet Street, where they put up at the hostelry known as Symson's. Most of the horses were sent back, with their grooms; but each of them kept one body-servant for his personal needs. Then they settled down to the laborious business of interviewing legal experts, entertaining officials who might be in a position to help, and doling out occasional purses in the pleasant and entirely open fashion of the day – which More seems to have been the first man of law to condemn. Mostly they travelled by boat, to Westminster or Lambeth, at a cost of 1½d. to 2d. If horses were needed, they could always hire one at 4d. a day.

The law, as usual, was in no hurry to decide. Weeks dragged into months; and still there was no sign of a verdict. From time to time their duties called them back to Cambridge, but they had always to return and try to speed up the elaborate machine they had set in motion. The year 1495 found them at another inn in Fleet Street, probably the George. As this academic year again drew to its close, the Vice-Chancellor had to get back for the ceremony of Commencement; but he left Suckling to carry on in London. They *had* to force a decision. And in Suckling's account of his expenses after Pentecost there comes the entry:

Item Tuesday for dinner and supper with master Skelton
because he was with the bishop of Sarum   5d.[22]

Suckling is a trifle apologetic at including the Poet Laureate in his expense sheet. What had he to do, it might be asked, with the processes of law that were detaining the Master of Godshouse? But then he was in the company of John Blythe; and Blythe was by this time not only Bishop of Salisbury, but Chancellor of the University. That was reason enough for the invitation, surely. And so the three Johns spent the day together, discussing business, no doubt, but relieving it with certain memories of the chimes at midnight, as is the way of university men when they forgather.

The following Saturday Suckling took Skelton out, as we should say, to lunch. (Men rose early in those days; the midday meal was usually taken at ten in the morning, with supper at five.) Again the amount goes down in the account-book:

Item Saturday for dinner with master Skelton at Symson's 4d.

Had Skelton turned out to be useful after all? He was on the spot, of course, at Westminster; he knew who was who, and where the judicious application of a little palm-salve might ease the passage of this intricate law-suit. Moreover, just at the end of Fleet Street, looking on to the river, lay the splendid mansion that served as the town house of the Bishop of Sarum. There, we may surmise, they went on to complete their business, after lunching to the hymn-tunes chimed out from the 'fair new tower of stone' which had recently been set up at Fleet Bridge.[23]

But, even with the combined help of poet and Bishop, the University was not yet to win its case. In due course Suckling had to return and confess defeat; leaving Skelton behind him in the unacademic bowers of Westminster.

§ 6. RANK PASTURE

According to La Bruyère, the courtier spends his happy life gazing at the king's countenance – a foretaste of the sight of God's. But Skelton, it is clear, found time for other activities. He was still young, and always vigorous; and in the strange parasite town of Westminster, living exclusively on its giant parents, the Abbey and the Palace, he would find ample scope for his leisure hours. No doubt, like Hoccleve before him, he soon grew familiar with the cooks and taverners of Westminster Gate. And some of his verses, too, more than hint at an acquaintance with 'Venus' lusty female children dear.'

The short-heeled ladies of the city were famous. 'Westminster, Westminster!' cries Nashe in *Pierce Penniless*, 'much maidenhead hast thou to answer for at the day of judgment!' The throng of idle courtiers was chiefly responsible: though, had the girls eyes to see, they might have read in the figure of Jane Shore the fate of 'the merriest harlot of them all.' The *Belle Héaulmière* of London, she was still alive, More tells us, in 1513; but then 'old, lean, withered, and dried up, nothing left but rivelled skin and hard bone.'[24]

More congenial, doubtless, to the little colony at Westminster was the strapping figure of Long Meg – whose name lived on long after the time of Elizabeth. We know her only from this late tradition, which presents her as a gigantic Lancashire lass, who had come to take up service in the capital, and was soon legendary for her brawn – only equalled by her limitless good humour. Meg became barmaid at the Eagle tavern, and there Skelton must have made her acquaintance. Years afterwards their pranks were remembered and written down, with the usual exaggeration, for popular enjoyment. How she arrived at the inn and was immediately picked out by Skelton as the ideal person to cope with the swaggerers of the court 'that, when they have eat and drank, will not pay what they call for.' How she proved it by laying low Sir James of Castile with one blow of her ham-fist. How later, disguised as a man, she fought a duel with Sir James and again got the better of him, so that he was forced to wait on her at table in the presence of Skelton and Sir Thomas More. The grain of fact at the core of this mythology is now impossible to discover. We cannot even tell how Long Meg ended her days, for while Veale says she retired to Islington to run her own tavern as an honest wife, the more general belief was that she became a notorious bawd and 'kept always twenty courtesans in her house, whom by their picture she sold to all comers.'[25]

But London had also less ingenuous characters to show. There was Mistress Anne, for example, the recipient of many good things from the poet:

> The umbles of venison, the botel of wine
> To fair maistres Anne that shuld have be sent,
> He wrate thereof many a praty line,
> Where it became, and whither it went,
> And how that it was wantonly spent;
> The balade also of the Mustard Tart:
> Such problemes to paint it 'longeth to his art.[26]

Skelton's behaviour was not quite so idyllic as it sounds. '*Elle alla bien à la moutarde*,' remarked Villon of one of his heroines; and an anonymous rondeau makes the inference clear:

> *En trop de lieux brassez moustarde*
> *Vostre mortier ne vault plus rien.*[27]

So that for Skelton to send Mistress Anne a tart full of mustard – if that is what he did – would be something more than the Retort Courteous.

Both these pieces have been lost, unfortunately. But another of Skelton's poems to Mistress Anne still survives. Printed (or reprinted) by Pynson some time in the 'twenties, it has the harsher note of early disenchantment:

> Womanhod, wanton, ye want,
>   Your medeling, mastres, is manerles;
> Plenté of ill, of goodnes scant,
>   Ye rail at riot, recheles.
>   To praise your port it is nedeles.
> For all your 'draff' yet and your 'dregges,'
> As well born as ye full oft-time begges.
>
> Why so coy and full of scorn?
>   Mine horse is sold, I wene you say;
> My new-furred gown, when it is worn –
>   'Put up your purs, ye shall non pay!'
>   By Crede! I trust to se the day,
> As proud a pohen as ye sprede,
> Of me and other ye may have nede. . . .
>
> Your key is mete for every lok,
>   Your key is commen and hangeth out,
> Your key is redy, we nede not knok
>   Nor stand long wresting there-about.
>   Of your dore-gate ye have no dout;
> But one thing is, that ye be lewd:
> Hold your tong now, all beshrew'd!
>
>   To mastres Anne, that farly swete,
>   That wonnes at the Key in Temmes Strete.

medeling=meddling, behaviour.   at riot, recheles=at random, recklessly. As proud, etc.=However proud a peahen you spread (your tail).   one thing is=i.e. is certain.   farly swete=wondrous sweetheart.   wonnes=dwells.

Remembering the fake address to the *Comely Coistron*, one is inclined to gaze with suspicion at the 'Sign of the Key in Thames Street.' The key was another popular symbol of the time, as may be seen from the light-hearted carol on Kit the serving-maid, with its refrain:

RANK PASTURE

> Kit hath lost her key, her key,
> Good Kit hath lost her key;
> She is so sorry for the cause
> She wots not what to say.[28]

Moreover, the word *key* then also meant 'quay,' and Thames Street was of course one long succession of quays. But a house called the Key (or the Hoop) did actually exist in the parish of All Saints in the Ropery during the fifteenth century: at one time it had been a brewery.[29] This would place it halfway down Thames Street, between the Steelyard of the German merchants and the Lady Margaret's town house of Coldharbour. Here, I believe, Mistress Anne was really living when she so enraged the poet with her airs and graces. Once again, as in the *Bouge of Court*, Skelton suddenly sets us down before a particular house in Early Tudor England – creaking sign and all.

But wherever she lived and whoever she was, Anne's character is not in doubt. She was the perennial pert miss, vastly proud of her rank and riches, and not at all tactful in her advertisement of them. The only other piece, however, that has been claimed as relating to her:

> Masteres Anne,
> I am your man,
> As you may well espie:
> If you will be
> Content with me,
> I am merie

is definitely not by Skelton.[30] 'Mistress Anne' was evidently one of the many type-names of the period.

Altogether, Skelton's view of the society flirt had small room for mildness. A glance at his other 'lyrics' shows that. He possessed none of Chaucer's smiling acceptance of men and women as they are. But if his verdict differed, and still more the language in which it was couched, Skelton's eye was just as keen and exact as that of his 'noble Chaucer.' While in and around the Tudor court there was, it is clear, material enough for his acid observation.

§ 7. ROYAL TUTOR

Court preferment, all the same, had been in Skelton's mind
from the beginning. Why had he chosen Diodorus for translation
if not for that historian's evident bias in favour of monarchy? The
opening books of the *Historical Library* would make an excellent
tract for princes. Even his demi-gods turn out to be great kings
apotheosised by the gratitude of their subjects. If King Henry
ever toiled through Skelton's 'dilated' version of the work, he was
bound to feel that it had at least the right idea.

By this time there were two little princes in the royal nursery;
and the problem of their education was one which called for
careful thought. Arthur, the heir, born in 1486, needed most
attention. Having mastered the elements, he was handed over to
John Reed, who later became doctor of divinity and, in the last
year of his life, Warden of New College, Oxford. Perhaps Reed
proved unsatisfactory; at any rate, the blind monk of Toulouse,
André (whom we know better as court poet), was summoned to
give, in his own modest phrase, 'some help.' Despite his blindness,
André was a teacher of experience; and he has preserved a list
of the works which Arthur had read, or at least examined, before
he was sixteen: 'in grammar Guarino, Perotti, Pomponio, Sulpic-
ius, Aulus Gellius, Valla; in poetry Homer, Vergil, Lucan, Ovid,
Silius, Plautus, Terence; in rhetoric the *Offices*, *Letters* and *Paradoxes* of Cicero, and Quintilian; in history Thucydides, Livy,
Caesar, Suetonius, Tacitus, Pliny, Valerius Maximus, Sallust,
Eusebius. . . .' Even if the Greek writers were read (as they almost
certainly were) in translation, it is an impressive phalanx of
names, with a marked tinge of the Renaissance about it.[31]

It has been suggested that Skelton too had a hand in the education of Prince Arthur.[32] This seems very doubtful. André does not
mention him; and however much he disliked the English Laureate,
he could not very well have avoided doing so in an official
chronicle. And nowhere else is there so much as a hint of the
English poet's assistance.

Prince Henry was another matter. Born on 28 June 1491, he
began life in the comparative obscurity of a second son. But
this does not mean that little Henry was neglected. Before he
was twelve months old he had been officially appointed Warden

of the Cinque Ports; and other honours followed thick and fast. As usual, there was sound policy behind his father's moves. Not only did they make it easier for the King to choose his own officials, but the fees provided handsomely for the Prince's household.

But events now demanded further action. Perkin Warbeck was abroad, claiming to be Richard, Duke of York, one of the ill-fated 'princes in the Tower.' There was only one answer to such pretensions. On 28 October 1494 the King 'sent to Eltham for to convoy the said lord Henry, which, with great honour, triumph, and of great estates, was convoyed through London, and received with the mayor, the aldermen, and all the crafts in their liveries, and so honourably brought to Westminster.' There, with divers other notables, he was made a Knight of the Bath – with a real bath, and a gorgeous bed to dry out in. On Hallowmas, 1 November, he was created, with splendid ceremony, Duke of York. [33]

There still remained the question of his tuition. And about this, suddenly, the canny monarch had a brilliant idea. Already the boy held some of the highest honours in the land. None the less, one had to think ahead. So long as Arthur was alive, Henry had no chance of ascending the throne. Then why not – why not make him *Archbishop of Canterbury*? The more he considered his plan, the better it sounded. With this key position in the family, the King would have no trouble with Convocation; and at the same time – a consideration never far from his thoughts – a princely income would be assured his son for life. [34] It was perfect. The only thing left was to consult his mother about the choice of a tutor.

This was his invariable habit. The minute figure of the Lady Margaret was one to conjure with at court. To the Spanish Ambassador in 1498 she was among the half-dozen people with the greatest influence in England. In personal matters her power over the King was so absolute that 'the queen, as is usually the case, does not like it.' And her interest in matters educational was pronounced. Already, at Collyweston, she was providing a home and a tutor for a number of young gentlemen; while, more significant still, the epitaph of her grandnephew, Sir John St. John informs us that 'as a boy the countess of Richmond brought him up, from his earliest years, with the royal children.' [35]

This cannot refer to Arthur, who was being given a separate education. But the others were brought up together, at Eltham;

and for the curly-headed Henry, in particular, the Countess always showed a special fondness. We see her begging the king to arrange 'that none of my tenants [on a certain estate] be retained with no man, but that they be kept for my lord of York, your fair sweet son, for whom they be most meet.'[36]

Education began early in those days – though not so abnormally as some would have us believe. The chronicler Hardyng has given us the ordinary timetable for the upper classes:

> . . . lords' sons been set, at four year age,
>   At school to learn the doctrine of lettrure,
> And after, at six, to have them in language,
> And sit at meat seemly in all nurture. . . .

In other words, they started on their alphabet at about four, and went on to Latin (and table-manners) a couple of years later. It was not usual for both to be entrusted to the same person: in the case of both Edward VI and Henry Fitzroy, bastard son of Henry VIII, Latin tutors were not appointed until their sixth year. So that when Skelton announces, later –

> The honor of England I lerned to *spell*,

I do not think we should take him too literally. Not until 1497 would a schoolmaster be required for the Duke of York.[37]

The Lady Margaret, we may be sure, warmly seconded Henry's plan for making a churchman of his son. Her mind filled with visions of a great crusade – at table she would often wish 'she were a launder unto them that should go against' the Turks[38] – she must have felt that here was a notable step towards that glimmering ideal. And the choice of a suitable tutor must have exercised her greatly. That John Skelton, then, was finally selected to bring up the future Archbishop is most revealing. There was evidently another side to the poet than the one that caught the popular fancy. Manners he must have had, and something of the clerical cut, before he passed the Countess's exacting scrutiny.

Fisher may have helped. It was in 1497[39] that he entered the Lady Margaret's household. But recommendations, however strong, were obviously not everything: a man had to be reasonably well qualified for a post of this kind. And in fact there are signs that, in addition to his various laurels, Skelton was by now a master of arts; perhaps, even, a candidate for the degree in theology. Bale, at least, says that he was a doctor of divinity (*theologie professor*); and in 1504-5 the Cambridge Grace-Book, under the heading 'Masters of Arts,' conceded Skelton the same status there as he enjoyed at Oxford. Unfortunately, the Oxford registers are missing for the period, so we cannot be sure just what that status was. But it must have been at least that of M.A.; and is there any good reason for refusing him, eventually, Bale's D.D.?

If our chain of evidence holds, then Skelton had a mistress as sweet as she was devout. All who came in contact with her felt the spell of the little woman's charm. Herself an avowed ascetic and severely dressed (except for the rings on her fingers), yet she saw to it that there was no gloom in her household. 'Her condition always,' says a former page of hers, Lord Morley, 'at the beginning of her dinner was to be joyous, and to hear those tales that were honest to make her merry.' At Christmas she kept open house for all comers, and her largesse – carefully graded according to rank, for with all her graciousness she was a stickler for etiquette – outwent the King's by far.[40] By her side on these occasions stood a man we shall meet later – William Bedell, Treasurer of her household – to dole out these munificent awards. Is it any wonder that everyone who knew her loved her – with the possible exception of her daughter-in-law?

One thing she insisted on for the new tutor. Before a year was out Skelton had himself entered the Church. Between March and June 1498 he was successively promoted subdeacon, deacon and priest.[41] (This was in London. At Marlborough, in the same month of March, a brilliant young Oxonian named Thomas Wolsey was also entering the priesthood.) The rapidity of this progress through the orders was in no way exceptional, as is sometimes thought.[42] All the more reason, then, for our spying a close connexion between Skelton's sudden but quite orthodox change of cloth and his recent appointment.

It is a new and somewhat unexpected Skelton that now confronts us. In place of the court poet, ruffling it with Anne and Margery and Long Meg of the Eagle, we have the grave divine, specially singled out for the privilege of instructing a budding Archbishop. Yet, in fact, there was really no such division. As we shall see, the new priest had by no means cast aside his human, poetic self. Skelton offers us nothing to compare with the transformation of Jack Donne into the ascetic Dean of St. Paul's. For him poet and parson were complementary, and – luckier in this than most poets – it does not seem that he was ever conscious of any violent conflict between them. It is only we, with our crude pigeon-holes, that find them hard to reconcile.

Certainly the clerical Skelton was no myth. Although nearly all the results have vanished, if we may trust the *Garland*, Henry's tutor took his duties with exemplary seriousness. To instruct his princeling in the rules of Latin he wrote a grammar – 'in English,' after the current fashion. For the cardinal subject of behaviour he translated that popular Latin treatise, the *Art of Dying*; compiled (or translated) a tract called *How Men should Flee Sin*; and produced the interlude of *Virtue*. The special duties of royalty called for a whole set of volumes: *Royal Demeanance*, the *Book of Honourous Estate*, and a 'noble pamphlet' on *Sovereignty*. The glosses make it pretty clear what these were like. They must all have followed the now well-worn text which Skelton quotes from Cassian: 'The nobleman is the man who is ennobled by his virtue.'

Those who care may, I think, still examine the original of one of them. The mysterious *Dialogues of Imagination*[43] was probably taken from a French prose work entitled *Imaginacion de vraye noblesse*. A copy of it, written out by Poulet, the royal Librarian, was presented to Henry VII in 1496: perhaps the king took a fancy to it and asked Skelton to turn it into English for his son. It relates how a Flemish knight, travelling from Lille, was met on the road by Dame Imagination, wearing a long, multicoloured mantle. She communicated only by signs; but after she had touched his eyes, ears, mouth, hands and feet he suddenly found he could understand her. Beginning with a lament upon the 'great outrages, abuses, mischiefs and inconvenients' of modern Christendom, she launched into a long sermon upon the nature of *vraye noblesse*. This, as we might expect, turns out to be, not birth or rank, but virtue.[44]

There is just one item which peers somewhat faunishly out of this sober array of titles.

Item, Automedon of loves meditacion,

it reads. This was not, as Brie thought, a translation from the Greek Anthology. Far from it. It refers to the poet Ovid – and to the least presentable of his poems, the notorious *Art of Love*. (As Automedon was the master charioteer, Ovid begins, I shall be known as the Automedon of Love.)[45] No Oxford grammarian was permitted to read this improper work in the schools. Yet here is Skelton, to all appearances, laying claim to a translation of it. Was it intended for the future Henry VIII; or did he merely slip in the title at this point to make up a rhyme? We shall never know. But it will serve as a reminder that the priestly cassock had by no means smothered in our poet the unregenerate man of the Renaissance.

§ 8. BOUGE OF COURT

From the first, Prince Henry had had his own establishment – at Eltham, near Greenwich. (Its nobly timbered hall is still standing to-day.) His elder brother, as befitted the Prince of Wales, spent most of his time on the borders of that country; but he also made frequent public appearances with his father. This was not the case with Henry. 'Formerly,' wrote Duque to Isabella in 1504, 'the king did not like to take [his second son] with him, in order not to interrupt his studies.'[46] With his two young sisters and the short-lived Edmund, he stayed for the most part in his Eltham manor-house, trying, with Skelton's aid, to fathom the mysteries of the Latin subjunctive.

At first sight his tutor's position seems far from uncomfortable. Two or three servants were at his disposal; and in modern currency his salary would be in the neighbourhood of £400 a year, all found.[47] The work, too, was by no means heavy: it gave him plenty of time for writing and relaxation. Whenever he felt like it, he could ride over to join his friends at Greenwich, Westminster or Sheen, where his position as royal poet entitled him to 'bouge of court' – free board and lodging. And at the same time he enjoyed all the advantages of living in the country – though, from his description of them, Skelton was not greatly enamoured of the wild heaths that formed his immediate neighbourhood.

The first year of his appointment turned out to be rather an eventful one. Perkin Warbeck was now in Scotland, threatening a descent upon the northern counties. Parliament had been assembled and had voted the usual subsidy for their defence. But down in distant Cornwall men began to grumble: why should they in the south pay for 'a little stir of the Scots, soon blown over'? As usual, there was no lack of ringleaders. A blacksmith and a lawyer, between them, coaxed these casual flames into a promising blaze. It was decided that they should march to London and deliver the King from the evil counsellors who had proposed this iniquitous levy. So the motley band of Cornish tinmen and peasants moved slowly east, and encamped on the high common of Blackheath, between Greenwich and Eltham.[48]

Queen Elizabeth had been on a visit to her younger son at Eltham. It was obviously no place for either of them now. So, on 6 June, 'came the queen with my lord of York, her second son, unto Coldharbour, where her grace rested till the Monday following.' Henry's tutor was no doubt one of the party; and he presumably went along too when 'her grace, with my said lord of York, removed unto the Tower of London' for greater protection.[49] But the authorities soon made their plans. The Earl of Oxford was sent to catch the rebels in the rear; Daubeney was given the main body of troops and ordered to Hounslow Heath; while the King took up his position with the reserves. By the time he came up next day the battle was over. Joseph, the smith, ran to Greenwich for sanctuary, but was caught before he reached the church. Lord Audley and the lawyer Flammock were taken in the field. The nobleman was beheaded on Tower Hill; the commoners were hanged, drawn and quartered at Tyburn.

This 'Cornish war, which was fought on the vast, exposed and moorish wastes near Greenwich,' formed an important item in one of Skelton's lost poems:

The tratise of Triumphes of the Rede Rose,
Wherein many storys ar brevely contained
That unremembred long time remained.[50]

Another, without a doubt, was the final overthrow of Warbeck, which happened in October of this same year.

Was it for celebrating these events that, on 3 or 4 December, the King paid the sum of £3 6s. 8d. (now about £100) to 'the king's mother's poet'; and was this unnamed poet John Skelton?[51] We cannot be sure. At any rate, during Christmas of this year the royal family held a joyful reunion at Sheen. The King and Queen were there, says the *Great Chronicle*, with 'my lady the king's mother, my lord of York, my lady Margaret' his sister, and a throng of noblemen and great ladies, all in high spirits at the victory. Probably Skelton was there as well; and had to tumble out hastily at the outbreak of a 'huge fire within the king's lodging,' on the night of the 30th. No one was killed, fortunately, but a good deal of splendid furniture was destroyed, and the building almost gutted.[52]

Such excursions, however, were exceptional. For the most part Skelton and his little charge seem to have been left undisturbed to the rural solitude of Eltham. It was, as we have hinted, a not unwelcome change from overcrowded Westminster. Besides, in the new solemnity of holy orders, Skelton did feel more aloof; it was in a way a break with the past, if not quite the turning of a new leaf. And he expressed his feelings in the most ambitious of his poems to date: the remarkable *Bouge of Court*. Published by Caxton's successor, Wynkyn de Worde, in 1499,[53] it must have been composed round about this period – probably between 23 August and 23 September 1498, when the sun (as the first stanza tells us) was in Virgo.

There was nothing revolutionary in the theme of the *Bouge*. The Court was used to hearing itself described as hell. (That, indeed, had been the subject of the opening chapter in Walter Map's famous *Vanities of Courtiers*.) More recently there had been Alain Chartier's *Curial*, translated by Caxton, and Pope Pius II's *Miseries of Courtiers*, soon to inspire the *Eclogues* of Barclay. Incidentally, no monarch would object to these diatribes against his large and unruly household; in fact, he would rather welcome them. They were a kind of moral talisman – like the sermons to which he listened, with surprising meekness, every Sunday.

Skelton's poem is cast in the most impeccable of official forms: the dream allegory. For the rest, the astrological dating, the rhyme royal, the self-depreciation, the aureate pleonasm – they are all here, as they had been in the visions of Lydgate a century ago. Skelton, once again, is not trying to be 'original.' Even his

central image, the ship of knaves, is only a variant of Brandt's
Narrenschiff, which had just been translated into Latin (in
1497) and, in its humanistic dress, become the rage of educated
Europe.

But for some reason Skelton was not born to conformity.
Following hard on the fine introductory stanzas, we are pulled up
short by the couplet:

> At Harwich port slumbring as I lay
> In mine hostes house called Powers Key.[54]

For the first time the medieval vision is given a strictly local
habitat. There was Langland, true, with his Malvern hills; but
Langland was *poetically* a nonconformist of the direst stamp.
Generally speaking, the medieval dreamer fell asleep in some
quite utopian garden, wood or vale. To bring him, as Skelton
does, out of the everywhere into Early Tudor Harwich was a
violent breach with tradition. But once this is done, the mercantile
flavour – an everyday smell of tar and seaweed – hangs about
the poem to the end.

At first sight the poem proper is little more than an extended
picture gallery. Seven Court vices are presented in turn – types
as old, for the most part, as the *Roman de la Rose*: Favell the
flatterer, pale Suspicion, Harvey Hafter the pickpocket, Disdain,
the threadbare gallant Riot, Dissimulation and fawning Subtlety.
To begin with, they will have nothing to do with the shy newcomer, Dread. Then, one by one, they come up and angle for
his confidence. There is little or no action; and monotony seems
inevitable. But those critics who accuse Skelton of formlessness
might do well to examine the tectonics of the *Bouge*. One can
almost graph the method by which he avoids a wooden repetition.

Nevertheless, the impact of the poem is not at all that of a
classical economy. Rather, its tone is of a Chaucerian realism,
sharpened – coarsened, if you will – to the point of satire. It
is not only the phrasing that is reminiscent of Chaucer. In the
Bouge we return, after a century, to the world of the senses.
The rogues, moreover, are not only individualised; they are
presented *dramatically*. Their richly flavoured speech betrays
them more clearly than their names. Here is Suspicion, for
instance:

'Spake he, a' faith, no word to you of me?
  I wote, and he did, ye wold me tell.
I have a favour to you, whereof it be
    That I must shew you moch of my counsel. –
    But I wonder what the devil of hell
He said of me, whan he with you did talk? –
By mine avise, use not with him to walk.'

The next figure is a not unworthy prototype of Autolycus:

Harvy Hafter came leping, light as lind.

Upon his brest he bare a versing-box;
  His throte was clere, and lustily coud fain;
Methought his gown was all furred with fox,
    And ever he sang *Sith I am nothing plain*.
    To kepe him from piking it was a grete pain.
He gased on me with his gotish berd:
Whan I loked on him my purse was half afer'd. [55]

lind=linden, lime.   versing=dicing.   fain=sing affectedly.   piking=picking
                purses.   gotish berd=goatee.

Harvey's prattle, too, is cunningly suggested in the flicker of
his monologue, with its sudden, ingratiating asides. But the
portrait of Riot is probably (and deservedly) the best known; it is
a brilliant sketch of the seedy, jazz-humming Early Tudor roué.
  As the conspiracy takes shape, tension mounts higher and higher
to the brief and admirable climax, sudden as the starting-up
from a nightmare:

And as he rounded thus in mine ere
  Of false collusion confetred by assent,
Methought I see lewd felawes here and there
  Came for to sle me of mortal entent.
  And as they came, the ship-bord fast I hent
And thought to lepe – and even with that woke,
Caught pen and ink, and wrote this litel boke. [56]

rounded=whispered.   sle=slay.   hent=grasped.

The romantic biographer has translated this allegory into
literal fact. Obviously, he says, it must represent Skelton's farewell to the corrupt and shameless court of Henry VII. The

leap overboard stands for his retirement to Diss, in faraway Norfolk, disgusted by the intrigue to which he had been subjected. It is a neat and charming theory; the only trouble about it is that it fails to correspond with the truth. For some time to come Skelton continued to live within hail of the iniquitous society that he derides.

Nevertheless, there is something to be said for it. The *Bouge* was not written completely in the air. The closing lines, with their challenge to the reader —

> I will not say it is mater indede,
> But yet oftime such dremes be found trew:
> Now constrew ye what is the residew. [57]

clearly reflect a conflict in the poet's mind. Skelton was at once revolted and fascinated by the rottenness of Court life; and the fascination continued for the rest of his life. But for the moment, in his quiet Eltham study, he only 'thought' to leap. Five long years were to pass before the dream was 'found true.'

Are we going too far if we associate this mental revulsion with the poet's entry into the Church? For, at the end of this same autumn, Skelton again rises into momentary view. On Sunday, 11 November 1498, the King, with his usual devoutness, attended divine service, contributing his customary 6s. 8d. But following on this came another, and special, ceremony, which he also honoured with his presence. The next entry in the royal account-book reads:

Item for offring at master Skelton' masse   20s. [58]

The sum offered – at least £30 in modern money – makes it plain that this was no everyday event. Presumably it was, in fact, the first Mass at which our poet officiated in the Palace. Skelton the priest had become a reality. It is in the aura of this consecration that the *Bouge of Court* should be considered.

But causes more mundane may also have been at work. In retiring to Eltham, Skelton had not left 'the court' altogether behind him. The Prince's household was itself a little court; and if we may judge by the next reign, this too could provide its examples of Riot, Favell and Disdain. The Rev. John Palsgrave, tutor to the young Henry Fitzroy, was 'sore despised at' by some members of that prince's retinue. Learning, they would snort, is a great hindrance and displeasure to a nobleman; 'every day more people call upon him to bring his mind from' it, carrying him off to hunt and hawk and ride, or to other, indoor amusements on wet days. After all this spoiling Palsgrave's successor found his young charge completely out of hand. His gentlemen ushers now taught him bawdy songs and encouraged him to laugh at the clergy. School hours went by the board: they even forbade his rising – like every well-bred boy – before daylight! With such companions Henry Fitzroy was the despair of both his tutors.[59]

One doubts if the Eltham circle was nearly as wild as that of Sheriff Hutton thirty years later. The Lady Margaret would see to that. Nevertheless, both as schoolmaster and as cleric, Skelton must have come up against the scorn and intriguing of his lay associates. And this too, it may fairly be guessed, went to colour the complex experience that lay behind the astonishing *Bouge of Court*.

CHAPTER THREE

LIZARD IN THE GRASS?

The court laugheth at the beginning on them that enter, and after she grimmeth on them, and sometime biteth them right eagerly.

CAXTON: The Curial.

§ 1. SKELTON MEETS ERASMUS

IN 1499 Skelton lost an old and valued acquaintance in Blythe, Bishop of Salisbury. But he also made a new one – and 'one far better known to history: Desiderius Erasmus the Dutchman. It was in the summer of this year that the young humanist crossed over to England with his elegant pupil William Blount, Lord Mountjoy, to see what this country could offer him. Mountjoy, he soon saw, had not exaggerated; England was definitely making up for lost time in the humanistic race. Erasmus found himself in a circle of scholars whose match he had not met elsewhere. An enthusiastic letter, written in December to Robert Fisher in Italy, gives us his impressions. He liked the country and the people; he even liked the climate; but the *learning* – that exceeded all his praise, and Erasmus could praise when he had a mind to. The scholarship of these men was an eye-opener to him; it was 'not hackneyed and trivial, but deep, accurate, ancient, Latin and Greek. . . .' Erasmus was almost pleased that he'd been unable to afford Italy.[1]

Thomas More had been one of the first men he had met. Quiet, moated Well Hall, the Eltham seat of the Ropers, was not far from Mountjoy's Greenwich manor; and More occasionally week-ended there, to get the smell of law-books out of his nostrils – he was officially studying law at Lincoln's Inn, and unofficially, with the help of Grocyn, mastering Greek as fast as he could. All his spare time was now spent in translating Greek epigrams, when he was not trying his hand as a playwright. (In a letter to Holt the grammarian in 1501, he talks mysteriously of 'those parts which I put into the comedy on Solomon.')[2] With his usual charm More

66

set himself to render this young foreigner's stay in England
as agreeable as possible. One morning he had a surprise for
him:

> I was staying at lord Mountjoy's country house [writes
> Erasmus] when Thomas More came to see me, and took me
> out with him for a walk as far as the next village [Eltham],
> where all the king's children, except prince Arthur, who was
> then the eldest son, were being educated. When we came into
> the hall, the attendants not only of the palace but also of
> Mountjoy's household were all assembled. In the midst stood
> prince Henry, then nine years old, and having already some-
> thing of royalty in his demeanour, in which there was a certain
> dignity combined with singular courtesy. On his right was
> Margaret, about eleven years of age, afterwards married to
> James, king of Scots, and on his left played Mary, a child of
> four. Edmund was an infant in arms. More, with his com-
> panion Arnold, after paying his respects to the boy Henry,
> presented him with some writing. For my part, not having
> expected anything of the sort, I had nothing to offer, but
> promised that on another occasion I would in some way
> declare my duty towards him. Meantime I was angry with
> More for not having warned me, especially as the boy sent me
> a little note, while we were at dinner, to challenge something
> from my pen. I went home, and in the Muses' spite, from
> whom I had been so long divorced, finished the poem within
> three days.

This was the *Description of Great Britain*, published with the *Adagia*
in 1500.[3]

Writing a quarter of a century after the event, Erasmus's detail
is not so clear as we could have wished. That he gets the children's
ages wrong is of no consequence; but we should have liked a little
more information about the company at dinner, and especially
a word or two on Henry's tutor, who was undoubtedly present.
As it is, we have matchless word-portraits of Colet and More
from this keen-eyed observer, but none of Skelton. It is obvious,
though, that the whole affair was prearranged – probably by More
and Skelton in concert. And as More came along ready armed with
his manuscript, it is highly probable that at the dinner table
Skelton too recited a carefully prepared Latin eulogy of their
learned visitor. Such 'impromptu' efforts were then much in

vogue. Accordingly, when Erasmus got home he not only produced his pæan on the royal family; he added an 'extemporal song' to Skelton for good measure. His draft of it may still be seen at the British Museum, with its stumbling attempt to spell the wretched name correctly – he would insist on writing *Stelkon*![4] And its opening lines make it quite plain that they are a reply to an earlier panegyric from the Englishman:

> O Skelton, worthy of eternal fame,
> Why should thy fount of speech pour on my name
> The meed of praise . . . ?[5]

Like so much else of Skelton's, this poem to Erasmus has been lost; indeed, its very existence has been doubted. But Erasmus is unequivocal; obviously he was not the initiator of this friendly log-rolling.[6] He made a pretty good second, though, it must be confessed. The *Description of Britain* also contains a word on the excellence of the royal tutor, and its introductory letter to Prince Henry ends by saying that Erasmus would urge him to grow in virtues, 'were it not that you are of your own accord already, as they say, under way with all sails set, and have with you Skelton, that incomparable light and ornament of British letters, who can not only kindle your studies, but bring them to a happy conclusion.'[7]

Far too much has been made of these exercises in polite flattery. When they were written, Erasmus was still a young and little-known scholar, hawking his pen about Europe and desperately in need of patronage. In Paris he had been heavily scolded by Gaguin for the way he laid on the butter. And here, in England, was the nearest he had got, so far, to a promising refuge. If not the English court itself, it was the court at one remove. England, too, suited him very well. He had never expected to find so many minds akin to his own among the ultimate Britons. Mountjoy wanted him to settle here. It only remained for the King to invite him. And nothing, surely, was more calculated to produce this invitation than an elaborate dose of humanist compliment. So it was not Skelton that Erasmus was praising in this sumptuous fashion; it was the tutor to the King's son. Whether he was being praised as a writer in English or Latin – and Erasmus is ambiguous here – does not really matter; for in any case the humanist could not understand a word of the former. He was merely engaged in suave and eloquent panegyric – and for a strictly business end.

What Skelton had written to instigate this amiable response we cannot say. But the poet too knew how to flatter: no doubt it was on much the same level of fulsomeness, and just about as sincere. There is no sign that the two men ever became friends – and a good many reasons to render it improbable. Although Erasmus was to spend several years in England – he even composed the inscription for the Lady Margaret's tombstone – he had nothing in common with our poet. Even their tastes in satire were different. And Erasmus's pacifism, his devotion to Greek, his prim humanist's love of accuracy and his contempt for the schools – all would have irritated the older man. After this, Skelton is never once mentioned in the whole voluminous correspondence of the great humanist, and the extemporal song was never printed: that remained buried in manuscript, to be finally resurrected as the work of Pico della Mirandola! While the only possible references to Erasmus in the works of Skelton are an attack on his *Praise of Folly* and another on his New Testament translation. [8]

Much the same may be said of Skelton's relations with More. Although later tradition represented them as boon companions, crowing with joy at Long Meg's overthrow of the Spanish knight, this was obviously a case of linking together well-known names for popular effect. They must have known each other at court, the witty King's councillor and the witty King's poet; but there is nothing to indicate that they were ever on intimate terms – not even when both found themselves summoned by Wolsey to write in defence of the Church.

No; the meeting of these three men, in 1499, has a different kind of significance. On this summer's day at Eltham, at the close of the century, Skelton, now nearly forty, was confronted with the Younger Generation. Whether he sensed it or not, More and Erasmus represented the coming victory of humanism in England: the new era (so sadly betrayed) of intellectual sweetness and light, based on the study of Greek and higher criticism of the Vulgate. Did he feel, as he listened to their enthusiastic chatter of enclitics and codices, that he was rather outmoded, with his obstinate loyalty to so much that these youngsters condemned out of hand? I doubt it. Skelton was never lacking in self-confidence. But there they were for all that, the men of the future, dining with the future King of England; and it was their intellectual standards, and not his, that were to prevail at the court of his pupil.

§ 2. PETALS OF THE WHITE ROSE

About the same time as this symbolic dinner-party was taking place, news reached the King that the Earl of Suffolk had taken ship and secretly fled the country. 'Stout and bold of courage, and of wit rash and heady,' this nephew to Edward IV, Edmund de la Pole, had long been simmering under various indignities. As a prominent Yorkist, Henry had taken special care to keep him in his place. But the final disgrace came in 1498, when, having killed a 'mean person,' he, a de la Pole, was actually summoned before the King's Bench to plead his case! Pardon or no pardon, this was an intolerable insult to one of the blood royal. One fine night in July 1499 the Earl slipped over to Calais and made his way, fuming still, to Guisnes, where he was welcomed by its captain, Sir James Tyrrell – soon (as we shall see) to be notorious as the murderer of the princes in the Tower. Henry was disturbed: he had quite enough on his hands without this new centre of disaffection. An emissary was sent across the Channel to talk Suffolk into reason. The Earl's temper had now subsided. He was persuaded to return as if nothing had happened, and was quietly received back into favour. The next year he accompanied the King and Queen on their state visit to Calais.[9]

Another plot had been averted. But the strain was beginning to tell on Henry VII. Before the end of 1499 no less than three executions took place. First came the wretched Wulford; Perkin Warbeck followed; and after him that most unfortunate of all claimants to the throne, the youthful Earl of Warwick. On 11 January 1500 the Spanish Ambassador wrote enthusiastically to his sovereigns: 'England has never been so tranquil as at present. There have always been pretenders to the crown of England, but now that Perkin Warbeck, and the son of the Duke of Clarence have been executed, there does not remain a drop of doubtful royal blood' in the kingdom.[10]

Dr. Puebla was exaggerating only slightly. But, as we have said, the incessant strain of fifteen years had left its mark on the King of England. The 'merry and smiling' features of Hall's eulogy had grown lined and worn; in 1499 another ambassador noted that he seemed suddenly to have aged twenty years.[11] The self-control had stiffened, become iron hard; the caution grown into something very like cunning; the penny-wisdom turned into a frank covetousness. Henry had won the battle for his dynasty, but it was at the cost of his self.

§ 3. THREE SUPPERS AND A QUARREL

Early in 1501 Suckling rode up from Cambridge with the Vice-Chancellor, in a renewed attempt to settle their age-old dispute with the town. Sir Reginald Bray, the privy councillor, was among those to be seen: he was renowned for his bluff handling of the touchy and not easily approachable King. The matter seemed trivial – some trouble about a meadow belonging to a Cambridge fishmonger. But it involved all the complicated privileges and counter-privileges that had made their lives a burden in 1495. This particular visit to London lasted for eighteen days. Much of the time was spent at Westminster, talking with the furred men of law; and on three separate occasions they rounded off an exhausting day by supping 'with master Skelton,' the bill coming each time to 6*d*. This was no lavish entertainment, like the 8*d*. banquet provided for the important Master Sampson; but, being just double what they paid for their own meal, it does show a proper hospitality.[12]

Naturally, the account-book tells us nothing of what was said at table. But we may fairly guess, from what followed, that Skelton was being used to gain the ear of the influential Lady Margaret. (Fisher, now her confessor, was no doubt in the plot. Indeed, it was through his interviews with her as Senior Proctor in 1495 that he had entered her household.) If we are right, then the gallon of strong ale consumed before the fire that final Thursday evening in their room, if it was for a toast to their success, apparently did its work. The Countess, who was on excellent terms with the good townsfolk of Cambridge (as she was with nearly everyone), decided to get this tiresome business settled once for all; and on 11 July 1502 she engineered an agreement that was satisfactory to both sides. Unhappily, it did not last, but that was hardly the Lady Margaret's fault.[13]

At this period – between January and March 1501 – Skelton seems to have been back in the cramped and swarming lanes of Westminster. He was soon to pay it another visit; but the results this time were a good deal less agreeable.

A flood of excitement was now sweeping the whole country. Catherine of Aragon was actually coming over at last, to marry Prince Arthur! Already the ceremony had taken place more than once by proxy – but then further difficulties arose over the marriage agreements. As Dr. Puebla wrote despairingly, it seemed as if they would never come to an end. But this time they really had; and word came from Spain that Catherine was to leave in the spring. At first she was expected in London by 25 May: the King had personally ordered the entire city to deck itself for that date. The most likely harbours for her arrival were Southampton or Bristol. Down to Bristol hurried the Bishop of London, to make the necessary arrangements; while to Southampton, as the more probable scene of disembarkation, it was decided to send the princess's future brother-in-law, Henry, Duke of York. But a nine-year-old boy could hardly be expected to supervise a royal reception himself. With him went probably his entire household, from John Reding, the Treasurer, down to John Goose, the Fool. And above all he would need the advice and assistance of his tutor, Master Skelton.[14]

Westminster was an obvious resting-place for the slow-moving cavalcade from Eltham. And during their halt there, for baiting and supplies, Skelton fell foul of one of the royal chaplains. Peter Ottley or Ottey was his name. As to the cause of the trouble we have not the slightest clue; but it is obvious that the short-tempered poet was the aggressor, for on 14 May –

> in the case of Peter Ottey versus John Skelton, it is postponed to the following day at the ninth hour in hope of agreement, and a term is set for the said John Skelton, on a penalty of forty pounds, to appear before the reverend father in Christ, Richard bishop of Ely, and others of the council of our lord the king, in London at the said ninth hour, if in the interim agreement shall not have been reached in the said case between the parties aforementioned.[15]

Starting as 'the court of poor men's causes,' the Court of Requests had soon extended its scope. Like the Star Chamber, it developed into an instrument for dealing summarily with all kinds of breaches of the law. With a handful of royal councillors for an impromptu bench, it was held wherever the King happened to be at the time. On this particular occasion Peter Ottley had ob-

viously appealed to it for protection. Against what? Who knows
what depths of black hatred (or mere trivial pique) lie hidden in
the curt memorandum of the clerk of the court? He condescends to
tell us only that Skelton was ordered to appear next day and
explain his menacing attitude. The bail, about £1,200 of our
money, sounds enormous; and, recalling that it was later the
sum demanded of Christopher Marlowe in a case of homicide,
we may be tempted to suspect the worst. But in fact, many of the
penalties imposed by contemporary justice were ludicrously
beyond the nature of the offence or the capacity of the defendant.
When Skelton's predecessor at Diss, the royal chaplain Peter
Greves, was ordered to attend more regularly to his palace duties,
the same obligation of £40 was demanded of him.[16] So we cannot
really infer very much from the money involved. And there is no
further mention of the case in the records. It must simply be left –
a reminder that the poet was no less truculent in life than he was
in his verse. Or, as Thomas Churchyard more tactfully put it –

> His terms to taunts did lean,
> His talk was as he wrate. . . .

§ 4. A PRINCE'S LOOKING-GLASS

Catherine's arrival turned out to be a false alarm. It was in
fact 17 May before she finally left her beloved Granada for the
last time; and the journey to Corunna, on the coast, took a full
two months. Another month slipped by at the seaside. Prince
Henry returned to Eltham: with him, we may presume, his faithful tutor, unabashed by his recent tiff with the law. August took
its usual sultry, showery way; and in the course of it news came
that the Earl of Suffolk had again made his escape to the Continent.[17] This time the step was irrevocable. Henry was not likely
to pardon him a second time. The peace so glowingly described
by Dr. Puebla seemed about to vanish again under the shadow of
yet another pretender.

It was in this atmosphere of heat and anxious rumour that
Skelton, on 28 August, sat down at his Eltham desk and scribbled
a little Latin homily for his royal pupil, who had just reached his
teens. *Speculum principis*, he called it: 'the prince's mirror.' One or
two pages have been torn out of our copy; but its general nature is
clear.[18] Its burden (as we have now come to expect) is the duty of

every prince to be a man of virtue..The famous trio of Republican
heroes is cited, Regulus, Cincinnatus, and Fabricius – who
resisted the bribes of the wealthy Pyrrhus. 'It is my opinion therefore,' concludes the poet, 'that princes should conduct their lives
rather by the unfading glory of virtue than the vain pride of
riches.'° Cato is brought in to confirm this worthy sentiment, and
after him Scipio, Horace, and the pseudo-Aristotle. There is
another break in the text, and then a queer little outburst of what
the Germans call *Reimprosa*.[19] This rhetorical device had persisted
all through the long history of Latin prose, though by Skelton's day
the true Ciceronian would have scorned the stanzaic jingle of:–

> Habes consiliarios
> scios aut nescios,
> illos incertos,
> istos inualidos.
> > Solus sapis,
> > O saxum, o lapis!
> Scias prodesse
> in numero esse.[20]

'You have councillors,' Skelton tells the Prince, 'learned or lewd,
some without trust, others without strength.' Then, borrowing a
tag from Erasmus's *Adagia* (which had just been published with
the letter praising Skelton),[21] he exclaims: 'You alone are wise,
O rock and flint! the rest are but shadows beside you! Nevertheless, know that it is an advantage to be one of the crowd.'

Then comes a remarkable passage, which we must quote at
length:

> Whosoever you are – I except no birth, no rank, no con-
> dition, no sex – even, perhaps, the most magnificent of
> princes, thinking that it befits me to restrain my unpleasing
> tongue and objecting against me the reverence of your an-
> cestors, the pride of your lineage, and a family emblazoned
> with wondrous splendour, glory, fame and royal titles, by
> which you promise yourself security: – yet, because I chance
> to seize upon a most deserving opportunity for censuring you,
> on that account I am unrepentant and only desire you to
> banish me to the company of Lucilius with his patriotic
> mordacity. But, by your leave, first let me make my reply,
> briefly and succinctly; for these blustering days of ours call

for a thunderbolt of words (witness Juvenal's 'it is hard
not to write satire,' etc.). Now I come girt for the reply.
Mark diligently, I beseech you.°

A thunderbolt of rhyming prose duly descends, warning the Prince
that it is not impossible he may suffer worse losses and exiles
than his father and grandfather before him. It is an astonishing
tirade for a Tudor schoolmaster to deliver a King's son; and one
notes with interest that Skelton, even now, sees himself as a
conscious satirist, side by side with Lucilius and Juvenal. Probably
the sudden report of Suffolk's second flight gave a topical edge to
the jeremiad. Nevertheless, one feels that this was how Skelton's
mind always worked. Just as in the *Bouge of Court* he had turned the
dream-allegory into satire, so he does here with the homily. From
the beginning he ranges himself with the masters of invective.

But for the moment Skelton feels he has said enough. He brings
his sermon to a close with a handful of precepts in the vein of
Petty Cato – couched once more in the peculiar *Reimprosa*. One
need only pause to remark that the future Henry VIII is urged to
'pick out a wife for himself and love but her alone (*coniugem tibi
delige, quam unice semper dilige*).'[22] If moral precept were the soul of
education, then Henry would have grown up the paragon of kings.

To some students the *Speculum* has proved a sad disappointment.
They had expected a treatise on kingship in the manner of
Aristotle – or at least of Poggio or Buonaccorsi. Instead, they are
faced with this quaint little halfpenny tract. But we should
remember that, unlike the former, this sermon was actually
intended for the boy of ten to whom it is addressed. When he sat
down to write it, Skelton had no eye on posterity. Its only interest,
then, should be in the glimpse it gives us of the schoolmaster in
action. At the same time, we cannot help noticing that the prose
is far from reaching any humanist standard. It is the oddest
mixture of medieval and Vulgate Latin, streaked with *Reimprosa*
and an occasional Ciceronianism. However gifted in other (and
more important) ways, Skelton was never able to reach the
flawless purity of the Renaissance stylist.

§ 5. A MARRIAGE AND A FUNERAL

Five days after Suffolk had been formally proclaimed a traitor
on 7 November, Princess Catherine arrived in London. Her

unexpected appearance, much buffeted, at Plymouth, had not prevented a tumultuous welcome. Anti-Spanish feeling was a growth of Mary's reign. Catherine 'could not have been received with greater rejoicings,' said an awed Spaniard, 'if she had been the Saviour of the world.' At Kingston she had been greeted by the sprightly Duke of York, with several hundred followers; and it was by young Henry that, next morning, the dazzled girl was 'right honourably conducted to her lodging at Lambeth.'[23]

This wedding marked the definite acceptance of the Tudor dynasty among the leading monarchs of Europe; and Henry made up his mind that it should be celebrated with fitting splendour. Bride and groom were in white satin from head to foot; and Prince Henry, in gold and white velvet, was deputed to escort Catherine as he had done the day before. A well-built girl of seventeen, with red-gold hair, pleasantly snub nose and expressive mouth in a neat, rounded face, she had a fresh peasant charm that appealed strongly to the boy at her side. He it was who led her back again to the Bishop of London's palace for the wedding feast. This stately ritual over, Prince Arthur and his bride were carried in a noisy procession to the bridal chamber. There, says Bishop West, the din was so great that no one could hear a word; but the couch was blessed by a solemn array of prelates, and the young couple left to one of the most disputed nights in history.

At the same time Henry was about to lose the companionship of his elder sister. On St. Paul's Day, January 1502, all the royal family except Arthur gathered at Richmond for Margaret's formal betrothal to the King of Scots.[24] The marriage itself did not take place until August; but before Margaret's departure the Court was stricken with horror to learn that, less than six months after his wedding, Prince Arthur had died at Ludlow Castle. The drenching rain that bedraggled the black trappings of the funeral cortège, and made the roads so deep in mud that 'in some places they were fain to take oxen to draw the char,' was symbolic of the general feeling.[25]

§ 6. ROYAL RESHUFFLE

Arthur's death, which occurred on 2 April, brought about an immediate change in Prince Henry's circumstances. As the new heir to the throne, all kinds of new arrangements had to be made for him. There was his marriage to be considered. He must go about more with the King. Naturally, there was no longer any question of his becoming Archbishop of Canterbury. And one of the first signs of his new elevation was Skelton's relinquishment of his post as tutor to the Prince. The royal account-book records in the last week of April:

Item to the duc of york' Scolemaster   40s.[26]

This was – an interesting comment upon 'status' – exactly half the gratuity received by Arthur's tutor two months later; and we know *this* to be a farewell gift because the Queen's Treasurer, in recording a similar present from her, adds that it was made 'at his departing.'[27] Prince Henry would be eleven in June – a good time to begin his more advanced instruction on the new level. And we duly find a certain William Hone in this exacting rôle. We know little about him except that he was an Oxford M.A., soon to be incorporated at Cambridge. Henry later made him one of his chaplains; and in 1514 thought him good enough for schoolmaster to his sister Mary. About the same time he was granted his B.D. at Cambridge.[28]

Henry was not actually created Prince of Wales until the following February – because, said some later, Catherine was thought to be pregnant. But from this time on, the boy lost whatever freedom he had enjoyed under Skelton. The King watched over him with the anxious fussiness of an aged duenna. He was given a room opening on one side into the King's bedchamber, and on the other, on a private staircase leading to the park. It was impossible to talk to him alone. All his meals were taken in private; and when he did appear – a giant of a lad, already outstripping everyone around him – it was always with the King or the Lady Margaret. He 'never opened his mouth in public except to answer a question from one of them.'[29] In addition to Hone, the King had entrusted Erasmus's pupil, Lord Mountjoy (in 1502 a young man of twenty-five or so), with the supervision of his historical studies.[30] Apart from these two, and the gentlemen of his chamber, the poor Prince saw no one – except on official occasions. This gloomy seclusion was the background to the first wild years of his entry into power; it also helps, among other things, to explain Wolsey.

The romantic story, that Skelton was removed from his post

'lest he teach his pupil less seemly things,' is quite unsupported. He lost his place in the automatic reshuffle that occurred when Henry found himself heir to the crown: that is all. There is no sign that he lost the royal favour at the same time. The almost complete absence of his name from the records is curious, but it cannot be dated from 1502. In any case, his salary as tutor was probably undertaken by the Lady Margaret – which may account for his attitude towards Bedell, her Treasurer!

Moreover, he was not sent away empty-handed. Among the benefices held by the King's Chaplain, Peter Greves, was the comfortable Rectory of Diss, in south Norfolk. This had come into the King's hands in 1494, through the attainder of Lord Fitz-walter; and in 1498 he gave it to 'Mr. Peter of the Closet' – who already held various other livings. Some while later (it is not clear exactly when), the King's mother apparently bought from him the manor of Diss for her own use. So, when the question of recompensing Skelton cropped up, the answer was easy. About this time Master Peter was not showing the diligence he ought in attending the King's Chapel. Perhaps he was too well off: his other benefices brought him in a round £60 a year (nearly £2,000 to-day). Then why not apply a small practical reproof by transferring Diss to Skelton? It was, I have no doubt, the Lady Margaret's idea, and a neat instance of her methods of justice. So Diss was tacitly removed from the erring Peter and handed over to her own protégé.[31]

No record was made of the change; or none, at least, that has survived. So it is not certain that it took place in 1502. But, all things considered, this seems much the most likely date for the transaction. Skelton had served the King faithfully, both as Court poet and as family tutor. He was now rewarded with a benefice. There is no question of the 'exile' that is so often posited. For one thing, Skelton did not leave town immediately his tutor-ship came to an end. It was not until 1504 that he finally seized the shipboard and leapt. Dread had not yet completely broken with Riot and Harvey Hafter.

§ 7. A MATTER OF PRISON CELLS

It was not long before he was in trouble again. On 10 June, says a Court of Requests record –

John Skelton appears before the council of our lord the king by virtue of an obligation in which the prior of St. Bartholomew and others are held by Reginald Bray and others in the sum of £200, and is committed *carceribus genitoris domini regis* until the privileges of the said prior are produced before the said council and otherwise determined after inspection by the same. And therefore it is decreed that the obligation remaining in the custody of the mayor of the city of London be returned to the said prior or declared null &c.[32]

In Dyce's day nothing was known of the case but the bald fact of Skelton's imprisonment. Now that we have details of its cause, it loses its attractive air of mysterious wrongdoing to appear as the result of a humdrum debt. William Guy, the Prior of St. Bartholomew's, Smithfield, and a few friends, had borrowed what would to-day amount to £6,000 from Sir Reginald Bray, the royal councillor, and others. Why, we are not told. (Had it been Guy's successor, William Bolton, we might have guessed it concerned matters architectural; for both Bolton and Bray were mighty builders.) At any rate, Skelton, as a respectable clergyman, was asked to stand as surety. It would be natural for him, as a priest at Court, to be on intimate terms with a London prior – as he was, later on, with the Prior of Westminster. But the money had not been repaid; and Skelton was duly summoned before the Council.

Now comes the interesting part of the affair. The defendant (says the minute) was committed *carceribus genitoris domini regis*. In 1592 an abstract of the entry was made which turned *genitoris* into *janitoris*; and this had been accepted without question by all later critics. No one seems to have thought the phrase odd: 'the prison of the King's gaoler.' *Custody*, one could understand; but *prison . . .*? It is not a conventional phrase of the records. But in any case, why should the scribe have gone wrong? Skelton, the defendant, had been tutor to Prince Henry – whose education, we have reason to believe, was in the hands of the Lady Margaret. The chief plaintiff was Sir Reginald Bray – who had been steward to the Lady Margaret's second and third husbands. What could be more reasonable, then, than to commit Skelton to 'the prison *of the king's mother*' until the dispute was settled? True, in this event the scribe ought strictly to have used the feminine *genetricis.* But there was no possibility of confusion; the Lady Margaret had been the king's 'onlie begetter' as long as anyone could remember. And besides, he was surely as capable of making this slip as of writing *genitoris* for *janitoris* – which doesn't even make very good sense. Great ladies were quite accustomed to dealing out their own justice, and even to guarding prisoners. And to cope with her vast domain, which spread into every corner of England, the Queen Mother would certainly have the right to her own dungeons.

In Skelton's case, we may be pretty sure, the 'imprisonment' would be the merest formality. 'Of marvellous gentleness she was unto all folks,' says Fisher of the Countess, 'but specially unto her own, whom she trusted and loved right tenderly.' Besides, the Court obviously expected the Prior to have privileges of immunity from such tiresome things as debt. It was merely a matter of waiting until these were produced. One may doubt whether the poet was even confined to his chamber. Probably he was just required to stay within call while the case was pending; and was quite free to join his friends of the Chapel Royal if they invited him to help dismember the fine buck given them by the Queen, with 20s. 'to drink at a tavern,' on the night of the 17th.

The most significant point in the whole case is the circumstantial evidence it gives that Skelton was now attached to the Lady Margaret's household. This fits in perfectly with our earlier evidence of the connexion; and it helps to explain how Skelton eventually found himself Rector of Diss. The poet, it is clear, owed a great deal to the generosity of this sweet old lady; and we can well understand him writing of her, in 1516, 'Maecenas has fallen asleep.' It may be doubted whether he ever found such another.[33]

§ 8. DEPARTURE

But the Tudor Court was not what it had been in those early, carefree days. With the turn of the century came a sudden crop of deaths, some of them, at least, of men well known to the poet. Blythe had been the first to go, in 1499; in 1500 he had been followed by More's patron, Morton, the shrewd Cardinal-Archbishop of Canterbury. Not even youth was immune, as Arthur had just proved. And now, in 1503, came in swift succession the deaths of Queen Elizabeth, Archbishop Deane, and Sir Reginald Bray. Following so soon on that of their son, the Queen's miserable end in childbed, at the Tower, had a noticeable effect on the King's temper. Never very demonstrative, from this time forth he grew daily more reserved and peevish: the only two things that brought light to his face, now, were his dynastic schemes and the enrichment of the privy purse.

From this time on, the notorious Empson and Dudley felt free to abuse their authority in wholesale plunder. Brilliant lawyers both, they had proved themselves invaluable to the King in devising means for cajoling funds out of his wealthier subjects. The plan itself – of checking baronial lawlessness – was excellent; and Empson and Dudley proved so good at it that they were turned into a sort of permanent sub-committee of the King's Council. But the vast network of spies and informers that they gradually perfected soon made their names dreaded by every man of substance.

One of the people they fell foul of was Master Cornish of the Chapel. As early as July 1504 he had expressed his opinion of Empson in an outspoken lampoon – and promptly found himself in the Fleet. The ballad credited to him in the *Great Chronicle* cannot be the one in question, for it was obviously written after the statesman's own imprisonment in 1509; but it will serve as a specimen of the indignation roused by these 'horse-leeches and shearers' of the later Henry:

> Thou pigman, thou garg'yle, most worst shapen visage!
>   (Saving reverence of thine order) thou knavish knight!
> That lady thy wife, that foul sow's image,
>   As vile filth among flowers, with gold she is dight;
>   Thy most proud son, that 'prince Empson' hight,
> He jetteth with his men like a lord of kind;
> But a knave go'th formest, and a knave foll'weth behind![34]

Skelton never found it easy to keep his mouth shut over political issues. With this kind of terrorism rampant, he must have felt that the purlieus of Westminster were growing rather too warm for comfort. At any moment an incautious word might result in his being laid by the heels. Moreover, a cause more purely physical made the capital an unhealthy place to be in during the summer of 1503. Plague had broken out there, and was slaying scores of people in its mysterious ravages.

So, I imagine, his thoughts turned to that country rectory of his in Norfolk. There were no longer any urgent ties to keep him at Court. Perhaps he lingered on to attend the ceremony at his old friend Blythe's palace when, on 25 June, Prince Henry was betrothed to his brother's widow, Catherine. But shortly afterwards we may picture the poet jogging at his ease along the brambly lanes of East Anglia towards the little market town of Diss. By 4 April 1504 he had proved himself that rarest of birds, a Court clergyman *in residence* – having just witnessed his first will.[35] And his opinion of the Westminster he had left may perhaps be gathered from the sententious little verse that he translated himself:

> Though ye suppose all jeperdys ar past
> And all is done that ye loked for before,
> Ware yet, I rede you, of Fortunes double cast,
> For one fals point she is wont to kepe in store,
> And under the fell oft fester'd is the sore;
> That when ye think all danger for to pas,
> Ware of the lesard lieth lurking in the gras.[36]

Book Two

PARSON

CHAPTER FOUR

PARISH PUMP

In the meane time, to liue in good estate,
Louing that love, and hating those that hate;
Being some honest Curate, or some Vicker
Content with little in condition sicker.
SPENSER: *Mother Hubbard's Tale.*

§ I. DISS

ABOUT THE same time as Thomas Wolsey left England
for Calais, a chaplain in the train of Sir Richard Nanfan,
the Reverend Skelton also said goodbye to London. But he
was riding off to no sleepy rural backwater. At the period of which
we speak, East Anglia was the most crowded and flourishing
corner of all England. Its prosperity came from the great cloth
trade, which was now (after a century's pause) again expanding at
a dizzy rate, filling every cottage kitchen with looms and decking
every high street and hillside with the grand new mansions of
successful clothiers. On his way from London, the poet would pass
long pack-trains plodding through the ruts laden with fine English
wool: their destination, the scores of country weavers that were
employed by such merchant princes as Jack of Newbury, Paycock
of Coggeshall and, wealthiest of them all, Skelton's friend to be,
'good Spring of Lanam' or Lavenham.[1]

Another indication of the district's importance was the clutter
of monastic buildings that pricked the horizon on every side.
Walsingham, of course, was, next to Canterbury, the most visited
shrine in the country; and there were Hoxne and others besides.
But local prosperity, alas! had not improved the quality of the
religious life that went on in these splendid erections. Little
Dunmow was spending far more than it ought on playing-men,

83

to entertain its many guests. In 1526 Hickling Priory was full of 'incorrigible, rebellious and disobedient' brethren. And the famed Walsingham itself was in a shocking state. In 1514 Prior Lowthe was letting a Mrs. Smith run the whole place. It was she who doled out the provisions, and the Prior's favourites spent half their time at her house in the town, drinking till eleven at night. Prior Lowthe had even paid her expenses for a pilgrimage to Canterbury. Erasmus's picture of the shrine, in the *Colloquies*, is the gentlest of satires in comparison with the reality.[2]

Skelton's new home, Diss, was a halt for pilgrims *en route* for the neighbouring Hoxne. On the borders of Norfolk and Suffolk, the town straggled untidily down its hillside to a large sheet of water (which still boasts several kinds of duck and a swan) known as the Mere. A little below this now stands a pleasant Elizabethan house, Mere Manor, which has replaced Skelton's rectory – though at least one tree in the grounds, a fine maple, looks as though it might have been there in the poet's day. South of this again lay Diss Moor, part of the common land of the village. To-day it is all enclosed, and bisected by a modern ribbon highway; but then Diss was a conservative place: the inhabitants viewed with strong dislike the new move to replace arable with pasture, and they stuck firmly to the custom which forbade those 'great devourers,' sheep, the use of their common.[3]

From now on, this small market town was to be Skelton's own kingdom. A not ungenerous domain. It brought him in a clear £33 6s. 8d. per annum – the equivalent of nearly a thousand a year in our day; besides which, he had twelve acres of glebe adjoining the house, where he could grow corn for sale (a profitable extra) and lay out his kitchen garden, feed his poultry, pigs and cattle, pasture his nags and set up his beehives. For every parson was half a farmer then. His tithes alone would compel him to it: the habit of converting them into money payments was only just beginning, and he had to know how to handle a squealing tithe-pig.[4]

In return he was expected to look after the spiritual needs of his parishioners. There was daily Mass – for the better-to-do, at least, still attended church every day of the week. There were baptisms at the font, weddings at the church door, and the elaborate funeral services, which often included a week's mind, a month's mind, and an obit at the year's end. Ashes had to be scattered over the congregation on Ash Wednesday, palms distributed on Palm Sunday, and the whole of the Passion reconstructed over the Easter week-end.

As a practised dramatist, Skelton must have made this as vivid a ceremony as possible, for at least a third of his flock was illiterate, and in any case, in default of an English Bible, it was their only means of grasping the central truths of their religion. That, and the Sunday sermon. It is to be feared that Skelton would also enjoy exercising his rehetoric on some of the themes that Myrc suggests – the vision of Hell, for instance, with 'souls bulming up and down, crying horribly, and a noise of fiends crying, "Slay, slay, slay, slay, slay, slay! Upon the broach! Roast hot! Cast into the cauldron! Seethe fast in pitch and cood [tar] and brimstone and lead!" '[5] Yes, the craft of Galfrid would come in very handy at sermon-time.

§ 2. CAMBRIDGE REVISITED

On 10 April 1504 Mistress Margery Cowper, of Diss, drew up her will. As witnesses she summoned 'master John Skelton, laureate, parson of Diss, and sir John Clarke, soul priest of the same town.'[6] This, as we have already noted, is our first sign of Skelton's presence in his new profession. Clarke, the other witness, was probably priest to one (or both) of the two trade gilds in the town, which had a joint chapel where masses were said for their deceased members. Perhaps he also served as Skelton's curate.

But such activities did not fill up the whole of Skelton's time. His first University was within an easy day's ride; and in the year 1504-5 it was set in a flurry by the announcement that the King's mother was to pay it a state visit. She had shown it such singular generosity that something unusual was called for in the way of hospitality. Accordingly, a grand procession rode out as far as Caxton to meet her; and on her entry into the ancient city she was greeted with fourpennyworth of joy-bells and a sumptuous repast, during which were delivered the usual Latin orations and a gift which cost the University 15s. 2d.[7] The Countess had come, no doubt, to settle with Fisher (now Chancellor of the University) the final details of her great new foundation. The licence for it was dated 1 May 1505; and by it the old Godshouse, of which our

PARISH PUMP

friend Suckling was head, expanded into Christ's College. Unhappily, Suckling only lived to be its first Master for a few brief
months.

There can be little doubt that it was for this festive occasion
that the University conceded Skelton 'the same status here that he
has at Oxford, and the right to wear the robe granted him by the
king.'⁸ What that status was, we have said, is not very clear –
though it was at least the rank of M.A. At any rate, his 'Calliope'
costume must have added not a little to the picturesque cavalcade
that clattered out to pay homage to the University's great
benefactress. Incidentally, the grant is evidence enough that the
poet had not retired in disgrace to the fastnesses of Norfolk. The
University would never have dared to honour an exile from Court,
however distinguished. Moreover, its High Steward at this
moment was Sir Richard Empson. Which suggests that, whatever
the poet's feelings might have been about the man who had, only
the previous July, flung his friend Cornish into prison, he had not
yet given them expression.

Whether Skelton was also present on May Day 1506, when the
King, his mother and Skelton's former pupil all descended on the
University, we can only guess. Very probably he was, resplendent
in his royal habit, while the schools obliged with verbal fireworks
and Chancellor Fisher made his famous Latin oration, from which
we have quoted earlier in this book. Probably, too, he partook of
the 'certen buckes' that His Majesty provided, with drink, 'for
their recreacioun' afterwards.⁹ But all we know is that, when his
Diss epitaphs began to circulate, it was in the hand of the University letter-writer, the Vicar of Trumpington; and that careful
scribe recorded the date when he finished them. It was 5 January
1507.¹⁰

§ 3. BIRTH OF A NEW VERSE-FORM

But if he did take a holiday now and then, Skelton did not spend
the rest of his time lamenting the lack of fashionable society in his
new abode. Far from it. Instead, he plunged wholeheartedly into
the career of a country parson. Having once accepted the rôle,
characteristically he made the most of it. With the exception of an
occasional visit to Cambridge, there is no sign that Skelton showed
any further interest in the affairs of the wider world up to the
death of Henry VII. All his energies were transferred to the

86

provincial sphere. And – as if to make the cleavage absolute –
even the verse he wrote took on a new and revolutionary form.
The Skeltonic (so far as we can make out) made its first appearance in literature shortly after Skelton's arrival at Diss.

The difficulty of describing this remarkable measure has been
somewhat exaggerated. True, it is so free that any rules must be
laid down with great caution. But one is not far wrong in defining
Skeltonics as short, irregular lines (usually of two stresses, though
often rising to three or more) linked together by alliteration,
parallelism and rhyme-run. But where did Skelton find this strange
form that he made so uniquely his own? The most elaborate recent
discussion[11] traces it to Latin rhymed prose – an example of which
appears in Skelton's own *Speculum principis*. Skeltonics, maintains
Dr. Nelson, are nothing but prose rhymed into poetry. He is
even able to show this change occurring – in English this time –
in the *Replication*.[12]

So far, so good. But to insist that *Reimprosa* is the sole parent
of the Skeltonic is, surely, to ignore the nature of literary growth.
A new verse-form, like a new animal, has more ancestors than
one. And again it is Skelton himself who has obligingly shown us
where to look. This time it is Latin rhymed verse – the medieval
leonine. His Diss epitaphs both begin with rhyming Latin hexa-
meters, and both tail off into English Skeltonics. Here is part of
the Trental for John Clarke:

> *Dentibus exemptis   mastigat cumque polentis*
> *Lanigerum caput aut   ouis aut vaccę mugientis.*
> *Quid petis, hic sit quis?* John Jayberd *incola de Dis,*
> *Cui, dum vixerat is,   sociantur iurgia, vis, lis.*
>   *Iam iacet hic* stark deed,
>   Never a toth in his heed.
>   Adieu, Jayberd, adue:
>   I' faith, Diccon, thou crue!
>   *Fratres, orate*
>   For this *knauate*,
>   By the holy Rode,
>   Did never man good. . . .[13]

The 'Skeltonic' character of the Latin has been noticeable
throughout. It has the rhyme-runs, starting in pairs, but rapidly

increasing to the final group of eight in the quotation. It has, too, the rich alliteration. In fact, Marshe actually printed it all in short lines like a Skeltonic poem. The only difference is that, by the very nature of hexameter verse, the lines are rhymed in pairs of unequal length; which makes it impossible to introduce the other feature of Skeltonics: parallelism. But, as if to answer our objection, Skelton shows us how the form can be adapted – not only in English, but in Latin. The poem is prefaced by some Latin lines which are an amazing rhythmical experiment. The freedom and variety of quantitative verse are converted into accentual rhythms, with a success one can only describe as triumphant. Again we get the rhyme-run and the alliteration; but now the third element – parallelism – is added. It *is* the Skeltonic form – in Latin. Similarly, at the end of the poem (partly quoted above), Skelton breaks away from the double constraint of Latin and the hexameter, to produce Skeltonics in English. Once again the transition is masterly. See how accent echoes quantity in the change-over:

> *Iām iăcĕt | hīc* stārk | dēēd,
> Nēvĕr ă | tōth ĭn hĭs | hēēd. . . .

We are actually present at the rise of this very un-Venuslike being, the Skeltonic, from the strict sea of the hexameter! And here, incidentally, we have one secret of the satisfaction that Skelton's 'irregular' verse gives the reader. It is the fruit of a marriage between accent and quantity. To-day, after the lapse of centuries, the trick is being rediscovered. As they would be the first to recognise, it lies behind much of the best verse of Pound, Eliot and Auden.

But this is still not the whole story. Much of Skelton's verse is written in the rhyme-royal stanza. But it is not Chaucer's rhyme-royal. Rhythmically, its basis is the line of four stresses, with a strong caesura. As always with Skelton, the measure is very free; and the number of stresses may rise to five or even six. But that the norm is a four-stress line is no longer seriously questioned. And it is still easier for this line to break in half and produce Skeltonics. Ramsay has given an illustration of its happening in *Magnificence*.[14] There is another in the *Garland*:

A SPORTING PARSON

> But who may have a more ungracious life
> Than a childes bird, and a knaves wife?
> Think what ye will
> Of this wanton bill:
> By Mary Gipsy,
> *Quod scripsi, scripsi!* [15]

So another of the Skeltonic's forbears has been identified. There are still others – the Latin sequence, and the goliardics of the Archpoet – but these will suffice.

Just one more question remains. Was the Skeltonic 'respectable'? There can be little doubt about the answer. It was not. In almost every case, it will be noted, it represents the breaking down of a more complex form. But there is something to be said for simplicity. The final test, however, is æsthetic – and the Skeltonic must have sounded even more undignified to the Early Tudors than it does to us.

> It longeth nat to my science nor cunning
> For Philip the Sparrow the *Dirige* to sing, [16]

announced Barclay cuttingly. And Skelton knew it perfectly well. Not only did he confine its use, in *Magnificence*, to the vices; he expressly describes one of its variants in the play as 'bastard rime, after the dogrel gyse.' [17] And whatever else doggerel may have been, it was not elegant.

The fact is, Skelton had realised the parlous state of formal poetry in his age. It observed all the conventions; it was courtly, it was dignified; but it was dead. And though he kept on trying to inject it with stiff doses of realism, satire or rhetoric, the results were not somehow satisfactory. So now, as he turned his back on the court, he dropped even its poetic traditions, and struck out a new one for himself. The Skeltonic may have lacked dignity, but it had something still more valuable to poetry – life.

§ 4. A SPORTING PARSON

Turning up at his church shortly before vespers, one 29th of August in the middle years of the decade, Skelton was surprised to find the door bolted and barred against him. Inside, he could dimly make out a tremendous hallooing, followed by the crash of objects tumbled over. It was an occasion for quick thinking. Diss Church was in most ways an ordinary Norfolk specimen of flint and freestone, rather solid than particularly graceful. It had one peculiarity, though. As the Early Decorated tower stood right upon the highway, an archway had been cut through it so that festival processions might make their round of the church without venturing on to the muddy road. Just within the archway a second door led up into the tower; and from there one could then get down again into the nave. Luckily, he had the other key with him. In an instant he had whipped it open, clambered up and was through.[18]

There on the high altar stood, booted, spurred and gloved, a man he recognised as a neighbouring clergyman, yelling like a fiend:

> He shoke down all the clothes
> And sware horrible othes
> Before the face of God:
> By Moyses and Aron's rod,
> Or that he thens yede,
> His hawk shuld pray and fede
> Upon a pigeon's maw![19]

clothes = altar-cloths.   Or, etc. = ere he went thence.

What had happened was only too obvious. In the heat of the chase a hard-pressed pigeon had swooped in through the open church door. The falconer, determined not to be cheated of it, had locked the door and was now busy trying to egg his weary hawks on to the kill. Perched beside him on the wrecked altar, one of them was working up its appetite on a raw bone he had thrown it; and as Skelton watched, she dunged on his precious Communion cloth. The other had flown to the top of the rood-screen, where it sat motionless, obviously tired out.

By this time the poet had recovered his voice. Marching forward, he confronted the intruder in all the majesty of Skeltonic wrath, To be locked out of his own church, and when he did get in, to find this infamous scene enacted by a 'parson beneficed'! A torrent of abuse poured from him. At first the falconer was undisturbed; he was more worried about the shortcomings of his two birds. Then his temper gave way too. . . . Somehow Skelton got him out of the building in time to put his altar to rights and make ready for the service. It was the Eve of the Decollation of St. John.

But it was not Skelton's habit to lie down under any injury, real or assumed. Getting no apology out of the offender, he summoned him before the ecclesiastical court; in fact, he avers –

> whoso that lokes
> In the officialles bokes,
> There he may se and reed
> That this is matter indeed.[20]

But no trace has been found of any such action. Possibly there is good reason for it, since the defendant called on an ancient ally in 'maiden Meed,' as Langland named her, better known to us as Bribery. If the case was allowed to lapse under this pressure, then it is quite conceivable that the scribe, for a small extra fee, went back and erased all mention of it from his records.

For some reason, Skelton refuses to reveal the identity of his sporting parson. 'He shall be as now nameless,' declares the poet in his account of the scandal, *Ware the Hawk*! But then, right at the end, he gives way to a curious outburst that seems to have no connexion with anything that has gone before:

> Mased, witles, smery smith,
> Hampar with your hammer upon thy stith
> And make hereof a sickel or a saw,
> For though ye live a hundred yere, ye shal dy a daw![21]

This is the first and only mention of the falconer in the guise of a blacksmith; and its only imaginable point is that the name of the 'lewd curate' was – *Smith!* It is the commonest of names; but obviously the man in question must have held a living not very far, as the hawk flies, from Diss. (*Curate*, it should be observed, had not yet taken on its modern meaning, but was the equivalent of 'parson' or 'rector.') And a glance through Blomefield's monumental *Norfolk* brings to light a certain John Smith who was appointed Rector of East Wretham on 13 March 1503 and held it until his death in 1517. East Wretham is a small parish only fifteen miles from Diss. Very possibly, then, it was the Rev. John Smith of East Wretham whose amateur falconry culminated in this unedifying incident.[22]

§ 5. PARISH PESTS

In every small country town there are one or two of the faithful who manage to give more trouble than all the rest put together. Diss was no exception to the rule. Here the chief offender was a well-to-do old skinflint called John Clarke: wealthy enough to buy up the whole place, and old enough to behave as though he owned it. His familiar goatee had won him the nickname among the villagers of 'John Jay-beard' – though they scarcely used it, one fancies, to his face. It had not taken long for this old martinet to get at loggerheads with his equally irascible new parson. Here were all the makings of a first-class parochial feud. Gleefully, the inhabitants settled down to see which of them would win.

But Skelton had one supreme advantage – age. When he reached the village, Clarke was already a venerable senior; and between February and April 1506 the quarrel came to a decisive end. John Clarke died. In his will, after the usual bequests to charity, he arranged for 'a pilgrim, a priest, to be in prayer and pilgrimage at Rome the whole Lent, there to pray and sing for me and mine children, my father and mother, Robert and Cate, John Kew and Maut, Steven Brightled, and John Payne, the which I am in debt to.'[23] One can imagine the smile of triumph on the old man's face as he dictated this clause: not many of his fellow parishioners could afford the luxury of being prayed for in the capital of Christendom. And, if Skelton is to be believed, he was in life a miserly snudge indeed.

Some confusion has arisen over the fact that there was at this time another John Clarke at Diss. He was the soul priest already mentioned. But, although Skelton calls his enemy *holy*, the two men are not the same. Actually (as Nelson has pointed out), the soul priest was named as executor of old John's will. He was presumably some relation; though if he were old John's son, one would have expected him to figure elsewhere in the will.[24]

To-day, death would have ended the dispute: *de mortuis*, one is

92

taught. . . . But Skelton's age had no scruple as to the propriety of dancing over people's graves. In his joy at this God-given victory Skelton promptly scribbled out a mock trental (a thirty days' mass) for John Jay-beard – mostly in Latin, as befitted the occasion, but bubbling over at the end into uproarious English. It is dedicated to –

> John Clerc so bold
> Of names manifold:
> 'John Jay-beard' hight for shame,
> But 'Clerc' the clergy do him name.
> This holy father crossed the Styx
> In Anno Domini Fifteen Six.
> In all the parish pale of Diss
> Lived there no man like to this:
> Doing ill his greatest bliss,
> Double tongue, and heart remiss:
> With old age confected,
> With all men suspected,
> With all hate infected,
> *Sepultus est among the weeds,*
> *God forgive him his misdeeds!*°

Old John's stinginess, it appears, extended even to his food. He preferred 'a sheep's head soused in ale'[25] to any more elegant diet. Finally, as we said, the poem breaks into a riot of hearty English abuse, which winds up to a superb macaronic crescendo.

But opinionated moneybags were not the only adversaries that Skelton found at Diss. Another of his sworn enemies was the manorial bailiff, a man called Adam Uddersall. The name is most uncommon; and, though Skelton speaks of him as Diss-born, he may have been a humble connexion of the London stationer and notary, John Hothersall.[26] No doubt Adam came into collision with the poet when collecting fees for the Lady Margaret. In Skelton's eyes, he was a merciless bloodsucker; and when he died, about the same time as John Clarke, the poet composed another Latin epitaph for 'Adam Uddersall, otherwise known as Adam All-a-knave.' Like old Clarke, he was a notorious anti-clerical; but his gravest fault was that of rack-renting the luckless tenants:

> This beery bailiff did never fail
> To play the lord, Diss, over thee;
> An ingrate and a Pharisee,
> His swinish soul will never thee.
> He fed him fat upon his prey,
> Accurs'd as Agag every way:
> Now may this Cacus cruel of Diss
> Lie buried in the foul abyss!°

Skelton took very seriously his rôle of watchdog over the economic morals of his little community. In his day it was not only sharp practice, it was a sin, to overreach a neighbour. Let us hope that Adam's fate was a warning to his successor, Matthew Baron of Shelfanger, husbandman, who appears in the 1509 pardon-roll as Bailiff of Diss.[27]

§ 6. SKELTON'S MUSKET

Priestly celibacy had never been a great success in England. Back in the eleventh century three successive bishops of Norwich had been, according to Dr. Jessopp, almost certainly married men. And later centuries saw little change. At the beginning of the fourteenth, says an authority, many of the clergy were married, and though this was concubinage to the Church it was not otherwise illegal. With the Lollardy of the next century came increasing pressure from the ecclesiastical courts – which simply meant a decline in illicit marriages and an increase in temporary connexions to correspond. Offenders usually escaped with the fine of a few marks; sometimes the curious clause was added that the priest should 'swear friendship with' the woman's friends and parents, to preserve the general amity among his flock![28]

It was of little use for Henry VII to confirm the Church's right to imprison clerks convicted of *advoutrie fornicacion incest ou auscun auter carnall incontinencie.* Custom was stronger than law. Gloucester Diocese alone, in Skelton's day, produced case after case in which clergymen accused of these sins wriggled easily out of their penalties. Parson Winston of Awre, for example, 'appeared almost every year before the court; over and over again he was summoned, confessed, and was ordered a whipping in Hereford cathedral and elsewhere. At one time it was on account of a married woman, whose children, begotten by him, were boarded out in the village: in another, the trouble was over a single one. In the first instance he escaped by getting the whipping commuted for a small fine: the other case was dismissed on his successful plea that the child was not born in his house, but beyond the Severn. . . . Yet not only did he end his days as rector, but was actually appointed Rural Dean.' And Parson Winston was only one of a multitude.[29]

The main difficulty was aptly put in the mouth of Scoggin, as an apology for a clerical friend. He needed a woman about the house, declared the wit –

> To wash his dishes
> And to gather rishes;
> To milk his cow
> And to serve his sow;
> To feed his hen and cock,
> To wash his shirt and smock;
> His points to unloose
> And to wipe his shoes;
> To make bread and ale,
> Both good and eke stale;
> And to make his bed
> And to look [in] his head –

in short, to perform all the endless daily duties of a busy rectory.[30] If she happened to be young and winsome, the difficulty was so much the greater. But, with our long Protestant tradition, we should not fall into the error of assuming that the wedded priest was looked upon more leniently than one with a mere *focaria* or fireside companion. A letter of Sir Thomas Tyrrell to Cromwell is decisive on this point. 'The vicar of Mendlesham, my neighbour,' he wrote, 'hath brought home his woman and children into his vicarage, openly declaring how he is married to her, and she is his lawful wife. This act by him done is in this country [district] a monster and many do grudge at it.' Nor was the feeling confined to rural Suffolk. Both Henry VIII and Elizabeth found the idea repulsive and scandalous in the extreme. A priest with a wife, indeed! A few casual mistresses were infinitely preferable to this breach of the established decencies.[31]

It is in this light that we must consider the story first told by the antiquary Braynewode and developed in the *Merry Tales*. Of Braynewode I know nothing beyond the fact that he was an ardent Reformer, like his follower, 'bilious Bale.' The chronicle of his age that he compiled about 1549 began with Skelton[32] – the main reason being, evidently, that he took the poet for a literary John the Baptist of the new faith. He was profoundly mistaken, as it chanced. There is not a sign in all Skelton's work that he approved of a single Protestant tenet, and every indication that he was a vigorous opponent of the new heresy in all its forms. How on earth, then, could the misunderstanding have arisen? In fact, it is not at all hard to explain. Like Bale and Foxe an anxious hunter after precedents, Braynewode took Skelton's attack on Wolsey and the idler bishops as a proof that he was 'one of us' – subtly mining away at the foundations of Romanism itself. As it happened, he was wrong; but the initial error led him to interpret everything he knew of Skelton's life in the same Reforming terms. And among other things, he recorded how 'under Richard, pseudo-bishop of Norwich, Skelton kept a woman whom he had married (secretly, for fear of anti-Christ) in the guise of a concubine. At death's door, however, he confessed that he had always regarded her as his lawful wife.'[33]

One need not question the facts. There is no reason to doubt that Skelton kept a woman at Diss, when so many of his colleagues did the same. Probably, too, on his deathbed he tried to ensure that the poor creature was properly provided for. But the rest is entirely Braynewode. Regrettable as it may seem to the modern reader, Skelton must have regarded the lady less as his wife than as his 'remedy' – to use the Abbot of Walden's convenient term[34] – an Ovidian cure for the pangs of love. The conception allows of any degree of tenderness and genuine affection. Simply, it excludes marriage: and marriage was by no means its emotional equivalent for the Early Tudor. At all events, we may be fairly sure that Skelton accepted his celibacy as established – proper to the cloth. Tiresome as it may have been, it was nevertheless law canon and not to be questioned.

Remedies were another matter. Being human, and very much of his age, Skelton did keep a 'musket' at Diss. And with the usual consequences. A brood of young Skeltons began to make their appearance; and the more correct (and hostile) of his parishioners, objecting to this violation of decorum, complained to the Bishop. There are two versions of what followed. The earlier (that in the *Hundred Merry Tales*) was actually published while the poet was still alive, in 1525; and tactfully glosses over the real cause of the dispute. But its detail is liable to be all the more authentic for that:

> It fortuned there was a great variance between the bishop of Norwich and one master Skelton, a poet laureate, insomuch that the bishop commanded him that he should not come in at his gates. This master Skelton did absent himself for a long season; but at the last he thought to do his duty to him, and studied ways how he might obtain the bishop's favour; and determined himself that he would come to him with some present and humble himself to the bishop; and gat a couple of pheasants, and came to the bishop's place, and required the porter he might come in to speak with my lord.

The porter refused him entry; so Skelton tried to cross the moat over a fallen tree-trunk and got well soused before he reached the palace.

> Then quod Skelton:
> 'If it like your lordship, I have brought you a dish to your supper – a couple of pheasants.'
> 'Nay,' quod the bishop, 'I defy thee and thy pheasants also! And, wretch as thou art, pick thee out of my house; for I will none of thy gift!'
> Howbeit, with as humble words as he could, this Skelton desired the bishop to be his good lord and to take his little gift of him. But the bishop called him daw and fool oftentimes, and in no wise would receive that gift. This Skelton then, considering that the bishop called him fool so oft, said to one of his familiars thereby that, though it were evil to be *christened* a fool, yet it was much worse to be *confirmed* a fool of such a bishop; for the name of confirmation must needs abide. Therefore he imagined how he might avoid that confirmation; and mused a while, and at the last said to the bishop thus:
> 'If your lordship knew the names of these pheasants, ye would be content to take them.'

'Why, caitiff?' quod the bishop hastily and angerly, 'what be their names?'

'Iwis, my lord,' quod Skelton, 'this pheasant is called Alpha, [that] is *primus*, the first, and this is called O[mega], that is *nouissimus*, the last. And for the more plain understanding of my mind, if it please your lordship to take them, I promise you this Alpha is the first that ever I gave you, and this O[mega] is the last that ever I will give you while I live!'

At the which answer all that were by made great laughter, and all they desired the bishop to be good lord to him for his merry conceits. At whose request, or they went, the bishop was content to take him unto his favour again.[35]

While the early part of the story is traditional farce,[36] the naming of the pheasants has a strong air of authenticity, with its studied wit and its general clerical flavour. Skelton must have known Nick, the Bishop of Norwich, while he was Dean of the Chapel Royal. They had a good deal in common, these two; for Nick was also reputed to have a tongue as witty as it was sharp. His character has suffered rather because of his zeal for burning heretics: 'impure and bloody-minded' is Dyce's verdict on him. But this seems to be largely Protestant mythology. Certainly he did not lack courage; and his citing of Wolsey's bastard, Arch-deacon Winter, to appear before him led a terrified agent to describe the fiery old bishop as 'a devilish man.'[37] In his diocese he was renowned as a strict and active visitor; while Hoxne, where he spent most of his time, was within five miles of Skelton's parish. On all counts, then, it is probable that Skelton's 'incontinence' landed him in trouble with Bishop Richard.[38]

But, characteristically, he seems to have got his own back on the tale-bearers. The most famous of all the anecdotes about Skelton tells how, the Sunday following his interview with the Bishop, he accused his parishioners from the pulpit of being 'worse than knaves.'

'. . . and why, I shall show you. You have complained of me to the bishop that I do keep a fair wench in my house. I do tell you, if you had any fair wives, it were somewhat to help me at need. I am a man, as you be. You have foul wives, and I have a fair wench – of the which I have begotten a fair boy, as I do think, and as you all shall see.

'Thou wife,' said Skelton, 'that hast my child: be not afraid.

Bring me hither my child to me.' The which was done. And he, showing his child naked to all the parish, said:

'How say you, neighbours all? is not this child as fair as is the best of all yours? It hath nose, eyes, hands and feet, as well as any of your. It is not like a pig, nor a calf, nor like no foul nor no monstruous beast. If I had,' said Skelton, 'brought forth this child without arms or legs, or that it were deformed, being a monstruous thing, I would never have blamed you to have complained to the bishop of me. But to complain without a cause! I say, as I said before in my ante-theme, *Vos estis*, you be, and have be, and will and shall be knaves, to complain of me without a cause reasonable!'[39]

With its somewhat illogical argument, the story is probably not far from the truth. When Bale came to revise his jottings on Skelton, he added that the poet 'left children behind him.'[40] And both the manner of the reproof, and the acute pinning down of the complaint to jealousy, are thoroughly Skeltonic. In fact the poet, one would guess, understood his parishioners rather too well for their liking!

In 1873 a poem was printed in the *Athenæum* which was declared to be one of Skelton's, written to his 'wife' when she was about to have a baby. There is not a shadow of evidence for this fanciful theory; indeed, the poem is specifically entitled a *lady's* lament at separation from her lover. Only the inveterate itch for romantic 'revelations' could ever have led to the ascription.[41] But in any case it is more than doubtful whether Skelton ever wrote poems to the lady of Diss Rectory. She formed a part of his domestic life; and one suspects that Skelton, in common with most writers of his century, kept that side of him strictly detached from his poetic activities.

Perhaps we had better sum up at this point. Skelton did not regard any woman as his 'lawful wife.' As he could not believe it lawful for him to have a wife, that is obviously impossible. But, like a great many clergymen in his day from Cardinal Wolsey down, he kept a mistress, who looked after his Rectory, and gave him children and a woman's care; and in return, I have no doubt, he was very fond of her, and did his best to see that she was not left destitute when he died. At the same time he knew quite well that he was doing wrong. Later, in the person of Colin Clout, he notes how the people complain against their parish clergy:

PARISH PUMP

Of parsons and vicaries
They make many outcries:
'They can nat kepe their wives
From them for their lives!'
And thus the loselles strives
And lewdely sayes, by Christ!
Against the sely priest.
Alas and welaway!
What eiles them thus to say?[42]

vicaries=vicars.   loselles=rascals.   sely=silly, innocent.

The lament is poor simple Colin's, who cannot understand all the anti-clerical feeling he senses around him. But Skelton, with a 'wife' of his own, could hardly avoid knowing that this complaint, at least, was justified. Yet he never attempted to defend the practice. His only plea is that of erring mankind throughout the ages: 'I am a man, as you be.'

§ 7. PARISH DISCIPLINE

But this sizeable beam in his own eye was far from blinding Skelton to the shortcomings of his flock. One Thomas Pickerell, undeterred by the fate that had befallen Clarke and Uddersall, was rash enough to try conclusions with his Rector. We are not told exactly what his offence was – it might have been anything from heresy to cheating over his tithes. But whatever it was, Skelton decided to make an example of the sinner. In due course a summoner appeared, 'with fire-red cherubin's face,' at Pickerell's door, and ordered him to appear before the Consistory Court, on 3 December 1509, for enquiry into the health of his soul. Perhaps Thomas did not take the order seriously; perhaps this summoner, like Chaucer's, explained to him that 'Purse is the archdeacon's hell.' At any rate, when the court opened he was not there; and (in the usual way) he was declared contumacious. Nevertheless, the enquiry went on without him, and on 4 January, rather surprisingly, Pickerell was absolved from blame. (Had he taken the summoner's hint?) Still, it was necessary to uphold Church discipline: he *had* been summoned and had refused to obey. So a further summons was issued, ordering him to be present in ten days' time, to hear the court's verdict in person. But – whether through obstinacy or otherwise – Thomas paid no attention. A third and last chance was given him on 4 February: but no Pickerell turned up. Under the circumstances there was only one thing to do. On the same day he was formally suspended – that is, forbidden to enter the church until further notice.[43]

The interesting side of the case, for us, is its indication that, by the end of 1509, whatever trouble had arisen between Skelton and his bishop was now satisfactorily settled. The reconciliation of the *Hundred Merry Tales*, then, may well have been a fact. And, two years later, we have further proof that Bishop Nick had been 'content to take him unto his favour again.' In November 1511 the poet was appointed as arbitrator in a court case which concerned a neighbouring rector. The Rev. William Dale of Redgrave (five miles from Diss) had been accused by Thomas Revet – no doubt one of his parishioners – of various misdemeanours. On 6 November he denied everything, and the following week his name was cleared except in regard to one article. The next Friday Bishop Nick, having obtained the agreement of both parties, appointed Master Simon Driver, Doctor of Decrees, and Master John Skelton, Rector of Diss, to arbitrate between them. The love-day seems to have been a success; for a week later the Rev. Dale turned up at court with a letter of correction in his hand, and the Bishop was able to dismiss the case.[44]

It is a pleasant change to find Skelton, for once, helping to keep the peace instead of breaking it. But at any rate we can no longer doubt that – apart from his brief tiff with the Bishop over the wench who presided at his Rectory – Skelton was accepted as a responsible, if rather eccentric, member of the diocesan clergy in Norfolk. What is more, he showed every sign of having settled down for life as a country rector – even to lamenting, in pious Latin, the disastrous fire which laid waste his county town in 1507.

CHAPTER FIVE

BEAUTY AND –

And thanne I am so simple of port
That forto feignë som desport
I pleie with hirë litel hound,
Now on the bedd, now on the ground,
Now with hir briddës in the cage.
GOWER: *Confessio Amantis.*

WE MUST now turn back a little in our story. In 1485, after a married life of nearly eighteen years, Eleanor, wife of Richard Scrope, Esq., of Bentley, Yorkshire – a brother of the powerful Lord Scrope of Bolton – had been suddenly left a widow. They had been wedded in the little private chapel of Sheriff Hutton Castle; and their union had proved almost too fruitful, for Eleanor found herself with a family of no less than seven daughters and, very soon, a baby son to look after. Little Stephen was probably an ailing child; at all events, he died before reaching marriageable age, leaving the household entirely to the women.[1]

Wealthy widows were in no very enviable position in those troubled days, so Eleanor was quite ready to marry Sir John Wyndham of Norfolk when he proposed to her. Sir John was one of the New Men.[2] His father had been a swashbuckler of the luridest fifteenth-century cut, no less ready with his dagger than his tongue, and with a cunning to match either. A great rival of the Pastons, he too had had to fight for property which was rather dubiously acquired. We have already touched on the incident in 1461, when his wretched wife was dragged out of her house by the hair; and that earlier and disgraceful Friday brawl in 1448, when he had assaulted the Paston chaplain and called the Paston women 'strong whores' outside the church, must have lingered long in Norwich gossip.[3] But Wyndham's star was in the ascendant. He had made an excellent match in Lady Heveningham. With the aid of his grand connexions, he finally got back Felbrigg and lived down his violent past, to die in the odour of prosperity, at peace with the Pastons and the world.

Meanwhile, his son was continuing the good work. At an early age he had married no less a person than Margaret Howard, daughter of the Duke of Norfolk. So cleverly, though, did he steer his way through the shoals of party that when the Tudors came he was not imprisoned, like his brother-in-law, Surrey; and at the Battle of Stoke, in 1487, he was knighted for his prowess. When, in 1490, Surrey (out of prison by now) was established at Sheriff Hutton as warden of the marches, Sir John must have followed in his train. At any rate, when his first wife Margaret died, he set out to woo the delectable Yorkshire heiress, Dame Eleanor Scrope.

But Eleanor would not let herself be hustled into any sort of union. She was no green girl, and she had a large number of daughters to look after. That skilled climber, Sir John, was faced with a hard bargain: he was forced to buy the Yorkshire manors that had descended to Eleanor from her former husband.[4] It was on this condition that she demurely consented to take the more modest name of Wyndham.

Then came catastrophe. We have told how the 'rash and heady' Earl of Suffolk finally fled the country in 1501. Immediately, a round-up of his friends and relatives took place. Now, Suffolk's wife was Margaret, daughter of a Richard Scrope.[5] The White Rose Earl was therefore related, though in what degree is uncertain, to Sir John Wyndham. This was enough for the King. By the 13 February Sir John was safely under lock and key, and with him Sir James Tyrrell, Captain of Guisnes Castle. Tyrrell, who had entertained Suffolk on his first flight overseas, was not a victim the crowd was likely to shed tears over. It was he who in the dark days of Richard III, when Lieutenant Brackenbury jibbed at the order to assassinate the princes in the Tower, 'rode sorrowfully to London, and, to the worst example that hath been almost ever heard of, murdered those babes of th' issue royal.'[6] It was while awaiting sentence, now, that he confessed the crime.

On Monday, 2 May 1502, Wyndham and Tyrrell were solemnly tried at the Guildhall and sentenced to be drawn, hanged and quartered, together with a servant of Tyrrell's and a nameless shipman – possibly the man who had smuggled Suffolk abroad. For the two gentlemen, as usual, justice proved comparatively lenient. 'Upon the Friday following,' notes the London chronicler,

'. . . the said sir James and sir John, knights, were brought out of the Tower on foot and so led unto the scaffold and there beheaded; whose bodies and heads were after borne unto the Friar Augustins and there buried.' The shipman, unprotected by his rank, was drawn to Tyburn on a hurdle 'and there hanged and quartered.' Only Sir James's servant was, rather unaccountably, spared.[7]

Among the hushed spectators on Tower Hill who witnessed the execution that morning in early May was, in all probability, a young lady called Jane Scrope. Lady Wyndham would be expected to attend, and no doubt she brought along her eldest girls: it was customary, for this was, in a way, a funeral. Jane could not help feeling excited, and secretly rather proud, as she watched the grim ceremony. After all, Sir John was her stepfather; and besides, only the best people had their heads cut off. It was a sure guarantee of blue blood to have a member of one's family beheaded. . . . All the same, she had to close her eyes as the bright blade swished down at Sir John's kneeling figure. When she opened them again the assistants had thrown a cloth over the headless corpse, and from the crowd a rough coffin could been seen approaching the scaffold, on the shoulders of half a dozen frieze-clad and barefooted friars. Into it were lifted the bleeding remains and the cortège moved off, swaying solemnly, towards the tall steeple of the Austin Friars in the distance. Her real father, whom she could scarcely remember, lay in the church of the Black Friars, at the other end of the city.[8]

But now came the question: where were they all going to live? The Queen had packed off Suffolk's deserted wife to stay with the Duchess of Norfolk.[9] Lady Wyndham, however, had her own ideas. Her daughter Anne was a nun in the fashionable Abbey of Barking; and the family had been excellently entertained there, always. But Barking was rather expensive. . . . Suddenly, the memory of Carrow crossed her mind. It was small and therefore cheap; it lay just outside the gates of Norwich, where she had much enjoyed her odd shopping expeditions from Felbrigg. . . . Yes, they would go to Carrow. She would take a vow of chastity – perhaps, even, the veil itself, like that namesake of hers a century ago, Eleanor Lady Scrope, who had risen to be Abbess of the Minories.[10] But that needed thinking over. Meanwhile, she and her daughters would have comfortable lodgings while she tried to marry them off to the Norfolk gentry. It was a good district, as she knew, for eligible husbands.

And so, very shortly, another little procession set off in the direction of Norfolk. Fortunately, it was much smaller than it would have been a few years earlier. Dorothy had died in 1491; Anne had taken the veil; Elizabeth was already Viscountess Beaumont, and Eleanor probably wife to Thomas Wyndham – as she certainly was in 1505. Which left the anxious mother with only Mary, Jane and Catherine Scrope, and her one daughter by Sir John, Frances – plus, of course, Sir James, her private chaplain and general factotum, three men-servants, two maids, and their not inconsiderable baggage. Even so, it was a tiresome journey; and they must all have been glad to tumble stiffly off their palfreys at the hospitable gates of Carrow Abbey, tucked away in its wooded hollow at the southern edge of the city.[11]

§ 2. A PET SPARROW

Jane rather enjoyed Carrow. It wasn't as if she was expected to live like her grave sister Anne at Barking (though Barking hadn't been too bad). Apart from attending daily Mass – which she would have done, anyway – she was not expected to observe all the complicated rules of the Benedictine sisterhood. She was far too old – Jane was at least nineteen in 1503, and for some time her thoughts had been wandering towards marriage – to follow the strict discipline of the little girls from Norwich who were being 'educated' by the nuns. Occasionally she would look in while a lesson was in progress; but the teacher never seemed to know the simplest Latin words: Jane could have done better herself. For the most part, she just sat about, embroidering, mending or reading the *Four Sons of Aymon*, the *Morte d'Arthur* or (rather more secretly) tales like the Wife of Bath's in Chaucer:

> How she control'd
> Her husbandes as she wold
> And them to despise
> In the homeliest wise,[12]

which gave her ideas she thought best to keep to herself. At her age Jane didn't relish a beating. And at Christmas-time she joined in with a will when the youngest of all the novices was elected Lady Abbess, to a vast deal of giggling, and when the whole day's collection was scattered by the minx in mock-solemn largesse, ending in a grand feast with goose and plum pottage, and mumming to follow.[13]

Jane's pet sparrow, Phip, was equally against the rules, but nobody seemed to mind. Indeed, the nuns made a great fuss of him whenever they came into the guest-house. Jane had taught him all kinds of little tricks – to sit quite still on his jointstool when she cried 'Philip, keep your cut!' and then, when she called, fly up and catch at her lip. In the tiny velvet cap she had made for him Philip looked a handsome bird. Sometimes she would even take him into bed with her, and watch him snuggle between her breasts, or swoop down down at her little toe as she wiggled it about. He was wonderfully clever, too, at hunting down the fleas that made sleep almost impossible in the warm spring:

> Philip wold seke and take
> All the flees blake
> That he coud there espy
> With his wanton eye.[14]

Yes, Philip was useful as well as decorative. And he was a great favourite with the Poet Laureate, Master Skelton of Diss, who dropped in occasionally to visit her mother when he was in Norwich on business. He had got to know the Wyndhams quite recently, at the Earl of Surrey's residence of Kenninghall, which was only six miles from his parsonage. It was kind of him not to forget them now that Sir John was gone.

But Atropos had another blow in store for Jane. One sad day she ran into her room to find no sign of Phip – and Gib, the convent cat, licking his lips with a guilty look of unconcern in his green eye. This was real tragedy – far worse (though she would never admit it) than the execution of her stepfather. For days she was inconsolable, mooning about red-eyed and silent, and sniffing occasionally. She even tried to design Phip, as she remembered him, on her sampler, but every thrust of the needle seemed a stab. Then, one afternoon, she sat skimming idly through Caxton's *Reynard the Fox*. It had been the first book they'd given her in real print, and it was still a favourite. At the point where poor Cop, the cock's daughter, was killed by the wicked Reynard, she came upon the words:

> Tho began they *Placebo domine*, with the verses that to-longen.
> . . . When this vigil was done, and the commendation, she was laid in the pit, and there upon her was laid a marble stone polished as clear as any glass, and thereon was hewen in great letters in this wise: COPPE CHANTEKLERS DOUGHTER, WHOM REYNART THE FOX HATH BYTEN, LYETH HIER VNDER BURYED, COMPLAYNE YE HERFFOR, SHE IS SHAMEFULLY COMEN TO HER DEATH[15]

A familiar voice broke in upon her reading. Master Skelton – the very man she wanted to see! Would he – he was a famous poet – would he write her an epitaph for Phip like the one in Caxton, only longer, so that everyone should know what a wonderful bird he was? . . . The poet looked at loveliness in distress, and smiled, and nodded his head.

And that, or something like it, was the genesis of what is undoubtedly Skelton's most imitative, most original poem.

§ 3. A POEM GOES ASTRAY

As he sat down to fulfil this friendly commission, a host of precedents welled up into Skelton's mind. Corinna's lament for her parrot he knew by heart, with its mournful gathering of the fowls and the epitaph written by the lady herself. Then there was Martial – hadn't he got an epigram on Publius's lap-dog, and the memorial portrait that was painted of the poor beast? Statius too had something in the *Silvae*.[16] And this recent collection they were making such a fuss of, the almost complete Catullus they'd found under a wine-butt, was it? – that had a sparrow in it somewhere, if only he could remember how it went. *Passer mortuus* – no! . . . He must look at it again. A dainty thing. And, of course, the medieval Bird-Mass: that would fit in beautifully with Ovid. Slowly the traditional themes wove themselves together in the poet's head. Why not follow Caxton's hint and make it a real funeral service, calling upon all the pageantry of the Church One and Indivisible to lay to rest the soul of a sparrow? Had little Phip a soul? The Fathers were not very optimistic. But are not two sparrows sold for a farthing? and one of them shall not fall. . . .

So he began his little poem for Jane with the impressive opening antiphon of the Office for the Dead.[17] And as the sonorous syllables rolled softly out in the gloom of Carrow Chapel, back from its shadows came a whispered echo:

> *Pla ce bo*
> Who is there, who?
> *Di le xi*
> Dame Margery.
> *Fa re mi mi*
> Wherefore and why, why?
> For the soul of Philip Sparow
> That was late slain at Carow
> Among the Nones Blake. . . .

It is a matchless opening to a matchless poem – pronounced as in French the rhymes are perfect, of course. 'Dame Margery' would be the senior nun, Margery Carrow, who had been in the Abbey since before 1492 and was still there in 1514, then the oldest of the faithful.[18] It is she Skelton imagines conducting the service for Philip, while Jane stands by as chief mourner. And while the vespers are murmured around her, Jane's attention flickers back over her memories of dear Phip with all the vivid inconsequence of her girlish mind until, mysteriously, the elegy becomes transmuted into its opposite – a pæan to life, its inexplicable and absurd loveliness:

> Sometime he wold gasp
> When he saw a wasp,
> A fly or a gnat
> He wold fly at that,
> And pretily he wold pant
> Whan he saw an ant;
> Lord, how he wold pry
> After the butterfly!
> Lord, how he wold hop
> After the gressop![19]

I know no other poem with this direct evocation of an existence so unlike our own. Wry, swift and tender, it catches the breath with laughter and homage at once. So far, there is no parody of the burial service: only the antiphon, 'Despise not the work of thy

hands, O Lord!' gains a sly and unexpected overtone, coming as it
does after Jane's defence of her sparrow's antics in bed.

We must pass over the wealth of classical allusion, the Mass that
is sung by all the birds of the air, and Jane's strictly rhetorical
exclamatio against the feline assassin, lovely and amusing though
they are. We must pass over, too, the making of Philip's epitaph,
with its long preamble, in which, to prove her incompetence in
Latin, Jane recites several dozen of the English books she has
read and at length confesses with grief:

> Yet I am nothing sped
> And can but litel skill
> Of Ovid or Virgil
> Or of Pluthark
> Or Francis Petrark,
> Alcheus or Sapho
> Or such other poetes mo,
> As Linus and Homerus,
> Euphorion and Theocritus,
> Anacreon and Arion,
> Sophocles and Philemon,
> Pindarus and Simonides,
> Philistion and Phorocides. . . .[20]

Critics have been found to miss the humour of this so completely as
to reprove Skelton for putting this pompous list in the mouth of a
girl! . . . But we are brought to a halt at the *Commendations*.[21]

It is not usually realised that, technically, this part of the
poem corresponds to the Commendation of the Soul in the Mass-
book. But the Rev. Skelton was 'a man, as you be'; and he had
been far from blind, all along, to the blonde, grey-eyed, very
English beauty of Philip Sparrow's young mistress. Naturally,
as a Catholic priest, he had no business with such matters. Nor
are we able any longer to excuse him by pretending that Jane was
a mere schoolgirl, as Dyce piously hoped. Her father had died in
1485, and she was evidently not the youngest of the family. When
the poem was written, some time between 1504 and her mother's
death late in 1505, Jane must have been at least twenty – was,
more probably, twenty-two or three. Her charms, in a word, were

at their ripest; and they had not failed to work execution upon the susceptible parson of Diss. So, audaciously, he now proceeded to turn the last section of his poem into a commendation, not of the sparrow, but of its fair owner!

By this time he has given up all pretence of following the service. His thoughts are no longer on the other world, but, frankly and avowedly, on the beauty that perisheth. With a courtly apology for his daring, and a plea against 'the lover's foe' Envy (borrowed from Ovid via the *Roman de la Rose*), he sets out to present the perfections of Jane Scrope. It is all done, as we have noted earlier, with the utmost regard for decorum: one is encouraged to see the rhetorical textbook at his side. Moreover, he has precedents in plenty for this praise of fair womanhood – though few of them have approached the ravishing simplicity of

> But whereto shuld I note
> How often did I tote
> Upon her prety fote?
> It raised mine hert-rote
> To se her tread the ground
> With heles short and round.[22]

tote=peep.   raised=razed, cut.   hert-rote=heart's root.

And the reference to Jane's wart – it was even fashionable, perhaps, at this epoch, seeing that His Majesty also carried a wart 'a little above the chin.'[23]

But, however much Skelton protested the innocence of his tribute,[24] nothing could disguise the fact that the whole of the *Commendations* were a supreme blasphemy. It was not only that Jane replaced the soul of the defunct; more than that, she was, quite literally, deified. To-day, Latin has so lost its meaning for us that not a single critic seems to have noticed the point, and the most recent edition ignores it altogether; but throughout this section Skelton has substituted *domina* for *dominus*, Jane Scrope for God, in every one of his quotations!

These punctuate his eulogy in a kind of refrain, the third line of which is taken from a psalm, and sometimes the fourth as well – though this is often a hymn-fragment, a snatch of carol, or the like. Thus Psalm 119, verse 97, appears as

O how I love thy law, O Lady![25]

After this the aim of each quotation is unmistakable. 'Deal bounti-
fully with thy servant, that I may live,' Jane is urged; 'my lips
shall praise thee.' And, 'Teach me, O Lady, the way of thy
statutes. As the hart panteth after the water-brooks. . . .' And
again, 'Remember the word unto thy servant.' (Here, so that
there shall be no misunderstanding, Skelton adds with quaint
candour: '*I* am thy servant'!)[26] There is no need to continue. The
most surprising thing is Skelton's own surprise that Mistress Jane
should have objected to this remarkable apotheosis.

Not that there was anything wanton about such behaviour –
poetically. All through the Middle Ages Love had provided a
rival religion to what Chaucer calls that 'other holiness,' the
Church. Skelton was simply carrying the woman-worship of the
chivalric code to its natural conclusion.[27] Jane herself has become
the merest occasion for an exquisite and touching tribute to the
fresh concinnity of Woman. And indeed, any poet who worked in
the tradition would find it hard to avoid blasphemy.

But in this case the poet's very triumph was his undoing. Had he
been writing in stately rhyme-royal, even his blasphemy might
have passed as mere courtliness. But he was not. And in the new,
unorthodox, vital Skeltonic the innocent phrases took on a reality
so sharp as to be, socially, an insult. So Mistress Jane was duly
insulted – together with the poet Barclay and a number of other
respectable people. As we shall see, in his old age Skelton was
forced to write an apology for the success of *Philip Sparrow* –
itself no less brilliant a *tour de force* than the rest of this vibrant
and graceful, indiscreetly secular poem.

§ 4. JANE ENTERS THE WORLD

Philip Sparrow was apparently the first of the poet's ventures in
his new 'Norfolk' measure. Brie's simple test[28] is confirmed by the
fact that Jane's mother died at the end of 1505 – after which loss
Skelton would never have dared to write her a mock elegy on a
bird. On 11 December, no doubt feeling her end near, 'Elianore
Wyndam, widow, late the wife of Sir John Wyndam, knight,
whole of mind and in good remembrance, being (God be lauded)
at Carrow by Norwich,' prepared her last will and testament.[29]
Detailed instructions were given for her funeral. She even arranged
for a priest 'to sing for me in the university of Cambridge by the

space of two years' – at a salary of eight marks a year. Her husband's town of Felbrigg was not forgotten; nor were the 'poor prisoners within the castle of Norwich.' Having had both a husband and a son-in-law in the Tower, Lady Wyndham felt a special sympathy for the incarcerated.

After all these obligations of piety, she turned to her family. But first her patron, the Earl of Oxford, was given a diamonded gold cross, and his wife a ruby ring. This was a prudent form of insurance: it might help to preserve that nobleman's goodwill towards her orphans. (Actually it worked better than she had hoped, for the Earl ended by marrying her daughter Elizabeth – whom he had sheltered under his roof at Wivenhoe, together with her insane husband, the Viscount, since 1495.) Her two married daughters were suitably provided for. Dame Anne was bequeathed ten pounds – hardly the kind of legacy, one would have thought, for a nun. Next came Lady Wyndham's three unmarried daughters by her first husband: the Scrope trio. They were all presented with gowns – Jane receiving a 'gown of black velvet lined with crimson velvet, a gown of black cloth lined with shanks and a kirtle of tawny velvet.' Various other Wyndham relations were remembered; and all the residue of her property went to Mary, Jane and Catherine Scrope.

As her chief executor, Lady Wyndham appointed Thomas, the son of Sir James Tyrrell – who had been beheaded with her husband after making a full confession of how he had murdered the boy princes. Evidently Lady Wyndham had no theories about heredity.

Such anxiety as she had was more concerned with ensuring that her children were not left without a roof. Her will made careful arrangements 'that my household be sustained and kept at Carrow aforesaid well and honestly by the space of a month next after my decease.' So, when her mother died at the turn of the year, poor Jane was at least assured of a shelter for thirty days. What she did then we do not know: probably she went to live with one of her married sisters. But it had become more urgent than ever, now, that she should find a husband of her own. And eventually she did what her mother must have had in mind from the beginning – she married one of the numerous well-to-do squires in the neighbourhood.

Thomas Brews, Esq., came of staunch old East Anglian stock. The eldest of the line had held the title of knight for a couple of centuries now, taking his turn as J.P. and sheriff with the other prominent gentlemen of the locality. His grandfather, Sir Thomas Brews of Salle, Norfolk, married the sister and heiress of Sir Gilbert Debenham, thus bringing the pleasant manor of Topcroft into the family. For a time the estate had been split up between his two sons, and then the broad Brews acres were united under Thomas's father, Robert. He seems to have divided his days between Topcroft Hall, in Norfolk, a few miles north of Bungay, and the fine old thirteenth-century manor-house of Little Wenham, Suffolk – still to be seen, its warm Flemish brick almost untouched by the march of time. At Robert's death on 7 September 1513,[30] his son Thomas was thirty-two.

It was Thomas's Aunt Margery who had married John Paston the youngest, and provided almost the only genuine love-letters in the vast correspondence of that business-like family. One wonders if Jane too fell in love with Thomas, and wrote her 'good, true and loving valentine' that 'if that ye could be content with that good, and my poor person, I would be the merriest maiden on ground'[31] or whether, as so often, she regarded him as a necessary evil in her career as a woman. Married they were, at all events; and in due course (as their funeral brass tells us) they begot five children – John, the eldest, and Giles; and three girls, of whom Ursula (like Jane's sister Anne) became a nun in Denny Abbey.[32]

But Mrs. Brews did not enjoy her husband's society for very long. He died little more than a year after his father. To 'Jane, my well-beloved wife' he left Topcroft Hall. His mother Catherine was to have Little Wenham and the neighbouring manor of Vaux as long as she lived; they were then to revert to his wife. Jane was also to have 'all my moveables, as well those that be at Wivenhoe as those that be at Wenham.' Wivenhoe suggests that she may have met him through staying with her sister at the Earl of Oxford's.[33]

Jane never married again. She saw her two Scrope sisters wedded in their turn, both to good East Anglian gentlemen. Altogether the orphans hadn't done so badly. As the wife of a prominent Norfolk squire, Jane herself appeared at Queen Catherine's coronation in 1509, together with her sister, Mrs. Jerningham. But on the whole she seems to have preferred the peace of Topcroft or Little Wenham to the petty rivalries of Queen Catherine's suite. Although

Mrs. Jerningham attended her on the glittering Field of Cloth of Gold, in 1520, Jane's name is not mentioned. She was still living, however; and, as we shall see, the Brews dignity was to cause our poet trouble as late as 1522.[34]

When she died I have not been able to determine. She certainly survived the most distinguished member of the family, Elizabeth, for on her death in 1537 the Countess left her a gilt basin and ewer.[35] Jane herself was buried side by side with Thomas in their church of Little Wenham, where their portrait brass still remains – Thomas clean-shaven and long-haired, wearing his elaborate suit of Tudor armour; Jane in the typical square-cut gown of her day, fur-bordered, with penthouse cap and a long chain ending in a sweetmeat pomander. Not unnaturally, perhaps, there is no sign of the 'wart upon her cheke' – nor, alas! of the loveliness which had so intoxicated Skelton in the days of his first coming to Diss.

CHAPTER SIX

THE BEAST

A tall old Hag, whose soul-gelding ugliness would chill to
eternal chastity a cantharidized Satyr.

COLERIDGE: Letter of 4 February 1796.

§ 1. A TAVERN IN LEATHERHEAD

ONE BRANCH of the Skelton clan resided at Reigate
in Surrey, and supplied attendants to the Duke of Norfolk. (They were still there in the time of Elizabeth,
when Robert Skelton is described as the Queen's servant.)[1]
Perhaps they were relatives of the poet, and it was during a visit
to them that he discovered the 'Running Horse' at Leatherhead
near by. But whatever brought him to the little Surrey township,
Skelton's nose for character soon led him to the disreputable
alehouse run by the immortal Elinor Rumming.

She was no creature of the imagination, Elinor – as Brie
thought. In August 1525 the Leatherhead aletaster certified that
Alianora Romyng, common tippler of ale, was selling 'at excessive
price by small measures'; she was duly fined 2d.[2] A 'Running
Horse,' partly dating from Skelton's day, still stands near the
town bridge and claims to be the scene of our poem.

Elinor's tavern had nothing in common with the fashionable
'Eagle' of Westminster, kept so strictly in order by Long Meg. A
dingy and squalid boozing-ken, this: just an earth floor littered
with stinking rushes, a couple of beer-stained trestle-boards and
benches, and a special table at one end for the quality. Elinor's
hens strutted freely in and out of the open door and, when the
alewife's back was turned, in would wander, snuffling and
grunting, her tribe of porkers.

Like every other taverner, Elinor made her own ale, and she
had an infallible formula for speeding the fermentation – picked
up, she averred, from a passing Jew. It was only a matter of
sending her chickens to roost over the mash-vat:

Than Elinor taketh
The mash-boll, and shaketh
The hennes dong away
And scommeth it into a tray
Whereas the yeest is
With her mangy fistes. . . .[3]

It always worked, she would tell you confidentially.

At any rate, she never seemed to lack customers. Skelton had dropped in during the morning, while most of the menfolk were busy, and all of Elinor's clientèle were women, slipping in for a quick draught before their husbands came home from work. And what a superb set of slatterns they were! Barefoot and blowsy, hair uncombed, dress awry, they came panting down the rise for a taste of Elinor's home-brewed, each carrying their bit of household stuff to swop for a swig of ale. It was like some unholy tithing ceremony! Nothing came amiss to Elinor, from a clothful of London pins to a wedding-ring.

And as the giggling and nudging rose to a frank hoot of pothouse laughter, Skelton found what he had been looking for. *Philip Sparrow* had told the world how a poet reacted to beauty. It hadn't been received too favourably either. Well, now it was Circe's turn. He would spin the coin to tails and show them the other side. How would they like *that*, he wondered, picking up his blackjack for the last time as Drunken Alice collapsed in her corner?

§ 2. PRECEDENTS

As usual, there was nothing extraordinary in Skelton's idea. Ever since Chaucer, the Querelle des Femmes had been the source of countless poems, arguments, treatises in England as in France. Was Woman the sublime paragon of medieval chivalry, flawless, inaccessible; was she, rather, very much like Man himself, an imperfect partner, neither impossibly good nor execrably bad; or was she in fact his inferior by God established – the *sexus sequior*, fit only to darn his stockings and dandle his children, meekly attending the while her lord's good pleasure? Several of the *Canterbury Tales*, as Jane knew, had dealt with this problem, putting forward ideals as different as the patient dummy Griselda and the shrewd, pentagamous Wife of Bath.

In his wise and smiling way, Chaucer had held for the moderate
solution; but his followers tended to see the question simply along
class lines. Lydgate's courtly allegories still gave one the dream-
lady of romance, much too good to be true or interesting. Only in
his *Mumming at Hertford* did he condescend to realism – and then
it was avowed comic slumming. The six men who appeal to the
King against their heavy-handed wives are all yokels. Such
behaviour was only true of low life.

All the same, it was well and amusingly observed. When Hob
the Reeve, for example, came home for the midday meal –

> Then sitteth Beatrice bowling at the nale,
> As she that giveth of him no manner tale;
> For she all day, with her jowsy noll,
> Hath for the colic pooped in the bowl,
> And for headache, with pepper and gingere
> Drunk dolled ale to make her throat clear;
> And cometh her home, when it draweth to eve,
> And then Robin, the silly poor Reeve,
> Find none amends of harm ne damage
> But lean gruel, and suppeth cold pottage.[4]

Any complaint immediately brought the distaff into play – a
weapon at which they were all equally skilled.

This tradition of the boozy housewife was as old as the miracle
plays. When Noah called his wife to come into the ark and escape
the approaching Flood, it was sometimes the cue for a Gossips'
Song, in which the neighbours urged her to stay for a parting
drink. And there were many popular ballads which took the
women's side and described with gusto their forgatherings at the
ale-bench.[5]

But sometimes the picture was less amiable. Following up the
portrait of the Veck (the famous crone of the *Roman de la Rose*),
the *sottes chansons* of fifteenth-century France delighted to evoke
the figure of some grotesque old harridan. Occasionally she was
an innkeeper of doubtful repute.[6] Such was the heartless and
flippant basis on which Villon erected his wonderful *Ballade of the
Fair Armouress*.

All of these were familiar enough to Skelton. And the sight of
Elinor Rumming, as she shuffled around her filthy den, gave him

THE BEAST

the notion of combining them in a riotous Hymn to Ugliness, that would be at once a description of the Witches' Sabbath he had just witnessed and a satire upon it. He would bring in the gossips, just as he had seen them; and Elinor would serve as a stupendous type or symbol of the gluttonous squalor over which she presided – as Jane Scrope had been his symbol for the delicate and evasive loveliness of life.

§ 3. A MAD MUMMING

This time the portrait came first – but there can be no doubt of its being a deliberate parallel to Jane's. The prologue, in fact, is nothing more than a lengthy and brilliant Discommendation of Elinor. Its detail follows, as strictly as before, the *schema* of Geoffrey de Vinsauf: only they are blemishes now instead of perfections that he is describing. Bit by bit the dreadful creature is unveiled before us, wrinkled and drivelling; yet with a verve that more than counteracts its horror. Caught up by the rapid jog-trot of the verse, we actually find ourselves enjoying the spectacle evoked by these fabulous rhymes:

> Her eyen gowndy
> Are full unsoundy,
> For they are blered;
> And she gray-hered,
> Jawed like a jetty.
> A man would have pity
> To se how she is gumbed,
> Fingered and thumbed,
> Gently jointed,
> Gresed and anointed
> Up to the knockles,
> The bones her huckels
> Like as they were buckels
> Togeder made fast. [7]

gowndy=mattery. unsoundy=unsound. gumbed=gummed. huckels=hip-bones.

But even Elinor has her share of female vanity. Her everyday cloak may be forty years old if it is a day:

118

And yet I dare say
She thinketh herself gay
Upon the holy-day,
Whan she doth her aray
And girdeth in her gites
Stitched and pranked with pletes. . . . [8]

gites=gowns, petticoats.

with a kirtle of Bristol red, and a Sunday headdress towering up,
over its penthouse frame, like some strange gipsy concoction.
The final touch, however, gives the game away:

Whan she goeth out
Herself for to shew,
She driveth down the dew
With a pair of heles
As brode as two wheles. . . . [9]

driveth . . . dew=cf. dial. 'dew-beater,' clumsy-footed person.

It is no use Skelton's appealing to Geoffrey here. Inevitably this
takes us back to the 'heles short and round' of Philip's dainty
mistress, and the havoc they wrought in the poet's heart. The
two portraits, we now see, form a diptych, a female January and
May, to illustrate the astounding range of which God is capable in
that most mysterious of his creations, Woman.

But Elinor's *descriptio* is only the prelude to the poem itself.
This is an uproarious account of her customers and their all-too-
human behaviour – in what is surely the most drunken verse
ever written. The seesaw changes of sound and rhythm have the
physical effect of alcohol:

Another sort of sluttes,
Some brought walnuttes,
Some apples, some peres,
Some brought their clipping-sheres,
Some brought this and that,
Some brought I wote nere what,
Some brought their husband's hat,
Some podinges and linkes,
Some tripes that stinkes.

THE BEAST

But of all this throng
One came them among,
She semed half a leche
And began to preche
Of the Tewsday in the weke
Whan the mare doth keke,
Of the virtue of an unset leke,
Of her husbandes breke;
With the feders of a quale
She could to Burdeou sail,
And with good ale-barm
She could make a charm
To help withal a stitch:
She semed to be a witch.[10]

sort=set.   keke, leke, breke=kick, leek, breeks.   quale=quail.

The surrealism is only an accident of time; it has sense enough when examined. And yet free association is beginning – under the nefarious influence, it seems, of Elinor's ale. Only Skelton never lets his rhyme quite get the better of his reason, which remains tart and pungent as Margery Milk-duck's cheese. It is on this account that all his gossips live and breathe, from halting Joan and onion-sided Maud to the last and rarest of the crew: the affected 'prick-me-dainty' who turns out to have no money. The headlong rhyme does not prevent this anonymous 'lady' from being caught with an accuracy more deadly than the camera's. One cannot do better, here, than borrow Skelton's own tribute to Chaucer: 'No word he wrote in vain.'

In the main, the critics have shown themselves rather baffled by *Elinor Rumming*. Coarse and vigorous humour of this sort will always lead to misunderstanding in Anglo-Saxony. Professor Berdan's is the orthodox reaction. 'The reader,' he says, 'has the unwilling conviction that descriptions written with such gusto show a familiarity with disreputable resorts unexplained in a scholar and an enjoyment of them undesirable in a Churchman.'[11] The familiarity needs less defence to-day than it did, perhaps, in 1920. As for the enjoyment, we may as well admit that Skelton was no more easily disgusted than Chaucer or Shakespeare. There is no moral obliquity in question: he merely accepted, with a laugh, the monstrous richness of experience.

A MAD MUMMING

Skelton was not always in this frame of mind; far from it. Indeed, at the end of this very poem he claims it is an object-lesson for the drunken sluts who may read it. But that is convention. In fact, *Elinor Rumming* represents an equilibrium which he attained all too rarely in his turbulent verse.

We must not lose æsthetic proportion in the moral issue. Much reprinted though it is, *Elinor Rumming* is far from being the poet's masterpiece. Mr. Richard Hughes would give it a peculiar status as 'abstract' poetry:

> I do not speak of it as a precursor of the 'realistic' school of poetry: it is more valuable than that. It is the processional manipulation of vivid impressions, the orchestration, the *mental* rhythm which strikes me. So far from calling it a realistic poem, I would call it one of the few really abstract poems in the language. Its aesthetic effect is that of a *good* cubist picture (or any picture dependent on form for its value).[12]

This is gallant but misleading. Rhetorically, the Skeltonic itself is sheer form: rhyme, *repetitio*, alliteration. But in the better poems these do not, it seems to me, overshadow what is stated; they merely underline it. And the effect of *Elinor Rumming*, caricature though it may be, is undoubtedly more realistic than, say, the *Bouge of Court*. With this poem Skelton has finally broken with the courtly tradition. Its vocabulary and syntactic freedom, no less than its subject and metre, make it a popular tract. But it is too jovial for a satire of low life, and too detached for a vulgar panegyric of drunkenness. On the other hand, it is the most indisputably *national* piece our literature had yet seen. 'Rhyming Rowlandson,' exclaimed Mr. Edmund Blunden: that is nearer the mark. No other country could have produced it, any more than a Rowlandson print. In *Elinor Rumming* Skelton worked, for the first time, a thoroughly native vein of broad comedy – with astounding success.

Yet we should never forget that deep down under its farce there *is* a realisation of the punishment visited upon gluttony, and, too, the harder punishment of Time's wheel – Jane Shore, once the merriest harlot of them all, and now nothing left but rivelled skin and hard bone. . . . Otherwise, why should Skelton have so consciously written his vulgar *Tunning* as a companion piece to the exquisite tenderness of *Philip Sparrow*?

THE BEAST

Which brings us back to biography. When did Skelton write the *Tunning*? Noting its resemblance to *Philip Sparrow*, most critics have agreed to place it with that poem, in the first decade of the century. And Brie's metrical test seems to clinch this finding.

But let us reflect a moment. When Skelton painted her portrait, Elinor was already a hag 'well worn in age.' Grey-haired, bleareyed, she has used the same cloak for forty years. That is precisely why he picked on her: a stooping crone to match his lissom Jane. Now, is it conceivable that a woman as decrepit as this in 1505-10 could have survived to appear before the court in 1525, accused of bilking her customers? Conceivable, yes; some women of the time did live to a great age. But, when every allowance has been made for poetic licence, it can hardly be described as likely.

When, thus cautioned, we turn to examine the objective test of Professor Brie, we find that in fact *Elinor Rumming* is much nearer *Colin Clout*, stylistically, than it is to *Philip Sparrow*. And *Colin Clout* we can date with certainty in the middle of the year 1522.[13]

This simple fact at once explains a host of anomalies. It removes from the Diss period the only poem which deals with events outside Norfolk. And it throws another and a startling light on that most personal of Skelton's productions, the *Garland of Laurel*. We shall be dealing with the *Garland* later. Meanwhile, in *Elinor Rumming* we have stumbled across one of the two main causes which begat that astonishing apologia of 1523.

In it, you remember, Skelton defends his claim to fame by reciting a list of his works. When he reaches *Philip Sparrow* he pauses to remark:

> Yet sum there be therewith that take grevance
> And grudge thereat with frowning countenance:

whereupon he plunges into more than a hundred lines of brilliantly clever but (one cannot help thinking) untimely defence of his poem . . . in Skeltonics. Ah, say the critics, a reply to Barclay's attack in 1508: written long before, and inserted here merely for ornament! Not at all. Skelton himself gives us the reason:

> Alas, that goodly maid,
> Why shuld *she* be afraid,
> Why shuld *she* take shame. . . ?[14]

Jane herself has joined the chorus of detraction! That is what has galled him into this belated reply. And the Latin lines at the end make it clear that this outburst was a recent one. 'Your obsequies,' says Skelton to the sparrow, 'were earnestly begged of me by the fair Jane Scrope. Why is she *now* ashamed of my song?' And Philip answers oracularly: 'It is indeed late – but so much the less the scandal!'° What had happened to make the middle-aged Mrs. Brews suddenly turn on the poet for having written *Philip Sparrow* nearly twenty years earlier?

The answer, we now realise for the first time, is *Elinor Rumming*. In the thick of his campaign against Wolsey, Skelton had turned for relief to this riotous grotesque. It had seemed merely good poetics to match it with his early piece in praise of a girl. But imagine the feelings of Mrs. Brews, now no longer a 'blossom of fresh colour,' when she came upon the description of Elinor! Ladies have never been distinguished for objective criticism; and Jane must have jumped to the conclusion, as she noted echo after echo, that the poet was engaged in a cruel caricature of – herself!

If we reread the *Garland* in the light of this discovery, we can understand why Skelton chooses to describe himself so repeatedly as 'glad to please and loth to offend.' We can understand why he gets the Countess of Surrey to stand up for him, specifically, as the ladies' panegyrist:

> For yet of women he never said shame,
> But if they were counterfetes that women them call,
> That list of ther lewdness with him for to brall.

And finally, we realise why, in the catalogue of his poems, he chose to lump together two poems as dissimilar as —

> Also the Tunning of Elinor Rumming,
> With Colin Clout. . . .[15]

In fact, as everyone knew, Skelton delighted to offend, while his portraits of women are almost all 'counterfeits,' unworthy of the name. His self-portrait in the *Garland*, indeed, is comically wide of the mark. Why? Partly, we now see, because he had been rash enough to complete his picture of Beauty, years later, with another of the Beast – and Beauty, conscious of her fading, had had a tantrum!

Book Three

ORATOR

CHAPTER SEVEN

ORATOR ROYAL

Though some saith that youth ruleth me,
   I trust in age to tarry:
God and my right and my duty,
   From them shall I never vary.

HENRY VIII.

§ 1. MAGNIFICENCE

THE SIGH of relief that went up on 21 April 1509, when Henry VII died at his new palace of Richmond, was untempered. Although only fifty-two, he had outlived his rôle; and in his place Englishmen saw a youth whose promise surpassed the wildest dreams of an age with a passion for heroes. Prince Henry really seemed to have everything. When full allowance has been made for the current idiom of adulation, he remains an astounding specimen of budding royalty. A splendid blonde animal, glowing with vigour, he caught the eye wherever he went. Yet his appetites were not limited like those of his athletic friends. Music moved him profoundly. Of course, he spoke French and Latin; even a little Italian. In his graver moods the family piety showed through: later he would argue endlessly with Wolsey over Thomistic quiddities, and write a book against Luther. But it was all done with the same boyish verve, the same enthusiasm, with which he flung himself on his adversary in the tiltyard, or played tennis until his skin gleamed through his shirt, or tired out relay after relay of hunters.

That was what struck everyone – the extraordinary range of Henry's talents. He captivated the women by his angel face, the courtiers by his love of sport, the clergy by his obvious devoutness, and the humanists by his modest declaration that 'without them we should scarcely exist.' Set against the drab background of his father's parsimony, the ardent youngster shone like a jewel.

Mountjoy was especially delighted. He had been watching Henry develop from the plump, auburn boy with the rosebud mouth and the boyish taste for fun and horseplay into the massive adolescent who came in sweating from the stables to compress that mouth over his Livy or Quintius Curtius. Like all of Erasmus's disciples, Lord Mountjoy had an unbounded faith in the power of the written word to mould character. And Henry responded with a touching zeal to his exhortations. If the boy was restive under the strict régime of the last few years – well, who wouldn't be? And in fact his behaviour in the first month of his reign lifted Mountjoy's hopes sky-high. 'The heavens laugh,' he wrote lyrically to Erasmus at the end of May, 'the earth exults, all things are full of milk, of honey and of nectar! . . . Our King does not desire gold or gems or precious metals, but virtue, glory, immortality.' And he begged the scholar to drop everything and hurry to the side of a prince who would say to him, 'Accept our wealth and be our greatest sage.'[1]

Mountjoy was not the only man to talk in superlatives of the change. Thomas More, too, wrote of the new Achilles in the woman's garb of his beauty, who combined the prudence of his father with his mother's sweetness and the pious zeal of his grandmother. While, away in quiet Diss, Henry's old tutor gave vent to his feelings in a simpler but more memorable image – an image from which was to spring the entire Tudor Myth:

> The Rose both White and Rede
> In one Rose now doth grow,

he sang. Soon, Edward Hall was to build up the whole of his capacious History on the basis of this 'godly matrimony,' this union of York and Lancaster which put an end to a century of strife and dissension. And Skelton felt about it in much the same way.

Even in this panegyric, though, Skelton found it impossible to refrain from 'patriotic mordacity.' Three of its eight stanzas are devoted to the foxes, wolves and bears that have been laying waste the land. But now, he cries, is the time of reckoning:

> Therefor no more they shall
> The commons overbace,
> That wont wer over all,
> Both lord and knight, to face. . . .[2]

No one could doubt who 'they' were – the beasts of prey Skelton
had in mind. Nor was his confidence misplaced. One of Henry's
first and most popular acts was to put in the Tower his father's
hated tools, Empson and Dudley. From there, on the flimsy charge
of having raised arms against their sovereign, they were hurried
to the block. If the strict justice of his proceeding may be questioned, at any rate the intention was unmistakable. Young Henry
was wiping the slate clean.

His marriage to his brother's widow, Catherine, their coronation, the death of his grandmother the Lady Margaret, followed
on each other's heels. The last event was symbolic. From now on
the presiding deity at the Court of Henry VIII was to be Youth.
Youth! – it is the theme of nearly all the songs he wrote so freely
in this period:

> Virtue it is, then, youth for to spend
> In good disports which it doth send. [3]

It was a natural reaction against the frugal ways of the previous
reign, with its perpetual darning and decorum. Catherine was
swept off her feet in a sudden carnival of merriment, as strange and
delightful to her as it was to her overgrown boy of a husband.
Now, it was banquet after banquet of 'sumptuous, fine and
delicate meats,' each of them sandwiched between a joust or day's
hunting, and a 'pageant' which had taxed all the resources of the
revels office. In his desire for novelty, indeed, sometimes the fun
became a trifle crude, as when a pageant was trundled in in the
manner of a park with palings of Tudor white and green, and real
deer crouched among the pastiche trees: 'the which park or device,
being brought before the queen, had certain gates thereof opened,
the deer ran out thereof into the palace, the greyhounds were let
slip and killed the deer; the which deer so killed were presented
to the queen and the ladies.' [4]

But however crude the fun, it was invariably clean. Henry was
almost embarrassingly definite about the moral tone of his
amusements:

> Pastimes of youth some time among,
>   None can say but necessary.
> I hurt no man, I do no wrong;
>   I love true where I did marry, [5]

he carolled, with more conviction than elegance. Indeed, even the extravagance of these early years has been somewhat exaggerated. The loving detail of his hero's festivities indulged in by Hall has tended to give a false impression. It was not until he embarked on the grander game of war that Henry succeeded in making much impression on the sixty million or so (in modern money) bequeathed him by his economical father. Meanwhile, he spent his time in a whirl of athletics by day and revelry by night – a good-humoured giant at play. And few people grudged him what he termed his 'innocent and honest pastimes.'[6] They were, after all, those proper to a young paladin of the Renaissance.

§ 2. POET'S COMPLAINT

Skelton, we have said, had to all appearances made Diss his permanent home. From the day he left London in 1503, none of his surviving poems goes farther than Norwich for its subject. He had even changed his style to emphasise the break. Unofficially, at least, he was a married man; and, now reconciled with his Bishop, there seemed every reason for his settling down for good in his East Anglian rectory.

But the news from Richmond set his pulse fluttering un-expectedly. So his pupil would be Henry VIII! For the past seven years he had seen little of the lad; but he had listened eagerly to the rumours of his fabulous strength and cleverness. This fine youth was partly his creation. Surely, now that he was King, he would show some appreciation of his old 'creancer'?

Possibly, like More and Hawes and the others, Skelton came up to London to present his *Laud and Praise* to the stripling monarch. If so, there is no sign of it now among the royal manuscripts: his autograph copy lies, as we have said, buried among the revels accounts. As for his advancement, most probably he pinned his faith on the Lady Margaret. It was she who had thought him good enough to teach her grandson, and who had rewarded him for it with his rectory. Henry, it was notorious, still relied on her ab-solutely. That pushing priest Wolsey was said to be in her bad books, and he had certainly not yet shared in the royal bounty. . . . But Skelton's hopes were to be rudely shattered. On 29 June, only a few days after the Coronation, the Lady Margaret breathed her last in the Abbot's house of Cheyney Gates at Westminster.

Henry was no longer his grandmother's darling echo; henceforth he stood upon his own sturdy legs.

Skelton soon perceived the difference. There was no official place for the old tutor at the Coronation, though half the country seemed to have been invited – yes, even Jane Brews. True, on 21 October the poet's name appeared on the royal pardon-roll which signalled every new reign: but there again no special favour was implied. Traitors and debtors apart, everyone who had in any way come into conflict with the authorities – and who, in those days, had not? – hastened to get his name included, from Master Thomas Wolsey down to Adam All-a-knave's successor at Diss.[7] Perhaps we can understand Henry's point of view. No one likes to be reminded unnecessarily of one's boyhood follies. Henry was young enough to wish to forget the past. It smelt too sharply of thrift and discipline and a long-faced older generation. How could he swagger comfortably before a man who personified all that? Besides, Skelton was hopelessly old-fashioned in his ideas. Mountjoy had spent half his time correcting the stupid notions he had so carefully drilled into his pupil's head. Henry was now all for Greek and the new eloquence: his Court was to be (among other things) a humanist academy. There was no room for his sharp-tongued old dominie in *that* society. They would only laugh at him.

Skelton persisted, however. Before 1512[8] – probably, as was the custom, on New Year's Day 1511 – he had made a conscious appeal to the new King's finer feelings. Going back to the little homily he had composed for him in 1501, the *Speculum*, he wrote it out carefully with his own hand; adding his first poem in Henry's praise (written when he was created Duke of York) and his last (apparently a birthday gift for 28 June 1509 or 1510).[9] These he had bound in leather, and presented the little volume to Henry.

If the King took the trouble to leaf it through, three things would catch his attention. The first was that Skelton had adopted a new motto. Set under each of his poems, it ran: 'Jupiter Feretrius grant that I waste no more time beside Eurotas!'° What could it mean? He was not referring, as has been thought,[10] to the 'chill Eurotas' of Ovid. No, as Henry would doubtless recall, Skelton had in mind a phrase from Polydore Vergil's *Book of Proverbs*: they had probably gone through it together soon after it was published in 1498. Polydore explains how in the Corinthian portico at Rome, near the Flaminian Circus, there was a famous fresco of the Spartan river

Eurotas. The idlers that haunted the place were said to 'sit beside Eurotas': and so the phrase came to be used for doing nothing.[11] In other words, Skelton was not lamenting an exile, but simply pointing out that his talents were being neglected. He could be of use to Henry; whereas now he sits twiddling his thumbs in idleness.

But possibly the hint was too roundabout. And Skelton had no intention of allowing his meaning to lie undetected. So the little collection closes with a prose *Complaint* which deserves translation in full:

> *Skelton Laureate, once royal tutor, in mute soliloquy with himself, as a man wholly given over to oblivion, or like one struck dead through the heart:*
>
> Alas for our trust in gods and men! How comes it that I am marked off from all others by such, and so singular, a fate – I, upon whom neither the king's munificence nor fortune's blessing has so far deigned to smile more richly? You skies, you seas, to whom shall I ascribe this? Ah, shall I impute it to the gods – angered with me perchance? Let me not commit so great a folly. But shall I then impute to so mighty and generous a king the conspicuous blemish of inadequate liberality? From such a thought may that god preserve us who, best and greatest, weighs all with the most scrupulous justice in the scale of his unsearchable liberality!°

The phrasing is still loftily circumspect – almost comically so; but it conceals the horns of a dilemma. Skelton's misfortune is due *either* to the gods *or* to the King. To accuse the former is blasphemous: *ergo.* . . ! Skelton could never resist a good defending argument.

Even as he makes his farewell bow, however, the dominie in him rises once more to the surface. 'Rule,' he bids his former pupil, 'be not ruled. Hark to Samuel; read Daniel. Banish Ishmael . . . banish . . . banish. . . !'° Here, as early as 1511, we meet for the first time what was to be the burden of his advice to Henry in the years to come. *Rule; be not ruled!* A rather superfluous message, some may have thought, for the eager princeling to whom it was addressed. But Skelton's eye, sharpened perhaps by jealousy, had spied an influence in the Palace that boded no good. In November 1509 Thomas Wolsey had been appointed Royal Almoner and

Counsellor to the King. And this smiling, obsequious, smooth-tongued cleric of humble birth and easy manners was already beginning that steady process of absorption which was to end by placing in his hands more power than any man had wielded in England before or since. In the solemn, thrice-reiterated *Banish!* of Skelton there was prophecy.

§ 3. IMPORTUNITY

There was no immediate response to Skelton's curious *cri de cœur*. Henry's finer feelings refused to be touched. Perhaps he was too busy enjoying himself – or, as he would no doubt prefer to put it, raising his country's reputation for magnificence. But the poet did not give up hope. In 1511 he was arbitrating, at Bishop Nick's request, in the case of the Rev. Dale in Norfolk; but before this, on 5 July, we catch a glimpse of him in London, and in good clerical company to boot. It was a fast day; and William Mane, Prior of Westminster, had guests to dinner. On the table in front of them were two plaice, two pair of soles, a couple of large 'conger snakes' that cost fourteenpence and formed the *pièce de résistance*, some salt fish and two dishes of butter. And among the diners were 'the suffragan and Skelton the poet, with others.'[12]

What had brought Skelton up to town on this occasion, we do not know. Certainly it did not mark his departure from Diss; for he was back there in November, investigating the conduct of the Rector of Redgrave. Perhaps it was something to do with his reinstatement at Court. If so, once again he returned empty-handed.

But by this time his blood was up. Our poet was an obstinate man: when he had once set his heart on a thing, he did not let go of it easily. And, like the importunate woman in the Bible, he decided on yet another appeal. No doubt he again chose the traditional day for presenting gifts to the King: the First of January 1512.[13] And this time too he had picked out a memento of Henry's schooldays. It was an old French chronicle, originally chosen because it dealt with the life of Richard the Lion-heart. There on the margins were still the Latin notes he had scribbled to draw attention to his hero. 'Here the child is born.' 'Now he is called to the throne.' 'Here he sets up his camp. . . .'° From time to time there is an indignant comment. When the chronicler remarks that Richard was jealous because Philip had the credit of

131

capturing Acre, Skelton breaks into a furious hexameter: 'Frenchman, hold your tongue: your words are all in vain!'° More
significantly, where the death of Henry II is mentioned, Skelton
devotes a couplet to explaining why the 'villain' died: the holy
relics of Becket afford an immediate answer.° Skelton's royalism
was far from being uncritical king-worship.

But that was the schoolmaster. Now, as he lays the tattered
manuscript before his prince, the most strenuous Henry VIII of
England, Skelton apologises for its *pagina trita*, its dog-eared condition. And his whole tone is strangely subdued. 'Go, my book, in
haste; prostrate yourself before the king and commend me to him,
his humble poet Skelton. Above all, recount to his majesty the
famous battles waged by England's greatest hero, Richard, first
of our race. . . .'°

Humilem Skeltonida vatem! – this is unexpected modesty from the
proud bard of all the Britons. And, knowing Skelton, we cannot
but suspect that it was modesty with a purpose. In that event, it
was shrewdly timed. Henry was three years older now, and much
more sure of himself. Perhaps his conscience was pricked. It was
true, the man *had* been his first teacher. . . . At any rate, in April or
May 1512 Skelton was once more formally recognised, by letters
patent, as Court Poet to His Majesty King Henry VIII.[14]

Here again, in the absence of the patent, we cannot be sure on
what terms he was readmitted. But there are hints. Actually,
Henry seems to have done no more than confirm his father's grant
– probably without fee, for there is still no sign of a pension in the
royal accounts. In a little poem of this period Skelton is asked,
'Why wear ye *Calliope* embroidered with letters of gold?' His
answer is that,

> Though I wax old
> And somdele sere,
>
> Yet is she fain,
> Void of disdain,
> Me to *retain*
> Her serviture.[15]

In other words, Henry has merely 'kept him on' as a servitor of
the heroic Muse – allowing him, of course, the special livery

that went with the privilege. This was probably all that Skelton wanted – re-recognition. At all events, his delight was unbounded. With engaging frankness, he signalled it by promptly taking on a new title. From now on, all his poems (unless there is good reason for it) are signed with the lofty name of Orator Royal.

Like *poet*, *orator* at this time meant simply 'man of letters'; and like *poet laureate*, the title of *orator regius* was not confined to Skelton. André used it too, and so did Giovanni Gigli.[16] But Skelton was not claiming anything exclusive; he was merely asserting his right to be ranked among the King's official poets, as he had been in the previous reign.

§ 4. RUMOURS OF WAR

Perhaps Henry's change of heart was not wholly disinterested. Of all the innocent and honest pastimes permitted to a king in the sixteenth century, war was recognised as incomparably the finest. And, with his father's millions burning a hole in his pocket, Henry was aching to play at it. But if he did, he would also need a Homer to sing his praises. What was a warrior without his bard? It is rather significant, to say the least of it, that Skelton's return to Court happened to coincide with Henry's first venture on to the playing-field of Europe.[17]

The balanced pacifism of his father had no meaning for the son. From childhood – and by Skelton as much as anyone – he had been suckled on the myth of England's right to France.

His title is true in France to raign

was the tutor's firm belief and hence, *a fortiori*, the pupil's. In Henry's eyes the previous century was an inglorious interlude in the classic struggle for his patrimony. Obviously, it was the rôle of Henry VIII to complete the work of Henry V and unite the two nations under a single crown. It was no accident that in 1513-14 the first English life of the latter was presented to him, with the avowed hope that he would be inspired 'to ensue the noble and chivalrous acts of this so noble and so excellent a prince, which so followed he might the rather attain to like honour, fame and victory.'[18] Against this ideal, the cold facts that England was a fifth the size of France and had no professional army trained, like hers, in the use of the new caliver, weighed nothing. So much the better. It would be Agincourt all over again.

Henry's first diplomatic move had been to appeal for a great coalition against Louis XII. So that when Pope Julius, in 1511, appealed to him for help against France, persuasion was unnecessary. Henry needed only this, the loftiest of motives, to quiet his conscience. Now his piety could run hand in hand with his lust for glory. With Wolsey to spur him on as they chatted after Mass, he enthusiastically agreed to take his place in the Holy League beside his father-in-law, Ferdinand.

On 8 June fifteen thousand Englishmen landed at Passajes, in northern Spain, under the command of the Marquess of Dorset. There they stayed, waiting for mounts and artillery, while the Spaniards, their flank neatly covered, streamed into the adjacent kingdom of Navarre. That was all Ferdinand wanted; and, by using his allies to hold off the puzzled French, he had got it for a scuffle instead of a campaign.

Henry had no idea what was happening: treachery was the last thing that entered his mind. But his army was not so sure. All the Marquess (Wolsey's old pupil) knew was that none of the promised help had come from Spain, while his men sweltered at San Sebastian on garlic, fruit and local wine. When Henry, still blind to the truth, ordered them to stay to the following spring, the homesick troops mutinied outright. Swearing 'that they would not abide and die of the flux in such a wretched country,'[19] they terrified their leaders into putting them on board ship; and an ignominious rabble landed back in England at the beginning of December. Not exactly an auspicious opening for Henry's new pastime.

But in May 1512 there was no hint of disaster in the air. On the contrary, everyone was rejoicing that soon, after a triumphant campaign in France, Englishmen would be able to hold up their heads again in Europe. Foreigners were astonished at the heartiness of their dislike for the French. Now that the people have a chance to get at them, Pasqualigo noted in 1513, 'they take part so willingly that it is incredible.'[20] And, as Henry was well aware, Skelton was thoroughly English in this respect. More important, he also knew how to curse. Henry must have expected an invective of respectable dimensions from his new orator.

Skelton was now spending more and more of his time at Westminster. He had not yet – as we shall see – wholly deserted his rectory in Norfolk; but he may already have rented from the Abbey the house under the Great Belfry where he was living in 1518. Decidedly he was on very good terms with the Abbey authorities. In 1511 we found him at dinner with the Prior; and in the next year he might have been seen several times in earnest discussion with the Abbot himself.

John Islip had an idea about the sumptuous new Lady Chapel – the apple of his eye – that was now almost completed and was to enshrine the bodies of Henry VII, his Queen and the Lady Margaret. It would be an artistic wonder, with its fan tracery dimly glowing overhead and its Italian tombwork of bronze and marble. As he took Skelton round to watch Torrigiano the Florentine at work on Henry's altar, the Abbot's thoughts turned to the single art that was still unrepresented – literature. Why leave that out? The solution was simplicity itself. As the tombs were completed, Skelton was to compose epitaphs for them – in Latin, of course – which would be inscribed on fair parchment and hung about the chapel. A poetic gallery, in effect.

They need not all be epitaphs, either. In fact, he might start with a panegyric. The young King would expect something patriotic from him at a moment like this.

But when Skelton sat down dutifully to write the *Eulogy of his own Time*, somehow it began, like *Philip Sparrow*, to take quite a different tone from the one that would be expected. Only in that case he had known very well what he was doing. In this – well, he was not sure. There was nothing wrong with an expedition to recover France: he was all in favour of that laudable object. But wasn't Henry a little young to plunge into a full-scale war? He was barely twenty-one. And most of the pressure seemed to be coming from the wrong quarter. A cleric like Wolsey ought to be in the peace party, like Warham and Fox. . . .

It began with the death of Henry VII. Instead of shedding tears, the nation was jubilant. Why? Because of his noble successor. The poem then goes on to emphasise young Henry's boldness in sounding the trump of war. But now, where Skelton should have soared to the traditional pitch of optimism, he proceeds to don the robe of a cautious Jeremiah. And, having recalled the fatal uncertainty of war, he ends with this extraordinary sentiment:

If the fates do favour thee
(And I pray that this may be!),
England, sing thou loud in praise:
If not, thou dost end thy days!°

As a celebration, by an official panegyrist, of the opening war
of any reign, the poem can hardly be called a triumph of tact. And
there can be only two explanations of its gloomy foreboding.
Either Skelton was still lecturing the schoolboy he had once
tutored – in which case he would have done better to keep his
mouth shut. Or else he was, for the second time, giving vent to
what would soon become his grand obsession: a profound distrust
of the new favourite, Wolsey.

But whichever reason be correct – and there may have been a
modicum of both – the good Abbot Islip seems to have suspected
nothing. In due course, the *Eulogy* was mounted on parchment
and hung up in the Henry VII Chapel, as he had planned. On
30 November it was joined by an epitaph on Henry VII.[21]

§ 5. 'MAKING A MASH OF EVERYBODY'

But it took more than a half-hearted eulogy to dismay Henry.
His first reaction to the Spanish fiasco was to hang all the mutin-
eers, which was clearly impracticable; his next, to plan a grand
frontal assault on France, led by himself in person.

Wolsey agreed. This time not a detail would go wrong. The
Royal Almoner made sure of that by supervising, with his own
hand, every single chit for supplies – every order, however trivial,
for guns, biscuit, hoys, cordage, beer or ammunition. It meant an
eighteen-hour day for months on end, and an appeal from Bishop
Fox to slacken off if he was to avoid a breakdown; but Wolsey
ignored the warning. If organisation could win a war, this campaign would be a classic.

And indeed the crossing must have been a brave sight. Having
first executed the pretender, de la Pole – that Suffolk who had
sent Jane Scrope to Carrow and immortality – Henry set out for
Dover with a glittering retinue. On 30 June 1513 he solemnly
handed over the rule of his kingdom to Catherine, leaving the
susceptible north in the care of the Earl of Surrey – who 'could
scantly speak' with indignation, almost seventy as he was, at

losing this chance for adventure.[22] Then the King took ship, with a guard of six hundred picked men, one hundred and fifteen members of the Chapel, and five hundred and seventy-nine grooms and secretaries, kitchen-men, clerks and pages – not forgetting his poet and luter, Carmeliano, who so infuriated Erasmus by his maltreatment of Latin. (It was also noted that Master Almoner appeared with a cortège of two hundred, though he was a mere fledgling dean, while Bishops Fox and Ruthal were content with half that number.)

On the other side the pageantry continued. Henry had agreed to meet the Emperor Maximilian outside Thérouanne. Maximilian had his reasons for the rendezvous; he wanted Thérouanne and Tournai moved out of French hands because they threatened the province of Artois, which belonged to his grandson, Charles. If Ferdinand had won Navarre by making use of this green princeling, why shouldn't he? Indeed, he went one better: pleading poverty (and in this case with entire sincerity), he offered to serve as a private soldier under Henry's banner – for a consideration. The offer was irresistible. Henry installed himself in a hundred-and-twenty-five-foot 'house of timber with a chimney of iron; and for his other lodgings he had great and goodly tents of blue water-work garnished with yellow and white' and surmounted by his heraldic emblems.[23] From these modest headquarters he proceeded joyously to extract the Emperor's chestnuts, one by one, from the fire.

Thérouanne was the first of them. Henry was unaware that the French had orders to avoid an open battle – Louis was too deeply committed in Lombardy. He was surprised to find how easy it all was. He rode round in the rain, inspecting and cheering his men. He led his army gallantly across a river. He received with dignity the King of Scots' herald, who came to tell him that his master objected to the invasion and would take part in 'defence of our brother and cousing the maist Christian king': sending him back with a sharp answer. On 22 August Thérouanne surrendered; at 9 a.m. on the 24th Henry made his triumphal entry into the town, splendid in gilt and graven armour; and on the 26th a council of war decided that 'the walls, gates, bulwarks and towers of Thérouanne should be defaced, razed and cast down.' After this Henry and his nobles spent a few days of relaxation with the Lady Margaret of Austria.[24]

Now it was the turn of Tournai. But while they lay before the town, on 15 September, a brief note reached Henry with the news of a great victory at home – against the Scots. Four days later came Surrey's full account, followed by a gauntlet and piece of coat belonging to the luckless James IV. The Scots had been up to what Hall terms their 'old pranks.' Without waiting for Henry's reply to his challenge, James IV had crossed the Tweed with a great army almost as soon as the King's back was turned. Norham Castle – an outpost of the Bishop of Durham's – had held out for only five days; but they were vital. They gave Surrey time to gather his forces in the north and march to meet the threat. On 9 September the Scots, who were strongly entrenched on a hill-side, were misled (by a spy, says Hall) into burning their camp and moving over to Brankston Moor, near Flodden Edge. It was a fatal error. Worn out as they were, the English with their terrible brown bills mowed down the flower of the Scottish chivalry, with James himself at their centre.

This was the great battle of the period – far more significant than the skirmishes in France. And Henry had the grace to recognise it as such. On 22 September (Hall is five days out here) 'the tent of cloth of gold was set up, and the king's chapel sang mass, and after the *Te Deum*; and then the bishop of Rochester made a sermond and shewed the death of the king of Scots, and much lamented the ill death and perjury of him.'[25] After this, the capitulation of Tournai on the 24th was something of an anti-climax.

But already a month before, a sharp eye, watching Henry's progress from far-off Italy, had been unimpressed. Machiavelli – it was the very year he completed the *Prince* – wrote to a friend on 26 August: 'with all his dash, all his great army, all his resolve to make a mash of everybody, the king of England has not yet taken Tarraone, which is a fort about the size of Empoli and should have fallen at the first assault.'[26] He was inaccurate – Thérouanne had in fact fallen; but it had taken the best part of a hundred days to reduce, and his comment offers a just verdict on Henry's first campaign. Interestingly enough, it was exactly that of his English disciple, Thomas Cromwell, only a few years later. In 1523 Cromwell averred that Thérouanne 'cost his highness more than twenty such ungracious dogholes could be worth unto him.'[27]

Still, no one could deny that Henry had enjoyed himself. On

the Sunday after the fall of Tournai *Te Deum* was again sung, this time in the town's Cathedral, and Henry resolutely knighted a group of 'valiant esquires,' among them one Christopher Garnish, before returning home with his slender but indubitable laurels.

§ 6. DISS CHOIR

It seems natural to assume that during such an expedition, when so many of the Palace staff crossed over into France, the new Orator Royal should have done the same. We have seen him attending Henry VII on just such a first campaign. This time Carmeliano went over, and so did Ammonio; so too did all the gentlemen of the Chapel. And in fact a most plausible and ingenious case has been made out[28] for Skelton's having gone with them. The idea has everything to recommend it. And yet – the obstinate truth is that Skelton, for the beginning at least of these stirring and martial days, stayed quietly at home in Diss. Obviously so remarkable an absence calls for demonstration.

Dr. Nelson's argument for Skelton's presence in France is really based upon three words. On 28 August the poet celebrated the fall of Thérouanne in some Latin verses. These include the phrase: '*mẹnia strauit humi.*'[29] Henry, cries Skelton triumphantly, 'has razed to the ground the ramparts of Thérouanne!' If we take him literally, then he must have written these words on French soil; for, as we have seen, the decision to destroy the city walls and fortifications was not taken until the evening of 26 August. This would give under two days for the news to travel from France to Norfolk: which is out of the question.

True – but *are* we to take him literally? Skelton's phrase is a cliché; it is regularly used by poets of any town taken in battle. One has only to look at Sackville's *Induction*, for example, with its figure of dread War, who 'razed townes, and threwe downe towers and all.' Talbot again, in *1 Henry VI*, threatens the citizens of Bordeaux that the English —

> in a moment even with the earth
> Shall lay your stately and air-braving towers

if they do not surrender.[30] Are Sackville and Shakespeare to be taken literally? Possibly they are. The point is, it was a fate liable to overtake any town that was captured by violence. But for that very reason it became common heroic parlance for the latter. Skelton, in fact, *need* mean nothing more than 'Henry has captured Thérouanne.' An event which occurred, not on the 26th, but the 22nd of August.

If we assume for a moment that Skelton was at Diss, the time is still amazingly quick, but far from impossible. News of the victory reached the Queen by the 25th, which allowed three clear days for it to get to Norfolk. And there are no other details in Skelton's poem which concern events later than the 22nd.

Once this doubt is established, the rest of Nelson's argument totters visibly. At the head of his poem Skelton declares that 'the *chorus de Dis* solemnly chanted this pæan . . . on the Eve of the Beheading of St. John.' There can be no question of a numerical misprint, then: the poem was definitely sung on 28 August. The next question is, by whom? Here Nelson frankly confesses bewilderment. And with some reason. For the only plausible translation of the Latin is 'the choir of Diss.' And if Diss Choir sang Skelton's poem on 28 August, it is reasonable to assume that the poet was at Diss to write it for them.

Reasonable, but not inevitable. There is the possibility that he was in London when the news came through, and promptly galloped off to Diss with the glad tidings. But on the whole we may dismiss this as unlikely. It suggests a zeal for his parish which is contradicted both by later events and by the nature of his office. For his behaviour shows that Skelton took seriously his duties as Orator Royal. He was, in effect, a publicity agent of the King's. In the pre-newspaper era, just as to-day, it was important to keep the people informed of the progress of a war they were paying for. And surely, if Skelton were in the capital, he would be expected to turn his talent to use *there* – among the populace of London.

There seems no escape from the conclusion that on this fateful eve Skelton was neither at Thérouanne nor Westminster, but away in his country parsonage. Why, it is impossible to say. He may have been recovering from an illness. But conjecture is a waste of time where we know so little. Every fact we do know, however, leads us to believe that Skelton, for reasons now buried in history, had stayed behind while Henry's grand expedition was in progress.

Nevertheless, he was still the Royal Orator. And he was certainly well enough, the moment news came through of a victory in France, to arrange for a public celebration. The form of his poem, with its opening words from the great hymn of Fortunatus, shows that it was intended as a processional piece. So, on 28 August 1513, we must imagine the entire population of Diss winding joyfully under the archway of their church, headed by the chanting choir, in the manner which so distressed the puritan soul of Latimer: 'They must sing *Salve festa dies* about the church, that no man was the better for it but to show their gay coats and garments!'[31] It was obviously an occasion for one's Sunday best.

§ 7. FLODDEN FIELD

Which brings us to the Scottish war, and Skelton's reaction to that. Here we have no less than three poems to account for. In English there is the *Ballad of the Scottish King*, with a later (and longer) version of it called *Against the Scots*; and, finally, another Latin hymn for the Choir of Diss.

Catherine had arranged with Wolsey – she was already a little in awe of Master Almoner – to exchange a weekly letter with him all the time her husband was in France. It is in her letter of 13 August that we get our first hint that the north was aflame. She talks with regret of 'going farther, where I shall not so often hear from the king.' Meanwhile, she was 'horribly busy with making of standards, banners and badges.' In this tense invasion atmosphere the news of Thérouanne must have sounded rather tinny and unreal, but Catherine's tact was perfect. Immediately she wrote off to Wolsey welcoming the news. Nothing like it had ever been seen before; it could only be a reward for Henry's extraordinary piety. . . .[32]

On 2 September she wrote that the Scots were busier than ever, 'and I looking for my departing every hour.'[33] Richmond was in a ferment, with rumours pouring in hourly. The Scots were over the Tweed; there were forty – sixty – a hundred thousand of them; they were attacking Norham; Norham had fallen; Chillingham. . . . But Isabella's daughter had been bred to the trumpet's alarum. Reserves totalling 60,000 were swarming to meet her as she rode out of London. By the 14th she had reached Buckingham. There Surrey's first brief despatch told her baldly of a victory which paled Thérouanne into insignificance. That same night Londoners were speculating on what had happened to the King of Scots. 'As yet,' wrote a Venetian, 'nothing certain was known of the king; he was supposed to be either dead or a prisoner.'[34]

For Skelton, away at Diss, these events must have sounded a clarion. Whatever had kept him out of France, his duty now was clearly beside the Queen. And that is where we duly find him. As Orator Royal he would naturally be shown whatever documents Henry (or his Council at home) thought worthy of publication. It was in this way, I conjecture, that the *Ballad* came to reflect the official correspondence of the King.

When he scribbled it down, Skelton knew little but the first vague rumours of the battle. Most of the *Ballad* is concerned with 'Jamie's' inept challenge to the English King, in France. Obviously Catherine had let him see an account of Henry's meeting with the Scottish herald, and a copy of his written reply. Echoes of these recur throughout the poem.[35] About the King of Scots' fate, however, he was cautiously ambiguous:

> For to the castel of Norham,
> I understand, to soon ye cam,
> For a prisoner there now ye be
> Either to the devil or the Trinité.[36]

This would cover either eventuality; it might mean that he was dead, or merely captured. Nothing was said about Flodden – for the very good reason that no one yet knew anything about it.

The important thing was to get the news broadcast; to circulate the *Ballad*, at once and as widely as possible. Was it Skelton's own idea to have it turned out, anonymously, in hundreds on a London printing-press? At all events a text came into the hands of a London printer, Richard Fawkes;[37] and the haste of its reproduction is only too evident in the one abominably printed copy that has survived the centuries. But at least it told the people something, and more effectively than a thin flurry of manuscripts, however accurately transcribed. So far as we know, this was the first ballad to reach the semi-permanence of print.

Uncertain whether to be more relieved or delighted, now that her heroic march was over, Catherine moved east to Woburn. It was there that, on the 16th, she was handed Surrey's complete narrative of Flodden, together with the glove and plaid that signified the wretched end of King James. In passing them on to

Henry, she could not resist the gentle boast that she was sending him, in exchange for a few banners, a King's coat. But her main anxiety was – what to do with the body? In the first flush she had 'thought to send himself unto you, but our Englishmen's hearts would not suffer it.' In the meantime, her duty was done, and she would 'now go to our Lady at Walsingham that I promised so long ago to see.'

Here, surely, is the explanation of another Skeltonic puzzle. Skelton's French hymn had been written only six days after the battle; his Flodden hymn no less than *thirteen*. But if we assume he was with the Queen, and accompanied her to Walsingham to kiss the heavenly milk of the Virgin, this would account admirably for his belated appearance with his victory hymn at Diss, on the 22nd.

And there is one fact which confirms everything we have so far concluded. No one (except Dyce) seems to have noticed that in two early editions, those of Day and Marshe, Skelton's hymn on Flodden is signed '*Regine orator.*' Queen's Orator – it is the only place in which the title occurs; and it was natural for Dyce to assume a mere misprint for *Regius*.[38] But let us think back a little. We saw how, when Henry embarked at Dover, he first declared his wife Catherine 'governor of the realm' in his absence.[39] It would not do to stress the fact overmuch – or perhaps it did not occur to Skelton on 28 August, when he hailed the taking of Thérouanne. In any case, that was the King's victory. But Flodden was Catherine's; and when Skelton got back to Diss, still enthusing over her vigorous handling of the crisis, he could not resist recording the fact. So his Flodden hymn is proudly and deliberately subscribed, 'Skelton laureate, orator *of the queen.*'

We could hardly wish for a neater proof of our main contention. On his own admission, the poet was in England and not in France when Thérouanne fell and Flodden was won.

§ 8. 'CLOSED IN LEAD'

From this date on, Skelton's fate becomes curiously linked with that of the unfortunate King of Scots. Let us turn, then, to the movements of that illustrious corpse. The most convenient account of them is to be found, of all unlikely places, in Stow's *Survey of London*. There we are told how –

after the battle the body of the said king being found, was enclosed in lead, and conveyed from thence to London, and so to the monastery of Shene in Surrey, where it remained for a time, in what order I am not certain; but since the dissolution of that house, in the reign of Edward VI, . . . I have been shown the same body so lapped in lead, close to the head and body, thrown into a waste room amongst the old timber, lead, and other rubble. Since the which time workmen there, for their foolish pleasure, hewed off his head; and Launcelot Young, master glazier to her majesty, feeling a sweet savour to come from thence, and seeing the same dried from all moisture, and yet the form remaining, with the hair of the head, and beard red, brought it to London to his house in Wood street, where for a time he kept it for the sweetness, but in the end caused the sexton of that church [St. Michael's, Wood Street] to bury it amongst other bones taken out of their charnel. . . .[40]

What became of the body Stow does not think fit to narrate. As it was, in Scotland rumour began to whisper that in fact James was not dead at all.[41]

But what had really happened seems clear. The Earl of Surrey was somewhat baffled at having the corpse of an anointed King on his hands – anointed, but excommunicated too; for James's unprovoked attack on his brother brought him under the Church's ban. His final decision was to have 'the body 'bowelled, embalmed and cered, and secretly amongst other stuff conveyed to Newcastle.' There it sat while he dealt with the last remnants of the invasion; after which he brought it down to Richmond, where he left his difficult charge in the care of the Prior of Sheen.[42] We have seen what Catherine, with her Spanish directness, wished to do with it. In default of that, nothing could be decided until the papal curse had been removed. Henry's first generous impulse was to have the body buried with regal honours at St. Paul's, and he wrote to the Pope from Tournai for permission to do so. Eventually, on 29 November, this was granted.[43] But by that time the royal fellow-feeling had evaporated; and James's now sanctified body continued to lie at Sheen until the Dissolution. The rest we have gathered from Stow.

But what, it will be asked, has the King of Scots' posthumous itinerary to do with Skelton? Only this: that it happens to confirm for us his speedy departure from Diss – this time, in all probability, for good.

For Skelton did not linger much after 22 September in his old parish. Very soon he was back in Westminster. His arrival is marked by a Latin quatrain that he appended to his epitaph on Henry VII; which hung, as we have seen, on the abbey wall. In English it ends:

> For him, the Lion Red,
> The Lion White struck dead:
> Yet, though his life is fled,
> He lieth unburiéd.°

The White Lion, of course, was Surrey's badge, as the Red was James's. But the final pentameter, with its '*non tumulatus humo*,' is ambiguous. To the casual reader it might suggest that the King's body still lay naked on the field. This would mean that Skelton was in London about 15 September. But in fact, we now realise, the statement would be true whenever it was written; for James remained unburied long after Skelton's death. We have to look for some other indication of date. And this is surely given in the very subject of the quatrain. There would be no point in adding it except when Flodden was still 'news.'

Here, then, we have convincing evidence that Skelton had once more deserted his rural retreat, and very shortly after his Flodden hymn was sung there on 22 September. Perhaps it was to welcome home his King, when he returned from France at the end of the month and 'rode to Richmond in post to the queen, where was such a loving meeting that every creature rejoiced.'[44] But whatever it was that brought him to town, he had left his Norfolk rectory for good. Henceforth, his duties at Diss were performed by deputy. On 6 May 1515 a will of Diss was witnessed by William Becket, 'parish priest,' and he performed the same function in 1517. Other names occur in 1522 and 1529, but Skelton's never.[45] Officially he remained Parson of Diss till the day of his death; but from now on his fortunes were once again entrusted to the good ship *Bouge of Court*.

CHAPTER EIGHT

FLYTING

He ran him in at the breast with a hit, which at once cut his
stomack, the fifth gut called the Colon, and the half of his
liver, wherewith he fell to the ground, and in falling gushed
forth above four pottles of pottage, and his soule mingled
with the pottage.

RABELAIS: *Gargantua.*

§ I. KING'S MINION

HENRY VIII was no snob. If he did not stoop quite
so low as his hero, Prince Hal, in his search for pastime
and good company, at least he refused to confine himself
to the narrow circle of the nobility. The annals of his early reign
are enlivened by the appearance of several names new to history.
Staffords, Veres and Howards still supported him in the lists and the
disguisings, but with them were not a few buoyant young figures
of humbler origin, who pleased the young King by their ability to
run and jump, drink and gamble and swear notably and with relish.

Among these companions of his leisure was the scion of a modest
but respectable East Anglian family named Garnish.[1] Through
the fifteenth century the Garnishes had followed, if in a less
spectacular way, the example of their Paston and Wyndham
neighbours. A convenient marriage, and a good deal of hard-
headed bargaining, had left Peter Garnish, Esq., high among the
local gentry when he died in 1451. His second son, Edmund, was
given the father's handsome manor of Roos Hall, near Beccles;
he married a daughter of the Mayor of Norwich, and their son and
heir was named Christopher – the man we are now concerned with.

Christopher must have been the family joy and pride. His father
determined he should have every advantage: he even sent the boy
to acquire a society gloss under the widow of Sir Thomas Brews,
who had retired to Hasketon Hall, near Ipswich. 'My lady Brews'
was grandmother to the man who married the lovely Jane
Scrope; and we find her still alive in 1501.[2] She was also, it is
interesting to note, that Dame Elizabeth of the *Paston Letters* who

146

behaved so amiably during the protracted courtship of John Paston and her daughter Margery. John, for his part, swore to his mother that 'there is not a kinder woman living.'[3] It was as a page to this benign and warm-hearted lady that Garnish got his first insight into courtly behaviour.

In sharp contrast to that, however, was his trip abroad to learn French and soldiering at the little garrison town of Guisnes, near Calais. Then, as now, the young Englishman expected the Continent to provide him with far other kinds of experience. And, if Skelton is to be believed, young Christopher did not return without a few amorous scars to his credit.

He returned at any rate, a finished specimen of the Early Tudor *rutterkin* – the contemporary gallant. In 1509 Henry promptly made this gay sprig one of his gentlemen ushers; and his success at the King's favourite sports may be measured by the gifts which were showered on him. A man who was always good for a masquerade, or a game of Pope July for high stakes, deserved recognition. Henry soon added the wardship of a London alderman's son, worth about £25,000 to-day; and, not content with that, found a rich widow for him in the person of Sir John Risley's wife. Garnish's successor felt impelled to point out that Christopher was 'no beggar, as I am. Sir, thanks be to the king's highness, he had cause, for the king gave him a widow with 400 marks land, and £1000 in her purse, and she had 500 marks in plate. . . .'[4]

It was natural that when the invasion of France took place in 1513, Garnish should have had a good staff appointment. His official title was Sergeant of the King's Tents – which at this time, significantly, included the revels office as well. But Christopher was far too important a figure to do the actual work. For this purpose he had a deputy, a man named Richard Gibson. It was Gibson who attended to the 'binding of males and fardels, trussing of coffers and trussers,' and who saw that the cloth-of-gold tent was in good repair for the victory celebrations.[5] Nevertheless, the credit went, of course, to Garnish: who in due course, as we saw, received the usual reward for his valour. On 25 September he knelt before Henry in the Cathedral of occupied Tournai, and rose Sir Christopher Garnish, Knight.

From now on Christopher's advancement was rapid. In 1514 the whole course of England's foreign policy received an abrupt check when Henry discovered, long after everyone else, that Ferdinand and Maximilian had been cheating him. It was his first, and final, disillusionment. Henceforth he would play the game according to *their* rules. He began by proposing peace with the hated enemy, France. To do this it was necessary to cement the alliance by marriage; and his sister Mary, who had been engaged to Maximilian's grandson, the fourteen-year-old Archduke Charles, was offered instead to the decrepit Louis XII, who was fifty-two. Everybody was scandalised; but, as Hall remarked, 'the voice of people let not princes' purposes.' The Duc de Longueville, still a captive, was conveniently at hand for the negotiations. By early August the treaty was drawn up and signed. A proxy wedding was performed at Greenwich on the 13th. On the 29th Docwra, the 'lord of St John's,' and Somerset, Earl of Worcester, were sent over to complete the arrangements at the Paris end. [6]

Sir Christopher Garnish, we are told by Leland, made one of this glittering embassy. The princess herself followed on 2 October, with 'all her wardrobe, stable and riches,' and an even more splendid train of noblemen, knights, squires, gentlemen and ladies. She had delayed too long, however. They ran into a Channel gale; and it was now that the incident occurred that Dyce so pardonably misread. Hall relates how –

> when they had sailed a quarter of the sea, the wind rose and severed some of the ships to Calais and some into Flanders; and her ship with great difficulty was brought to Boulogne, and with great jeopardy at the entering of the haven, for the master ran the ship hard on shore. But the boats were ready and received this noble lady; and at the landing sir Christopher Garnish stood in the water and took her in his arms, and so carried her to land. . . . [7]

Garnish was not escorting Mary, as Dyce thought, when he performed this gallant exploit. It was from the shore that he waded to lift his Princess out of her tossing cockboat; for he had already been in France a month making preparations for the wedding. [8]

At the same time he certainly ranked as one of her attendants – a fact which is of some significance. For, despite all his proofs of devotion, he was not invited to be present at her marriage to the French King. [9] A further shock was coming, moreover. On 10 October – the very day after that brilliant wedding – 'all th' Englishmen except a few that were officers with the said queen, were discharged: which was a great sorrow for them . . . in so much some died by the way returning, and some fell mad, but there was no remedy.' [10]

Queen Mary (as she now was) had no doubt as to the reason for this swift axing of her retinue. Though it came in the form of an order from her husband, she at once blamed the Howards – the old Duke of Norfolk (for so Surrey became after Flodden) and his son. In a furious letter she complained to Henry of Norfolk's behaviour, ending bitterly: 'Would God my lord of York had come with me in the room of my lord of Norfolk; for then I am sure I should have been left much more at my heart's ease than I am now!' (My Lord of York was Wolsey, now an archbishop.) And the story has every sign of being authentic. A few jewels from her doting Louis soon made the feather-headed Mary forget her pique; but her outburst reveals an undercurrent of personal and political passions in the English Court that was shortly to come to the surface. [11]

Of that, however, later. For the moment we are concerned with Sir Christopher. Garnish was among that disconsolate crew of Mary's retainers who were ordered to leave on 10 October. In January he had been appointed a commissioner of the peace for Kent. Twice renewed in March, this honour suddenly lapsed during the spring and summer, but it was renewed on 18 October. [12] In other words, Garnish was now back in England, nursing his resentment against those insolent Howards.

That is all we know; but it immediately suggests a reason why Henry decided, in the summer of 1514, to set Sir Christopher and his orator, Skelton, at each other's ears in a poetic flyting. For everyone at Court knew, perfectly well, that the two adversaries were divided not only by temperament, but by an irreconcilable political hatred. In the phrase of Suffolk, Garnish was one 'of Wolsey's choosing.'

§ 2. 'BY THE KING'S MOST NOBLE COMMANDMENT'

In Renaissance Italy the vituperative art reached almost unimaginable heights. The early humanists had found this freedom of railing in their beloved Latins, and it became a point of

loyalty to prove their *virtù* in scabrousness. But it was more than a
mere copying of antiquity. Italy had herself reached the stage of
culture corresponding to the old city-state; a stage in which the
social unit was compact enough to retain a personal flavour.
Everybody was known – known, that is to say, as a fallible and
sometimes ridiculous human being. And so the invective was
born. The *invectivae* of Italian humanism would fill a library:
Poggio and Filelfo, Poggio and Valla, Trapezunzio and Poggio,
Valla and Fazio, Panormita and Valla exchanged pleasantries
about each other's person, habits and family with which Villari
refused to soil his page; and even the despatches of Pulci are enlivened with most undiplomatic caricatures.

The Scottish poets had the same astounding liberty of speech.
Dunbar's *Wooing of the King*, in which James IV hides from the
rage of the husband he is betraying, has no parallel that I know of.
It was in Scotland, consequently, that the 'flyting' first established
itself in our island. The *Flyting of Dunbar and Kennedy*, which was
printed in 1508, is only one of a series; but it is important because
it looks very much as though Skelton, in his battle with Garnish,
took it for a model.[13] Quite possibly he had actually met the great
rhymer of Scotland. Dunbar was definitely in England during
the year 1501; though it is less certain that he wrote the famous
poem on 'the flower of cities all' that Christmas in London.[14] But
we know he had a weakness for the south – 'In Ingland, oule,
suld be thyne habitacione,' railed Kennedy[15] – and we can
imagine that, if they did meet, the two masters of abuse got
along very well together.

All this, however, is conjecture. But somehow (we can only
guess how) a copy of the *Flyting* fell into Skelton's hands, and it
must have delighted him hugely. Perhaps he read it aloud to
Henry, and made a convert of him. If he did, it struck Henry
a novelty that should definitely be naturalised. For it was 'by
the king's most noble commandment' that in 1514 the first
English flyting was organised – between Skelton and Christopher
Garnish.

Most unfortunately, Garnish's contribution to this strange
contest is no longer extant. If it were anything like Skelton's, it
would have given us, in among its scandal, some priceless information about our poet. For the English match differed from
its original in being a good deal more realistic. But as no one

thought fit to preserve the knight's venture into the realm of poesy, we must make the best of what we have.

The flyting had at this time quite definite rules. It was a literary duel, in four rounds, between a challenger and a defender. Each had the right to appoint a second. In the English case, only Garnish availed himself of the privilege; Skelton preferred, as he usually did, to stand alone. The challenger began by reciting his first piece; his object being to overwhelm his antagonist with every conceivable insult that came to hand. They did not need to to be true, provided only they were pungent enough. The defender then replied in kind. The duel continued in this way until each of them had taken the floor four times. Finally, the audience was invited to decide, in the Scots phrase, 'quha gat the war.'

As it chances, the date of our English scolding can be fixed with some exactness. As Miss Stearns acutely noted, the incessant jeers at Garnish's title would have point only while the honour was still green; she therefore dated the poems 1513-14.[16] But one small detail enables us to limit them much more closely than that. In Skelton's third contribution occurs the phrase:

> Now upon this hete
> Rankely whan ye swete . . .[17]

A temperature that makes one sweat is not very common in England. One is pretty safe in saying that it only occurs between June and early September. This at once cuts out 1513; for the royal party did not re-embark at Calais until 21 October.[18] Which leaves us with the summer of 1514 – up to 29 August, when Garnish again departed for the Continent. It is possible that Henry arranged the match as a jovial preliminary to his setting-off. Certainly, there are signs of something like a heat-wave in this particular August; for on the 13th (the day of the proxy wedding) a Venetian comments that the King and his nobles danced in their doublets, and that his Ambassador was sorely tempted to do the same.[19] Very probably, then, it was in mid-August 1514 that Garnish and Skelton entertained a perspiring Court with their diatribes.

Garnish began the contest. The burden of his first piece seems to have been that Skelton was a knave – in the phrase of the time, a 'mean person.' However true this may have been, it gave the poet an easy opening. His reply looses a withering fire of knightly names from old romances – obviously aimed at the recently acquired title of the carpet knight. No doubt Garnish had had to put up with a good deal of chaff about his gallantry in looking after the King's tents in France. And Skelton's refrain points the moral:

> But sey me now, sir Satrapas, what autorité ye have
> In your chalenge, sir Chesten, to cal me a knave?

In return, Skelton gives us – in caricature, of course – a very detailed portrait of Sir Christopher. His skinny legs, his bald pate, his hairy back, and above all his prominent nose, are all rammed mercilessly home. The last is pilloried for all time in:

> Nosed like an olefant,
> A pikes or a twibill[20]

where the very obsolescence of the terms makes them sound the more damning. Nor is his background forgotten. In the line –

> Sir capten of Catywade, catacumbas of Cayre,

he is ironically greeted as the great soldier of Suffolk – Cattawade being a remote hamlet in that county which was famous for its shrine (the 'great God of Catwade,' as Heywood calls it). For Garnish, Skelton implies with crushing obscurity, this rural chapel was one of the Seven Wonders of the World – a veritable Mausoleum of Halicarnassus.[21]

From the start, the unfortunate Garnish must have felt that he was rather outmatched. At any rate, for his next round he called in a supporter – a 'scribe' whom Skelton dubs Gorbellied Godfrey. It has been suggested (I think very plausibly) that Garnish's second was no other than the poet, Stephen Hawes. Hawes was a Groom of the Chamber; he was the only Court poet with an *English* reputation at all approaching Skelton's; and everyone knew the obscene dwarf, Godfrey Gobelive, in his *Pastime of Pleasure*. Hawes was also, it appears, a Suffolk man, like Garnish. There seems every reason why he should have been brought in, however reluctantly, to help his unliterary neighbour. The objection has been made that as Hawes 'evidently disapproves of' his dwarf, they are not likely to have been identified. On the contrary, it was ideal flyting technique. And as the dwarf Godfrey is specifically described as pot-bellied or 'boln in the waist,' this would seem to clinch the argument.[22]

In the absence of all material from Garnish's side, we cannot tell how far Hawes' appearance improved the odds. Godfrey Gobelive shows that the romancer had some talent for invective. Is it fair to detect in the formless abuse of Skelton's second piece a touch of confusion? Certainly the note becomes sharper, more testy.[23] And it may not be without significance that in round three Skelton abandons the rhyme-royal in favour of his suppler and now well-tried Skeltonic.

This unquestionably brings a new vigour into the contest. Skelton's own 'living' has, it seems, been reprehended; and in return he drags to light a number of unsavoury scandals about Garnish. First, we get the grotesque picture of him as a dirty page-boy, gobbling up his salt pork in the kitchen of Hasketon Hall. Then we switch to his early days across the Channel, a 'slender spear,' still kept desperately short of pocket-money and with only one frieze coat to his back, which he had to turn inside out for holidays. (This is plausible enough: much the same thing happened to young John Paston, who, when approaching twenty, wrote urgently from North Wales – where he was attending the Duke of Norfolk – for money to buy another gown; 'since one gown without change will soon be done.'[24] Tudor fathers did not believe in pampering even their sons and heirs.) But apparently this had not deterred the hopeful Christopher from letting his eyes rove. . . .

Garnish's final rejoinder, like his first piece, seems to have been made without the help of his scribe. At least, when he sets out to answer it Skelton remarks: 'I have received your *secund* rime.'[25] More libels are now introduced about the gentleman usher's exploits with the fair sex. But to go over all the poet's charges would be tedious. As it is, there can be little doubt about the verdict of the audience in this novel entertainment. The odds were surely all in favour of the professional. Garnish had won his reputation in the tiltyard and the gaming-room, not in his study. While, for his part, Skelton was already a hardened satirist. He must have found his new-fledged knight the easiest of game.

For all its amusing scurrility, however, the battle has a significance which goes far beyond its immediate occasion. In its mimic combat clashed the two great influences that, from the very beginning of his reign, had been struggling for control of the young King. Behind Skelton there stood the Old World of fixed status and privilege, the conservative nobility, led by the Howards. Behind Garnish were massed all the rising bourgeoisie of the New World, the Comptons, the Brandons – and Wolsey. To-day, quite naturally, our sympathies go out to the latter. It is they who represent the movement forward, the liberating of gigantic new energies as yet untapped by the nation. Beside them the others seem to stand for an obstinate looking-back, a blind attempt to preserve a dying past. But Garnish may help to remind us that the picture was not a simple one of Progress *versus* black Reaction. The torrent of the new carried with it not a little worthless and unpleasant flotsam.

Though Garnish's future was to mark a temporary triumph for Skelton's party, for the moment he remained high in the royal favour. In December 1515 our gallant was sent north to welcome Henry's other sister, Queen Margaret of Scotland, who had just been driven out of her kingdom. It was Garnish who consoled her, on Henry's behalf, with the richest dress materials that London could supply; and he describes her rapture at their shimmering folds.[26]

But eventually the gay group of favourites about the king was broken by its own excesses. Its sway lasted for another five years. Then, in May 1519 –

> the king's council secretly communed together of the king's gentleness and liberality to all persons; by the which they perceived that certain young men in his privy chamber, not regarding his estate nor degree, were so familiar and homely with him, and played such light touches with him, that they forgat themselves. . . .Then the king's council caused the lord chamberlain to call before them Carew (and another who yet liveth, and therefore shall not at this time be named), with divers other also of the privy chamber, which had been in the French court, and banished them the court for divers considerations, laying nothing particularly to their charges: and they that had offices were commanded to go to their offices. Which discharge out of the court grieved sore the hearts of these young men, which were called the King's Minions.[27]

AN ABBEY EPITAPH WITH A DIFFERENCE

By some accident Garnish was not with the band on this occasion. Nevertheless, the Council had their eye on him. In the following year he was sent over to help organise the pageantry of the Field of Cloth of Gold. At the same time he let his house at Greenwich to the King for ten years;[28] and from henceforth he remained in honourable but undoubted exile at Calais, where he died as Knight Porter in 1534. His fellow minions were luckier than he: Carew, Bryan and their friends were soon back at Court again, in as high favour as ever.

One last incident, which took place in Calais the year before his death, may serve as our farewell memory of Sir Christopher. It seems that in the course of his duties there he had lost his temper and given a buffet to a certain 'lewd fellow' – who promptly complained to the Deputy against this infringement of a Britisher's rights. The case was brought before the King's Council. After solemnly debating the matter, in the end they decided to exonerate Garnish, 'perceiving the said stroke was given but only for correction and for none intent to break any law, statute or ordinance of that town of Calais.'[29]

To the end of his life, it would appear, Garnish remained the same hectoring cavalier who had threatened to use his sword on Skelton's royal livery in 1514.[30]

§ 3. AN ABBEY EPITAPH WITH A DIFFERENCE

Being a satirist, our poet seldom found himself without a target. In most cases, perhaps, there was a grim good-humour in the curses that he bestowed upon them. Enemies were the breath of life to Skelton, just as a mistress is to the love-poet. At the same time we should not fall into the error of assuming that Skelton nursed a friendly feeling for any of his victims. There was nothing fake, nothing trumped-up in his quarrels. Even in the flyting, as we have seen, there is every reason for believing that Skelton cordially detested his adversary. And in the case of William Bedell, likewise, the reasons for a genuine dislike are not far to seek.

Bedell[31] had been Treasurer of the Household to the Lady Margaret. Some of his accounts may still be inspected at Westminster Abbey; and from one of them we learn that the Countess, for some time, paid the wages not only of the Chapel Royal, but of Prince Arthur's household as well.[32] It may fairly be presumed,

I think, that she contributed to her favourite Prince Henry's expenses, too. We have already noted that Diss came under her authority. So, both as tutor and as parson, Skelton might have had dealings with Master Bedell. And it is easy to guess how a touch of hauteur, or a misplaced condescension on his part, would rouse the hostility of the cantankerous Laureate.

Even after the death of his mistress in 1509 Bedell continued to prosper. Henry made him bailiff for life of Cheshunt, Herts, where he now spent most of his time, and keeper of a neighbouring park. In 1517 his standing in society was assured by a licence to 'use any garments and chains, and to keep and shoot with cross-bows and handguns. . . .' He was thus officially exempted from Wolsey's strict new law of apparel, at the same time as Richard Rokeby, comptroller of Wolsey's household.[33]

Bedell, in fact, was by now a Crown official of some importance. To the Countess he had been a kind of Malvolio; but with the vanity of Shakespeare's steward he seems to have combined the morals of Garnish. At least, an obscure incident at Oxford in 1498 casts a peculiar light upon his private behaviour.

In that year the University wrote to the Lady Margaret in great agitation. According to their story, the Proctor –

> having taken a wench of evil life, and that in the city of Oxford, he was about to inflict punishment upon her – a matter entirely consonant with his office in that area – when, in fear of his authority, she clandestinely removed herself to the neighbouring village of Cowley: not however with the intention of remaining for any length of time, for she had no residence there, but in order to dupe the good man by hiding for a little. But when at length she returned to the city, she was chastised both in body and purse by the proctorial authority.

So far all seems clear. The Proctor had caught a prostitute and punished her, as he had every right to do. But his action had apparently roused the wrath of William Bedell – who, as the Countess's steward, was not a man to get on the wrong side of. Unfortunately, we are not told *why* Bedell intervened in this matter of a doxy's thrashing. I have found no sign of his possessing any land nearer to Oxford than Watlington, fifteen miles off. But angry he certainly was. The letter continues pathetically:

Therein, we consider, the proctor did nothing which could in any way offend, or contravene the authority of, the excellent and most amiable W. Bedell – a person whom, for your grace's sake, we shall ever hold in the highest esteem. . . . [34]

But whatever his relations with Oxford lights-o'-love, Bedell had more dignified connexions elsewhere. He was friendly enough with the Master of St. John's College, Cambridge – Robert Shorton, M.A., D.D. – to make him overseer of his will. And at Westminster, where his mistress died, he was a familiar figure. In 1512 he bought four tapers at St. Margaret's 'for th' year's mind of mistress Hungate'; and his own funeral is also recorded by the churchwardens.[35] It was here, possibly, that in 1518 he collapsed in the street. At any rate, his will requests that he may be buried 'at the lower end in my Lady's chapel at Westminster called *Scala Cęli*' – that is to say, the new Henry VII Chapel, which also held the body of the Countess. That he could make such a claim at all shows that Bedell was a personage of considerable worship.

With one of the sentiments in his will Skelton was in hearty agreement. He had no doubt that Bedell's was indeed a 'most sinful and wretched body.' His Latin epitaph makes this abundantly clear – though for all that one cannot see Abbot Islip hanging it on a tablet over his tomb! The cacophonous cataract with which it begins can hardly be reproduced in English, but a rough equivalent would be:

M.D.XVIII

A Devout Epitaph on Bedel, sometime Belial Incarnate

God grant Bedel, the Ishmael,
No honey'd dell but hell-gall fell,
Perfidious Achitophel,
Lurid lurdain and lorel!
   Lo, here lies stinking this Jebal,
This rebel Belial, knave Nabal,
Whom all and some, with sure accord,
Abominate before the Lord.
   For in the street this cursèd rutter
Did spout his soul out in the gutter:
Against the men of God he railéd,
Whereat his mind and breath both failéd. . . .°

One can never be sure, with our poet, whether the charge of being a priest-hater means anything more than a lack of proper respect to the Rev. Skelton. It may be that the real Bedell lies in his will, so beautifully replete with piety; or it may be that Skelton and the University of Oxford were nearer to detecting the man as he was. But while the latter muffled up their disapproval in the formulae of the *Dictamen*, Skelton had the courage to speak his mind. Behind the pompous steward with his gold chain he saw a figure like the Belial of the morality plays, black, boistous and bold.[36] And not even death could prevent him giving rein to that grotesque vision.

Book Four

SATIRIST

CHAPTER NINE

THE RED HAT

Then hath he servants five or six score,
Some behind and some before,
    A marvellous great company;
Of which are lords and gentlemen,
With many groomes and yeomen,
    And also knaves among.
        ROY: *Read me and be not wroth.*

§ 1. WITCHCRAFT

'FOR,' READ Jane in her favourite *Reynard the Fox*, 'when a covetous man of low birth is made a lord, and above his neighbours hath power and might, then he knoweth not himself, ne whence he is comen. . . . All his intent and desire is to gather good, and to be greater.' It is a classic statement, in contemporary idiom, of Thomas Wolsey's hubris.[1] This big intelligent son of an Ipswich butcher[2] had watched his father rise to wealth and the dignity of churchwarden while breaking every by-law in the city. Why shouldn't he do the same – on a scale, naturally, befitting his brains? He was clever, and had no objection to hard work. At fifteen he was being pointed out in Oxford as the 'Boy Bachelor.' Magdalen made him its Junior and then Senior Bursar, until he lost patience with academic red tape and paid for its new Tower without waiting for official authority. That was Wolsey: speed, and a native contempt for his superiors which was all too often justified. He could do it so much more efficiently and quickly himself!

The Marquess of Dorset, whose sons he had tutored, gave him his first living. Within a year he had added two more, and the right to be absent from all of them. He became chaplain to the Archbishop of Canterbury – who promptly died. Undismayed, Wolsey transferred his services to the Deputy of Calais, where he worked harder than ever. When Nanfan died he recommended his right-hand man to Henry VII. Before the King died he was Dean of Lincoln and of Hereford.

That death, like Archbishop Deane's, was a setback. The Lady Margaret, he suspected, did not approve of him. Wolsey waited for the renewal of his chaplaincy: it did not come. Was he to be thwarted now, so near? But the luck of the age was on his side. Every week after his grandmother's death in June showed a difference, a rising self-confidence, in the young Henry. He liked this modern spirit that Wolsey personified, of smooth and smiling efficiency. Old Bishop Fox approved of it too. By the end of 1509 the Dean was Royal Almoner – a key position – and the youngest member of the King's Council.

At last his plan was beginning to bear fruit! Ever since he accepted the tonsure, its seed had been growing in Wolsey's brain. He knew to a hair the depth of the new King's piety: did he not say Mass before him every morning? If England was to rise to greatness, she must do so *as champion of the Holy See*. That was the dream he nourished in his master's avid mind throughout their long confidences at Richmond or Windsor. To throw England's weight on the side of the Pope would not only bring glory to Henry in this world; it would be to his eternal credit in the next. Moreover, the papacy being elective, what was to prevent an English cardinal from receiving the honour as a proof of gratitude? An Englishman, one of Henry's subjects, the spiritual head of Christendom! Lightly touched upon – it would not do to stress the other man too much – this was exactly calculated to stir up Henry's misty idealism. It also gave him the best of excuses for marching off to a holy war. While before the Almoner's own mind, as he argued so persuasively, there danced the tantalising vision of the triple tiara.[3]

The young King needed careful handling, however. Ambassador Carroz, with all his diplomatic *naïveté*, realised this; he warned Ferdinand that it was advisable to 'put a bridle on this young colt' now, before he understood his strength.[4] But Wolsey was better aware of it than anyone. If he were to gather the reins in his own capable fist, it would call for all the skill he possessed. For Henry meant to follow Skelton's advice: he had no intention of being ruled.

Fortunately, affairs of state are exacting in their demands on a young man's time; and Henry was equally determined to make that time a good one. If Elis Gruffydd is to be believed, some of his little games went a good deal further than Hall thought fit to record. His cutting the purse of a respectable nobleman, for instance. This made an excellent bit of sport for his gay companions. 'As a result,' says the Welshman, 'the stealing of purses became so common that . . . if anyone had the chance to do it so skilfully that the owner did not notice or catch him in the act, or know that others had seen him, then the owner would never see one penny of his money again, and even if he caught him in the act he could only treat it as a laughing matter.' The stupid craze soon had to be checked on penalty of death; but if true, it indicates that Henry was at first inclined to play Prince Hal more thoroughly than he has been given credit for.[5]

Wolsey, at all events, wholeheartedly approved of such gambols. He himself had all the aplomb and high spirits, as well as the polish, of the born courtier – the 'common accent and the coarse red face' of a recent study are wide of the mark.[6] Even his enemy Polydore grants him distinction. And he knew exactly how far to go in his encouragement of Henry's boyish dissipation. An artist in good living, he made his large and handsome residence in Fleet Street, overlooking the Thames – it had been Empson's until Henry gave it him in October 1509 – what Polydore calls a 'shrine of all the pleasures';[7] and he took care that the King's pilgrimages there were frequent and well rewarded.

That silver voice of his had magic in it. 'He had a special gift of natural eloquence,' says his usher Cavendish, 'with a filed tongue to pronounce the same, that he was able . . . to persuade and allure all men to his purpose.' At intervals in the merrymaking he would set it to work on the flushed and flattered Prince. Who could resist such proffers, couched in that honeyed rhetoric by a man who showed so perfect a comprehension of what was due to royalty? Very soon Wolsey's study was the centre of the diplomatic web in England; while Henry continued to play, secure in the confidence that this man was his, body and soul.

Magic or no, Wolsey's ascent of Fortune's wheel made the onlooker rub his eyes. When he came back from France late in 1513 he was still Master Almoner, with two or three deaneries to his credit. Early the next year he became Bishop of Lincoln; to

which Henry, in defiance of the Lateran Council, added Tournai
as well. But a brace of bishoprics was no longer enough for the new
favourite. In mid-July 1514, Bainbridge, Cardinal-Archbishop
of York, died at Rome – by poison, rumour had it, and at the
instigation of some great prelate in England. The case was
hushed up; but the moment the news reached London Wolsey
was given the temporalities of York. Even this, however, was
merely another step upward. Before Bainbridge died, Wolsey
had sent Polydore Vergil back to Rome on a highly confidential
mission. He was to try to arrange for Wolsey's nomination as
cardinal. At the same time another of his agents, Gigli, was urging
the Pope to make him legate *a latere* for life.

Possibly his tactics were wise, if he were really asking for more
than he expected. But was he? Wolsey's opinion of himself already
passed all bounds. When a French claimant turned up at Tournai
in 1514, he wrote confidently to his agent there: 'the pope would
not offend *me* for one thousand such as the elect is.'

For his part Leo felt, rather pardonably, that Lincoln, Tournai
and an archbishopric were good measure for one year; he preferred
to bide his time. But as soon as Wolsey scented delay he became
frantic. By now he was capable of adding threats to his agents'
coaxing. If Henry decided to change his policy, he bluntly
reminded Leo, the latter would be 'in greater danger on this day
two year than ever was pope Julius.' It was blackmail – backed,
providentially, by the French descent on Italy in July 1515. We
need hardly be surprised that on 10 September Leo gracefully
yielded him his cardinal's hat. As some compensation for the
legacy he was created 'cardinal sole' at a special election.[8]

A cardinalate – here at last was a dignity of becoming magni-
tude! As the first churchman since Morton to bear the title in
England, Wolsey determined on a display that would impress even
the scoffer with a sense of his eminence. The red hat had been sent
over, as was customary, in the charge of a papal protonotary. But
in Wolsey's eyes it was a slight on his rank to have it 'conveyed
hither in a varlet's budget, who seemed to all men to be but a
person of slight estimation.' On his arrival at Dover, the bewildered cleric found himself seized and held until 'he was newly
furnished in all manner of apparel, with all kind of costly silks,
which seemed decent for such an high ambassador.'

Only then was he allowed to proceed to Blackheath: where a

long cavalcade, headed by an earl and a bishop, met him and escorted him in triumph, with all the pomp that the City could provide, to Westminster Abbey. There the precious hat was borne in state to the high altar, where it remained till the following Sunday. Issuing from York Place (now Whitehall) with all his retinue, Wolsey then proceeded to the Abbey. Warham sang Mass, assisted by two Irish archbishops, eight bishops and eight abbots. Colet, Dean of St. Paul's, delivered a sermon on humility, as sincere and as effectual as his earlier one to Henry, in 1513, on the injustice of war. Eighteen noblemen, headed by the Dukes of Norfolk and Suffolk, conducted the new cardinal back to his palace, followed by an innumerable throng of lesser dignitaries. An immense banquet ended the celebration.[9]

Only one thing was lacking to complete Wolsey's triumph. He had received the hat, but the habit was still on the way. Knowing the Roman genius for procrastination, he had written to Leo explaining that he must have it in time for the opening of Parliament on 3 November. In fact, Parliament was not due to meet until the 12th. Even so, the courier bearing the coveted robe was held up at Calais, first by arriving after the gates were shut and then, when he had made his mission clear, by the weather.[10] He was three days late in delivering his burden; and Wolsey was obliged to make his formal entry in unofficial rochet.

Still, he was Cardinal Wolsey now: nothing could take that away from him. Characteristically, his first act was to ensure the withdrawal of Warham's cross from the ceremony at the Abbey. His next was to dissolve Parliament; and Parliament met only once more while he remained in power. Wolsey left no one in doubt as to who was now ruling England.

§ 2. LETTERS ON A TUNIC

Some time (according to Ramsay) between 1515 and 1516 appeared an obscure and rather dull little poem by Skelton entitled *Against Venomous Tongues*.[11] The title suggests one of those invectives against backbiters which were so common in fifteenth-century France. It is in Skelton's most official manner, which is by no means his happiest; but otherwise there is little resemblance. Skelton's poem is not a general satire, but a reply to some unnamed slanderer of the poet. He has been accused, it seems, of daring to—

> Control the cognisance of noble men
> Either by language or with my pen.[12]

Skelton loftily rebuts the charge; then he launches into a diatribe against tale-bearers and their poisonous tongues. They ought to be torn out by the roots, he declares indignantly.

Most of this is familiar ground. It was a Renaissance convention to defy one's enemies, real or imaginary. But in this case there was, evidently, specific cause for the outcry. Skelton is said to have insulted a certain magnate – whose servants had 'Roman letters' inscribed on the back and front of their livery. It was one of these servants who had reported him for it. And in his reply Skelton makes the curious statement:

> For before on your brest and behind on your back
> In Romain letters I never found lack:
> In your cross-row nor Christ-cross you spede,
> Your Paternoster, your Ave nor your Crede.[13]

The point of this is not made any clearer by the pun on *lack*, which then also meant 'blame.' He seems to be saying: 'No, I don't object to the letters on your clothes, as you accuse me of doing. It's the lack of them in your mind that I dislike. You, an illiterate fool, have the cheek to calumniate me, Skelton!' (The last two lines enumerate the contents of the schoolboy's hornbook.) A Latin gloss then explains that 'here he is referring to Roman letters woven in bright colours, front and back, on the liveries of followers.'°

A little further on there is a similar ambiguity, or looseness of phrasing – it is hard to tell which:

> There is no noble man wil judge in me
> Any such foly to rest or to be.
> I care much the less whatever they say,
> For tunges untay'd be renning astray;
> But yet I may say safely, so many wel lettred,
> Embrawdred, enlaced together and fettred,
> And so little learning so lewdly alowed –
> What fault find ye herein but may be avowed?[14]

Does *so many well lettered* mean 'a man with so many fine letters,'

164

or 'so many men with fine letters'? We shall see the answer in a moment.

Meanwhile the general situation is clear. To repeat ourselves once more, some great man's servant has charged Skelton with jeering at the cognizance (or badge) he wears. This consists of Roman letters embroidered on the livery, both in front and behind. Skelton admits that he has talked about it, but not in such a way as to insult the nobleman in question.

Such is our solitary clue. Now comes the question: is it possible for us, to-day, to identify so slight a target? As it happens, it is. Let us look into Cavendish's *Life of Wolsey* at the point where his usher is describing, with fond detail, the stately retinue of the Cardinal-legate as he left London in 1527. There we read how he moved 'over London Bridge, having before him of gentlemen a great number, three in a rank, in black velvet livery coats, and the most part of them with great chains of gold about their necks. *And all his yeomen, with noblemen's and gentlemen's servants, following him in French tawny livery coats; having embroidered upon the backs and breasts of the said coats these letters: T. and C., under the cardinal's hat.*'[15]

The letters of course stood for *Thomas Cardinalis*. And Wolsey, as we have seen, was created cardinal on 10 September 1515. But that is not all. We have seen, too, the unexampled pains taken by Wolsey to ensure a fitting splendour for his investiture. He even took the trouble to reclothe the papal envoy. Is it likely, then, that he would have neglected the livery of his retinue? There can be no doubt whatever that coats of black velvet, and others of French tawny with TC embroidered back and front, were all ready long before the final procession to the Abbey on 18 November. In all likelihood, Wolsey's men wore them from the moment that Leo's bull reached England in September.

We can imagine the effect of all this ostentation on Skelton. Seeing one of Wolsey's men swaggering by in his belettered jacket, he must have let drop a gibe about 'more letters than learning.' The witticism got back to Wolsey – not a man, now, to offend unscathed. Prudence counselled an apology: only, as so often with Skelton, the palinode soon turns into something quite different – a vigorous assault on 'trattlers.' Such, at least, would seem the only conclusion from our data. *Against Venomous Tongues* turns out to be the first poetic result of Skelton's hostility to Wolsey.

This reading at once elucidates the poem's obscurities. It explains, for instance, why Skelton insists in both poem and gloss that the embroidered letters were *Roman*. They were Roman because Wolsey's new dignity was Roman. It explains his emphasis on the *religious* elements in the hornbook. A cardinal's servant, implies the poet, ought to be versed in those at least. It explains the odd word *post-ambulonum* in the Latin gloss. Cavendish tells us categorically that the men in lettered livery came *after* Wolsey, not before him.

And lastly, it suggests that *so many wel lettred* was deliberately ambiguous. Even in his apology Skelton cannot resist a dig at the unconscionable number of servants in Wolsey's household. The fact was notorious. We have seen how in 1513 he crossed over to France with twice the train of a bishop; and in later years their number swelled to 'little if at all short of a thousand.'[16] According to Cavendish, Wolsey scoured the country for likely retainers – with such zeal that 'well was that nobleman and gentleman that might prefer any tall and comely yeoman unto his service.'[17] Such a weakness was too blatant to ignore.

There is one difficulty about this interpretation, however. It is the one that has misled all previous critics – the use of the word *nobleman*. To a modern ear it immediately implies one of the lay peerage; and in Skelton's time too this was the most common acceptation of the term. But it was not the only one. Skelton himself describes *Why Come Ye Not To Court?* as 'the relucent mirror for all prelats and presidents, as well spiritual as temporal. . . .' Both, then, are included in the exhortation that follows:

> *All noble men*, of this take hede
> And beleve it as your crede.

Even to-day, though we are inclined to forget the fact, Bishops still sit in the House of Lords. So, obviously, in *Against Venomous Tongues* Skelton was using the term quite properly to mean a lord not temporal but spiritual. As Cardinal, indeed, Wolsey was the greatest nobleman in the realm.

But the real reason why Skelton picked on the term goes deeper. *Nobility* was the catchword of the age. We have seen how many of his textbooks for Prince Henry dealt with it. And always, in

166

deciding its true nature, the answer was: 'only the praise and surname of virtue.'[18]

There was genuine subtlety, then, in Skelton's declaration that—

> There is no noble man wil judge in me
> Any such foly to rest or to be.

No one, argues the poet, who is *truly* noble could possibly take offence at this sort of tittle-tattle. In other words, if Wolsey takes action against him, he proves himself neither an aristocrat by birth nor possessed of the virtue that made one of nature's noblemen. It is a dilemma – of the kind he had posed the King in his *Complaint*. And by spending the rest of the poem heaping curses on the villain in French tawny who had given him away, Skelton shows his confidence that Wolsey is logically trapped. It is the true atmosphere of the *Merry Tales*, where a quick answer so often averts disaster.[19]

CHAPTER TEN

THE MAGNIFICENT MAN

Take heed, therefore, ye great ones in the court, yea, though ye be the greatest of all, take heed what ye do, take heed how ye live.

ASCHAM: *The Schoolmaster.*

§ I. SKELTON AND THE STAGE

THOUGH ONLY one of his plays has survived, that is not because Skelton was above exercising his talent in this rising art. Its possibilities for the man of letters were just beginning to appear. Up to now, the stage had been left in the hands not of the poet, but of the humble clerk or chaplain, who occasionally turned out a morality in the course of his miscellaneous other duties. And the quality of the individual plays, with rare exceptions, was as trivial as might be expected under these conditions. It is no matter for surprise that, in 1494, Cornish could march into the King's hall and cut short an interlude that was still in course of presentation. The drama was a very minor art indeed; not to be compared, for entertainment value, with a mask or a pageant.

For all that, its place in the hierarchy was winning slow recognition. The classical revival made men realise that the stage, after all, had a distinguished pedigree. And, with Medwall and More leading the way, a genuine secular school of drama established itself in Skelton's lifetime, with John Heywood at its head.[1]

Skelton himself contributed to it in various ways. His *Achademios*, we have seen, was perhaps only a Latin comedy in praise of the University, written to justify his laureation: though its gloss in the *Garland*, 'There is no fear of God before their eyes,' hints at a certain satirical saucing of the piece.[2] Then there was *Virtue*, his 'sovereign interlude' – no doubt a variation on the theme of aristocracy. While during the war a fragment was unearthed of what may have been Skelton's *Good Order*, a Lenten *pièce d'occasion*, which dealt with the revolt of Hazarder, Gluttony, Riot and Perjury against their liege lord, Old Christmas.[3]

Among the lost plays, however, the most tantalising is the *Necromancer*. It has been suggested[4] that this was a satire on Wolsey, based on the charge of wizardry which dogged the Cardinal throughout his career. But Warton, who is our only authority for its existence, says that this 'moral interlude' was printed by Wynkyn de Worde in 1504 – while Wolsey was still an obscure chaplain in Calais. Warton's account of the play is extremely circumstantial and interesting:

> The characters are a Necromancer, or conjuror, the devil, a notary public, Simonie, and Philargyria, or Avarice. It is partly a satire on some abuses in the church; yet not without due regard to decency, and an apparent respect for the dignity of the audience. The story, or plot, is the tryal of SIMONY and AVARICE: the devil is the judge, and the notary public acts as an assessor or scribe. The prisoners, as we may suppose, are found guilty and ordered into hell immediately. There is no sort of propriety in calling this play the Necromancer: for the only business and use of this character is to open the subject in a long prologue, to evoke the devil, and summon the court.

Warton goes on to provide a large number of details – an amusing proof that the play was acted in the morning, a stage-direction giving Beelzebub a beard, and a sample of the sulphurous curses evoked by the devil against Simony – all of which sound authentic. Too authentic, indeed. It has been proved only too clearly that Warton had the eighteenth-century weakness for enlivening his fact, now and then, with playful invention. Whenever this occurred he always grew meticulous; and in this case Skelton was himself the source of almost all this lavish detail. Philargyria and Simony, ugly Eumenides and the other furniture of hell, even Beelzebub, may all be found elsewhere in our poet.

There can be small doubt, I fear, that Ritson was right in dismissing the *Necromancer* as a picturesque fabrication.[5]

§ 2. 'WANTON EXCESS'

But *Magnificence*, at least, is no figment. We still have it, and in an unusually careful text from the press of the elder Rastell. And in it we see what the most brilliant poet of his day could do with the somewhat intractable material of the Early Tudor morality.

The occasion arose in 1516.[6] That year witnessed something like a crisis in England. We have already watched Wolsey's giddy rise to the proud heights of the cardinalate. Even that, however, did not halt his progress. In another month he had replaced Warham as Lord Chancellor – supreme head of the country's legal system. It was almost the climax of his career. One by one the others dropped out of the race: it was useless trying to compete with Wolsey's daemonic energy. Of the younger men, the Duke of Suffolk had finished himself politically by his secret marriage with Queen Mary of France. Young Surrey, indeed, was spoiling for a fight, but the odds at Court were too much for him. Together with Abergavenny and Dorset, he was actually 'put out of the council chamber' in May, and retired to nurse his fury in the country. The only person who showed no concern whatever in all this turmoil was the King. Still a healthy young millionaire of twenty-five, he 'devotes himself,' an envoy noted, 'to accomplishments and amusements day and night. Is intent on nothing else, leaving business to the cardinal. . . .'[7]

The Cardinal's conception of 'business' remained obstinately European. Louis XII's collapse on 1 January 1515 had swung into power another and even livelier princeling than Henry VIII. Gay, active, and quite unburdened with a conscience, Francis I had ambitions too, and more than twice the population that Henry could call on to realise them. He had the further advantage of being a good deal nearer Italy. By September the 'battle of giants,' Marignano, had made him master of all Lombardy – and, automatically, of Pope Leo's warmest regard. It looked like the death-blow to Wolsey's hopes. If Rome was to be saved for England, something would have to be done, and quickly. Yet how was this possible, in face of the unanimous disapproval of Henry's Council?

At this point Wolsey found a heaven-sent ally: Henry's extraordinary vanity. The King was jealous as a girl of his dashing French rival. The news of Marignano brought real tears of rage to his eyes. Henry was all approval at the prospect of putting a spoke in Francis's triumphal car. The only question was: where were they going to insert it?

Direct intervention in Italy was impossible. As for an invasion of France, Henry's appetite for that was visibly sated. In the end it was decided to hire twenty thousand Swiss, who were to recapture Milan under the Emperor Maximilian. By 25 March 1516 the army had got to within nine miles of the city. Suddenly, without a word, the Emperor turned tail and vanished into the Tyrolean mountains. It was the *volte-face* of his career; and, as if to cap it, his grandson Charles, who had just entered the concert of Europe by succeeding Ferdinand of Spain, signed the Treaty of Noyon with Francis in the following July.

Francis had won all along the line. Poor Sir Robert Wingfield, the Imperial Ambassador – 'Summer-shall-be-green,' as Pace dubbed him – could hardly believe that the Emperor he so trusted had let him down. But that wily pauper had an answer even for his retreat before Milan. As for young Charles's treaty, that, he agreed, was an outrage. Obviously it had been signed against his will. He, Maximilian, would march up to the Netherlands and overthrow the boy's wicked councillors – if Wolsey would supply him with another 40,000 crowns. Incredible as it sounds, Wolsey gave him a quarter of this sum in advance. With his travelling expenses safely paid by the one side, he now turned to the other. Francis willingly granted him a further 75,000 for adding his signature to the Treaty of Noyon.

Fifteen-sixteen, indeed, was Wolsey's black year. In the pursuit of his Continental ambitions, he had flown dead in the face of every politician in the realm: and with what result? The royal treasury, already depleted by the wars of 1512 and 1513, had been practically emptied. The insatiable demands of Maximilian and the Swiss had almost doubled the expenditure of the previous year – and had left Francis, in January 1517, stronger than ever. If ever a policy had proved itself a failure, it was the Cardinal's. The chorus of detraction was nation-wide. The resignation of Warham and Fox was as plain a gesture as the scowling retirement of Surrey. Even rising diplomats like More and Tunstall thought the whole scheme expensive and futile – as, of course, it was. . . . But Wolsey was not content with an unpopular foreign policy. No sooner was the great seal in his grasp than he began a drive against domestic corruption. In May the Earl of Northumberland was examined in the Star Chamber and sent to the Fleet; and one after another the magnates of the

Court were summoned before him and fined, reprimanded or dismissed. Like Skelton's Ishmael, his hand was against every man, and every man's hand against him.

It was now and only now – between Marignano, in September 1515, and Maximilian's final treachery in January 1517 – that Fancy's reference would apply, when he comments on the change in French manners since the death of Louis XII:

> For sith he died, largesse was litel used.

Later in the play he illustrates what was now likely to happen to any Englishman travelling through France:

Fan.　By God, at the see side,
　　　　Had I not opened my purse wide,
　　　　I trow, by our Lady, I had ben slain,
　　　　Or elles I had lost mine eres twain.
Mag.　By your soth?
Fan.　　　　　　　Yé, and there is such a wach
　　　　That no man can scape but they him cach.
　　　　They bare me in hand that I was a spy
　　　　And another bade put out mine eye,
　　　　Another wold mine eye were bler'd,
　　　　Another bade shave half my berd;
　　　　And boyes to the pilery gan me pluck
　　　　And wold have made me Frier Tuck. . . .[8]

Such was one consequence of the new policy. But its most serious aspect was the economic one. To Wolsey's enemies, the Cardinal was deliberately egging on a young King to squander his entire fortune over a selfish chimera. And it is this view of the situation that Skelton attempted to portray in *Magnificence*.

§ 3. A PRINCE'S TEMPTATION

For his purpose, he chose one of the four standard plots of the morality: the conflict of Virtues and Vices over a hero.[9] But in Skelton's play we notice a significant change. Where his models set their hero against a background of eternity, our poet keeps strictly to this world. Magnificence is threatened not by Death, but by Poverty – a very considerable difference indeed. We are no longer in the realm of theology, but of Early Tudor politics.

This change, of course, involved a whole series of problems. Obviously, it was impossible for Skelton, even had he wished, to turn his play into direct personal satire. If he was to deal with the theme at all, his characters must remain safely abstract. Where, though, was he to find them? For answer Skelton turned to 'the master of them that know,' Aristotle; and in his beautifully ordered system of ethics (as interpreted by the Middle Ages) he duly found those virtues and vices 'that have to do with property.' This was Skelton's chosen ground; and here, sure enough, was his central figure: μεγαλοπρέπεια, a fitting munificence. This was the special virtue becoming a great man, a prince. Magnificence, indeed, is no other than an abstract Henry VIII, seen from the economic angle.

After this *trouvaille* the rest was easy. It only remained to group round his hero the necessary virtues. Measure, as the very keystone of the Aristotelian conception, was the most important of them. But in order to stress his particular slant, Skelton added the two vital figures of Felicity and Liberty. Felicity, whose second name is Wealth, represents the happiness to be attained by a measured use of riches. Liberty, who is also called Appetite, includes all that side of a man that is omitted when one talks of material felicity. Both are necessary to the worldly success which is Skelton's theme; but neither is possible without Measure.

When it came to the vices, however, Skelton found himself at a loss. What he wanted to portray was Wolsey; but he knew only too well the danger of anything approaching a personal portrait. So, in his natural anxiety for concealment, he rushed to the other extreme and multiplied his figures in a way that is somewhat bewildering. His two fools, Fancy and Folly, stand for the Aristotelian *incontinence* and the *lack of understanding* which is evil. But as they were too generalised for his purpose, he added a special quartette of court-vices, with the highly-coloured names of Counterfeit Countenance, Cloaked Collusion, Crafty Conveyance and Courtly Abusion. These were entirely new to the drama, which had never before been pinned down to a milieu so precise. They remind us that Skelton is no longer thinking of life in general, but of the Court and its more limited problems.

Of the play as a play this is not the place to speak. Opinions of *Magnificence* have varied widely. Professor Ramsay is not alone in regretting its 'intrinsic dullness and monotony'; but for all that it has given inspiration to at least one of our recent verse playwrights. In 1932 Mr. Auden noted the skill with which its metre was adapted to character; and he added: 'Skelton solves this problem of the verse play successfully, and I believe *Magnificence* to be an excellent acting play. The subject is of topical interest to any age; the verse is easy to understand, an important advantage in poetry to be heard; a great deal of scope is left for action: and, though the names of the characters may seem rather teasers to us, a sympathetic and intelligent producer could make them very significant.'[10]

Certainly, when we remember that *Magnificence* was performed by the usual troupe of four men and a boy, the sheer dexterity of it commands our admiration. But we are here concerned less with its purely literary merits, or its place in the history of the stage, than with its value for biography. And, after noting the professional skill of its construction – which has not yet received its due – we must turn to its effect on the audience for which it was originally written.

At its first performance *Magnificence* must have staggered the courtiers who looked on. No one could miss its application. The struggle between the 'party of prodigality' and the 'party of economy' was going on in their very midst. They had just seen the old counsellors Measure and Circumspection driven out or kept away from the court by Wolsey. And, for minds trained in ethical analysis – a fact which is implicit in the very vogue of the morality – the crowd of conspirators was a transparent screen enough. Besides, Wolsey was not in practice the lone figure we have made him out to be. This 'gay finder out of new pastimes,' as Tyndale called him,[11] had no lack of instruments in his task of distracting the King. If we seek individual models for the court-vices, we need go no further than the King's Minions. In that dissipated crew were some highly concrete originals for the fops, intriguers and dandified lechers of *Magnificence*.

Moreover, slipped in here and there, the audience would find more direct hints of where they were to look. Late in the play, Folly remarks:

I have another maner of sort
That I laugh at for my disport,
And those be they that come up of nought
(As some be not far, and if it were well sought);
Such dawes, whatsoever they be,
That be set in auctorité.
Anon he waxeth so hy and proud,
He frowneth fiersly, brimly brow'd;
The knave wold make it coy, and he coud; . . .
All that he doth must be alow'd,
And 'This is not well done, sir; take hede!'
And maketh him besy where is no nede. . . .

There is nothing here that could be taken exception to. It was the traditional sketch of the beggar on horseback: even the sly transition from plural to singular was normal enough. But the whole passage echoed the popular conception of Wolsey, with his bumptious and *parvenu* arrogance. And, cautiously as it is phrased, a clever actor could point it to perfection as he mimicked the familiar 'Take heed!' of the lofty Cardinal. There may be other touches too, which time has erased for us. But one we can still recognise, in the passing hit:

A carter a courtier! it is a worthy wark,
That with his whip his mares was wont to yark;

for Roy shows us that among Wolsey's many nicknames was 'the Carter of York.'[12]

But the chief impression that a spectator took away from *Magnificence* must surely have been awe – awe at the portrait of the hero. Once again, Skelton was within the safety-zone of tradition – if not dramatically, then ethically – when he set out to depict his imaginary ruler. Technically, Magnificence stood for the man in great place. It was not necessary to picture him as a king; the term covered any person of exalted rank, in so far as he was obliged to spend on a princely scale. Indeed, the Earl of Northumberland – to whom, at the age of twelve, Skelton had once dedicated his pen – was actually given the name of the Magnificent on account of his ostentatious lavishness.[13]

Nevertheless, no one seeing Skelton's play on the stage could have taken Percy for its hero. It was not so much its detail, perhaps, as its obvious application inside the royal Palace. The greater overshadows the less. Skelton, too, had been Henry's tutor for years. All that time he had been accustomed to reading him lectures on the perilous nature of his high office. And for him, clearly, the twenty-five-year-old monarch was still little more than a boy. At the moment, all the people he had gathered about him were men that Skelton detested. They were taking advantage of a young man's inexperience for their own greedy ends. Henry's very virtues – his heedless generosity and animal high spirits – were being slyly converted into extravagance and dissipation. So in his old fashion Skelton proceeded to illustrate, in terms of a modern morality, the decadence that he saw taking place in the Tudor court.

And his version, we must admit, is convincing. At times, indeed, he breaks into a realism that appals. The scene in which Courtly Abusion teaches Magnificence to fly into a royal rage must have scared the onlookers, it is so characteristic of the Henry they knew:

> *Mag.* Alas, my stomake fareth as it would cast!
> *Clo. Col.* Abide, sir, abide; let me hold your hede.
> *Mag.* A bole or a basin, I say, for Goddes brede!
> A, my hede! – but is the horson gone?
> God give him a mischefe! – Nay, now let me alone.
> *Clo. Col.* A good drift, sir, a praty fete!
> By the good Lord, yet your temples bete!
> *Mag.* Nay, so God me help, it was no grete vexacion,
> For I am panged oft-times of this same facion.[14]

bole=bowl.   brede=bread.   horson=whoreson.   praty fete=pretty performance.

Henry had never found it easy to control his feelings. The French herald's account of how he received the news of Marignano is ominously convincing: 'it seemed, to look at him, as if tears would have burst from his eyes, so red were they from the pain he suffered. . . .' It took all the ingenuity of Surrey and the other lords to cover up his undignified petulance.[15] And here Skelton takes us behind the scenes and shows us how Wolsey – himself notorious for his 'fume and haste' – was developing his master's wilfulness into an utter unrestraint that was to darken the whole of his reign. We glimpse here in embryo the gigantic bully of the 'thirties and 'forties, who greeted his first minister with buffets and sent two queens, a duke, a cardinal and scores of humbler individuals to the block.

§ 4. SANCTUARY

There is no clue as to where *Magnificence* was actually performed. It is hard to believe that so barbed a warning could have been inflicted on Henry himself. It is not impossible, however. The freedom of speech he permitted is no less hard to credit than his occasional savage punishments. A preacher could say almost anything before the King. 'Latimer,' as Froude points out, 'spoke as freely to Henry VIII of neglected duties, as to the peasants in his Wiltshire parish.'[16]

Skelton himself had a double defence to fall back on. He had been the King's schoolmaster; and he was now a minister of the Church. But, even if Henry was prepared to listen, there still remained Wolsey. And the Cardinal had no respect whatever for these antiquated traditions of free speech. Skelton must have known what had just happened to Polydore Vergil. Having lived in England as papal sub-collector for the better part of a dozen years, this witty, good-natured Italian was familiar to everyone at Westminster. In 1514 Wolsey chose him for a secret mission to Rome. Unhappily, while he was away, Wolsey and Henry decided to put Ammonio, their joint secretary, in his place. No one enjoys being supplanted; and when he got back to London in 1515, Polydore expressed himself pretty bluntly in a letter to Cardinal Adrian, his superior at Rome. The King, he said roundly, was a mere boy, ruled by others; he even signed letters without knowing what was in them. As for *le. mi.* (as Polydore dubbed Wolsey) he was hateful to heaven and earth, a tyrant abused by all England. . . .

Polydore's letter was written on 3 March 1515. It was intercepted and sent back to Wolsey's secretary; and Polydore was promptly put in the Tower. For the gay and laughter-loving humanist this was a catastrophe of the first order. Polydore was not built for imprisonment. But he was still there, pale now and spiritless, when the news reached him that Wolsey had received the hat. In desperation, he threw all scruple to the winds. One morning the Cardinal was handed a message addressed 'to the

most reverend lord my God, most worthy lord cardinal of York.'
It was from Polydore; informing him of the prisoner's ecstasy
when he heard the glorious news. If only the Cardinal would give
him the opportunity to fly to his feet and rejoice in him 'as in
God my saviour'! And more to the same effect.

Despite himself, Wolsey purred. Where the Pope and the
University of Oxford had pleaded in vain, flattery succeeded –
gross and blasphemous as it was. Before Christmas the Tower gates
had clanged to behind a free Polydore. And, as his *History*
reminds us, it was the Italian who had the last word in the
encounter.[17]

Now Skelton had said much the same things as Polydore about
King and Cardinal – though, it must be admitted, with rather
more circumspection. All the same, after *Magnificence* it was as
well to take precautions. Perhaps, when he wrote it, he had had
hopes that the Cardinal's policy would soon land him in failure
and disgrace. If so, he was rudely mistaken. Nothing in Wolsey's
career was cleverer than his swift about-turn after the fiasco of '16.
Cutting his losses, he set to work to restore the French alliance
that Mary's marriage had started in 1514; and two years' steady
negotiation – aided by the natural fragility of the bond between
Charles and Francis – brought about the triumphant pacifica-
tion of 1518. It left Wolsey stronger than ever: 'the best deed,'
wrote old Bishop Fox, 'that ever was done in England; and, next
to the king, the praise of it is due to you.'[18]

Our poet had now definitely made Westminster his home. In
1516 his elegy on the Lady Margaret was added to the other
poems hanging in the Abbey. For some time – perhaps, off and
on, ever since he became Orator in 1512 – he had been living in
one of the Abbey houses that lay under the grim shadow of the
Sanctuary Tower – where, to-day, stands the Middlesex Guildhall. This gloomy Norman pile rose, squat and solid, a little to
the north-west of St. Margaret's. It took the unusual form of two
churches one on top of the other; the ground floor entered by a
vast door, plated with iron, the upper by a small outside staircase. From its flat roof – covered with a wilderness of crazy hovels
– could be seen the rambling Palace beside the river, where
Canute had once bidden the tide recede. Since the disastrous
fire of 1512 a large part of it lay blackened and derelict, though

the Great Hall still stood proudly, beneath whose magnificent timber roof so much history had been and was yet to be made. West of it stretched the long nave of the Abbey, looking strangely lopped-off without its twin towers; but here again the eye was caught, beyond St. Margaret's, by the white loveliness of the new Henry VII Chapel, gleaming over Old Palace Yard.[19]

Within the Abbey precinct, though it lay at his very doorstep, the King's writ did not run; it was sanctuary. This privilege was not in essence religious, as we tend to think. It had originated in a royal grant – a voluntary relinquishment of legal rights, which even secular lords had occasionally enjoyed. But that was history. Now, only the Church still clung to the favour; and here too it was being hard pressed by a monarchy of unequalled strength and confidence. Even so, its terms were not unlimited. Men already condemned, or taken with the stolen goods on them, were excluded. Every Church building was a refuge from the law – but only for forty days. After that the fugitive had either to surrender or abjure the realm.

Westminster, however, was one of the few places which could offer *perpetual* sanctuary. Among the people who jostled Skelton in these twisting lanes were men like Marquess Berkeley, his would-be assassin, Chamberlen, or the Italian swindler, Grimaldi. Their names were all down in Abbot Islip's sanctuary register, but he could do little to check their behaviour. Together with the Abbey-lubbers attracted there by the monastery dole, they made up a floating population that could sting as well as stink. It is somehow in keeping, one feels, that the very charter that protected them was a forgery.[20]

But neither Wolsey nor the King was content to ignore this ancient loophole for the erring. Ever since the previous reign test case after test case had been brought up; and in 1516 the Prior of St. John's privilege was challenged. By this time Wolsey, as Lord Chancellor, was determined to bring sanctuary into line with Tudor justice. His chance came in 1518. The Pope had sent Campeggio to England, to sign the peace treaty and collect funds for a crusade. Wolsey blandly held him up at Calais, on various pretexts, until Leo had agreed to make Wolsey legate *a latere* too. This was inexcusable presumption: the legate *a latere* was a special ambassador sent 'from the pope's side' on a particular mission. All the same, out Campeggio stayed until Wolsey, on 17 May, received his legacy. That granted, there came a further demand: power to reform the monasteries. What could Leo say? All he wanted was peace, and above all good English pounds for his beloved St. Peter's. On 27 August 1518 the commission duly arrived. It made the new Legate as all-powerful in the English Church as he was in the State.[21]

All this manœuvring could not pass unnoticed in England. Rumours of an impending visitation must have reached Islip months before. And in fact, according to Polydore, Westminster was the first to suffer from the Legate's new authority. 'To give greater weight to his words,' writes the historian, 'he suddenly invaded the monastery of Westminster and made a severe investigation into the conduct of the monks. He peered and pried and turned everything upside down without any measure. . . .' The wretched monks had to bribe him heavily, adds Polydore, before the Legate's vanity was placated.[22]

Shortly before this ruthless descent, the lease of Skelton's house in the Abbey precinct fell in. On 8 August 1518 a lady by the name of Alice Newbury took it over – some relation, perhaps, of Henry VII's Yeoman of the Buckhounds.[23] In the jargon of the indenture, it was 'a tenement situated within the sanctuary on the south side of the Great Belfry of the said monastery, with the dwellings solars cellars and all appurtenances relating to the same, in which tenement John Skelton laureate is now living.'[24] The rent demanded was 7s. 8d. a quarter – nearly £50 a year in modern money; sanctuary rents were, for obvious reasons, rather high. Unfortunately, no attempt is made to describe the building: it was evidently thought sufficient to call it 'the house that Skelton lives in.' Nor is there any hint that the poet was being ousted from his shelter. As a sub-tenant, he was merely changing his landlady; that was all.

But, as Canon Westlake has noted, there is another, and more significant, gap in the lease. Normally, when renting a house within the sanctuary, 'the tenant had to agree not to harbour fugitives or malignants beyond one day and one night after due warning.' In Mistress Newbury's indenture, however, there is no such clause.[25]

What does this omission mean? Are we to follow Canon Westlake and take it that Skelton was already in hiding from Cardinal

Wolsey, his powerful enemy? I think not. For in April 1519 that most peppery of schoolmasters, Robert Whittinton, decided to show what he could do, for a change, in the way of panegyric. On the 22nd of that month he published a slim volume containing, among other things, a Latin poem in praise of Wolsey and another in praise of Skelton.[26] Now Whittinton, to judge from his *Vulgaria*, was definitely in London at this time; perhaps he was already teaching the 'henchmen' or royal pages at Court.[27] Surely no such person, if he were in his right mind, would have dared to put between the same covers two eulogies, one of a great statesman and the other of a man he had just driven into flight! No; we may take it as certain that in 1518 Skelton was still able to appear at Court whenever he felt so inclined.

But the missing clause has still to be accounted for. And the most natural reason for it is surely – just caution. Skelton saw the way things were moving: that needed no great acumen. He knew, too, his own weakness for speaking his mind. So, when his lease came up for renewal, it would do no harm if the Abbey conveniently overlooked its sanctuary provision. As a friend of Islip and the Prior, that was easily arranged. Now, should there be trouble in the future, Wolsey would have no document to which, in his damnable juristic way, he could appeal.[28]

As it was, his card came within an ace of being trumped. In November 1519 Wolsey finally staged the grand assault he had been meditating upon sanctuary. Henry himself was brought into the Star Chamber to thrash the matter out. Wolsey reported that – during, I suppose, his recent visitation – he and Abbot Islip had concocted a special oath for the use of sanctuary-men. But here Abbot Islip stuck gallantly to his charter. Once a man entered his precinct he was, to all intents and purposes, in a foreign land. Even if he took this oath and broke it, it would make no difference. From time immemorial Westminster had been a refuge for the needy, and neither oath nor Cardinal-legate was strong enough to prevail against it.

And, after two days of argument, Wolsey was obliged to give way. His was the longest arm England had ever known, but it could not reach over the wall of Westminster Abbey.[29]

CHAPTER ELEVEN

PARROT SPEAKS

A parable is properly one thing
That of another doth conceiving bring;
Yea, oftentimes, as parables are scann'd,
One score of things by one be understand.

HEYWOOD: *The Spider and the Fly.*

§ 1. BIRD OF PARADISE

'OF PARADISE,' begins Sir John Mandeville with exemplary if somewhat unexpected candour, 'ne cannot I
speken properly: for I was not there.' Nevertheless, in
the Middle Ages wise men had got to know, at second hand, a good
deal about this mysterious corner of the Near East. Paradise was
the highest point on the earth's surface; this is how it had escaped
the Deluge. From the exploring foot of fallen man it was guarded
not only by a gigantic moss-covered wall with a single gate, barred
with fire, but by the craggy desert that stretched round about it.
The garden inside was irrigated by a spring from which flowed the
four paradisal rivers – Pison, Gihon, Euphrates and Tigris. This
was the more necessary since (as Dante reminds us) its lofty peak
was 'raised clear of the exhalations of the water and of the earth,'
and so was rainless. Within this blessed coign death could not
enter. Report had it that Elias and Enoch still lived on amid its
delectable groves, which rang to the marvellous harmony of
innumerable birds.[1]

But among these light-hearted carollers was one bird that did
not sing – the parrot. And the reason for its being there at all is a
fascinating illustration of how the medieval mind looked on the
universe. In Europe parrots were known only as delicate house-
birds from the parched Orient. Obviously, then, they could not
be expected to stand rain: as was proved by the racket they made
during a downpour. 'For the parrot swiftly dies,' decided Alexander Neckam, 'when its skin is much moistened by water.'

To Neckam, therefore, it was plain that such a bird must live in an area of complete drought. Of these there were comparatively few; and Neckam himself plumps for Gilboa. Gilboa was forever dry because of David's curse after the death of Jonathan: 'Ye mountains of Gilboa, let there be no dew, neither let there be rain upon you!' Could anything be more beautifully logical? . . .

But Neckam had overlooked Paradise. That mount too, we have seen, had no dew neither rain upon it; and it was doubtless for this reason that English poetic tradition, at least, maintained the parrot's home to be Paradise.[2]

This in turn involved a further consequence. As Bartholomæus remarks, no living thing could die in Paradise. Hence the bird was immortal. Parrot, in fact, was now qualified for the grander regions of mythology. It was but a short step to confounding the creature *psittacus* with the legendary hero Pittacus – as we actually find them in Boccaccio.[3] The son of Deucalion and Pyrrha, the giant survivors of the Flood, this worthy visited the sage Ethiopians, most distant of men, and lived with them to a great age. At length, in his ripened wisdom, he implored the gods to remove him altogether from human affairs: which they did by turning him into a parrot. So ran the legend. The rare and beautiful bird from the East, with its plumage of perennial green and its mysterious gift of tongues, was now more mythical than the phœnix.

But parrots have an inconvenient habit of actually existing. And a second layer of natural observation thus arose, which added its own curious flavour to the above.

Long ago Aristotle noted that the bird had a weakness for wine; and an echo of the tradition lingers on, half-consciously, as late as *Othello*: 'Drunk? and speak parrot? and squabble? swagger? swear? . . . O thou invisible spirit of wine, if thou hast no name to be known by, let us call thee devil!' But Shakespeare has named it already: Parrot, the spirit of bacchic enthusiasm. The bird's aimless prattle had long linked it with the demented liberation of alcohol; with the frenzy of Dionysos – or the Devil. And side by side with this avatar, there was also the spoilt domestic clown of so many wealthy and aristocratic households. 'Its cleverness is amazing,' comments Neckam on this point, 'and it is better than a troupe of actors at raising a laugh. For its flattery is such that, when made a pet of, it is always asking to kiss a person it knows. And if a mirror is presented to it, like Narcissus it grows entranced with its own image and, now rejoicing and now grieving, with a lover's mimicry seems longing to embrace itself.' In the last detail we glimpse something very near the phallic symbol of the Vedas, the green parrot ridden by Kâmas, Hindu god of love.[4]

It is now, perhaps, more understandable why Skelton's contemporary, Jean Lemaire de Belges, should have picked on the parrot when he wanted to pay a delicate compliment to his patroness, Marguérite, Duchess of Burgundy. His two *Epistres de l'amant verd* use this convenient figure of the cherished pet, with privileges that are denied to ordinary mortals. Lemaire was much read in England at this date: even Barclay was not above borrowing from his work. A good many readers of *Speak, Parrot*, we may safely guess, would start with his Green Lover somewhere at the back of their minds.[5]

§ 2. 'SHREDS OF SENTENCE'

It is no mere bird, then, that confronts us in this strange poem of Skelton's. Yet how richly the opening stanzas convey the reality of a handsome, strutting lady's pet:

> My name is Parrot, a bird of Paradise,
>   By nature devised of a wonderous kind,
> Deintily dieted with divers delicate spice,
>   Til Euphrates, that flode, driveth me into Inde,
>   Where men of that countrey by fortune me find
> And send me to great ladies of estate:
> Then Parot must have an almon or a date,
>
> A cage curiously carven, with silver pin,
>   Properly painted, to be my covertour,
> A mirror of glass, that I may toot therin.
>   These maidens full merily, with many a divers flowre
>   Freshly they dress and make swete my bowre,
> With 'Speke, Parrot, I pray you!' full curtesly they say,
> 'Parrot is a goodly bird, a pretty popagey!'

'SHREDS OF SENTENCE'

With my beck bent, my litel wanton eye,
  My fedders fresh as is the em'rawd grene,
About my neck a circulet like the rich ruby,
  My litel legges, my feet both fete and clene,
  I am a minion to wait upon the quene.
'My proper Parrot, my litel prety fole!'
With ladies I lern, and go with them to scole.

flode=flood. covertour=coverture. toot=peep. freshly=elegantly. em'rawd
              =emerald. fete=neat. proper=dainty.

Parrot confides to us that his life has not always been this cosy
imprisonment. Like Man himself, he was born in Paradise and
nourished on its rarest spices until, rather obscurely, one of its
rivers bore him off to the outside world. The geography may seem
a little confused; but in Skelton's day *India* was frequently used to
cover the whole of Asia.[6] But, however he made the deafening
descent from his mountain peak, Parrot is now a captive in some
lady's boudoir, with an elegant cage, a mirror to admire himself in,
and a bevy of girls to make a fuss of the gay prisoner. And he rather
deserves it, thinks Parrot, preening his fine feathers complacently.

For a time it is all happily abstract and ethical. Parrot is simply
repeating, in his own allusive way, the oldest of medieval clichés:
measure is treasure. But finally a proverb pulls us up with a jerk:

> But Reason and Wit wanteth their provincial
> When Wilfulnes is vicar-general.

It seems to be Parrot's own invention: 'When Will is pope, then
Wit has no bishop left.'[7] This curious aphorism, he remarks, has
hit the nail on the head. Shut your mouth, he warns himself
instantly, and say no more!

Fresh from reading *Magnificence*, we now begin to suspect what the
wise bird is after. And the following stanzas confirm our feeling:

> Besy, besy, besy, and besines again!
>   *Que pensez voz*, Parrot? what meneth this besines?
> *Vitulus in Oreb* troubled Aron's brain;
>   Melchisedeck merciful made Moloc merciles.
>   To wise is no virtue, to medling, to restles;
> In mesure is tresure, *cum sensu maturato*;
> *Ne tropo sano ne tropo mato.*

Aram was fired with Caldyes fier called Ur;
  Jobab was brought up in the land of Hus;
The linage of Lot toke support of Assur;
Jereboseth is Ebrue, who list the cause discus –
  Peace, Parrot, ye prate as ye were *ebrius*!
Houst thé, *lever God van hemrik, ic seg!*
  In Popering grew peres whan Parrot was an eg. [8]

cum, etc=to the ripened sense. *Ne tropo,* etc.=*ne troppo . . . matto* (not too sane and not too mad). linage=lineage. *ebrius*=drunk. Houst=Hist! *lever,* etc.=*dear God of heaven, I say (Flemish).* peres=pears.

Business, we must recollect, had not yet won its Puritan aureole of virtue; in Skelton's day it was still the busybody's concern. In *Magnificence* it is the wilful Fancy who is 'busy, busy, and ever busy'; while, more ominous still, the Vulgate speaks of a certain devil whose name is *Negotium* – 'a devil,' as Sir Thomas More explains somewhat tautologously, 'that is ever full of business, in tempting folk to much evil business.' So all this activity in the land, for Parrot, smacked of no good. What does it all mean? he asks himself. And, like a good Christian, he turns for instruction to the Old Testament. On Mount Horeb it was a golden calf that seduced Aaron from his duty to God. Melchisadec . . . Moloch. . . . When a 'king of peace' grows *too* mild and good-natured, that is the chance for the monstrous bull-god of Phœnicia to rear its evil head.

Seeing that Henry had already been compared to Melchisadec in *Against the Scots,* and that Wolsey was popularly known as the son of a butcher, Parrot's drift is becoming gradually less obscure. Excess of virtue, he concludes, may be a danger to the State when you have wild animals to reckon with, who have thrown off all the restraints of reason. [9]

The next stanza begins with an interpretation of Gen. xi. 28: 'And Haran died . . . in Ur of the Chaldees.' Since the name *Ur* means fire, the commentators explained that the Chaldees, being fire-worshippers, burnt Haran to death for refusing to bow the knee before their false god. The following line reminds us that Jobab (as Job was sometimes known) lived in the land of Uz. Parrot then refers to a great rising of her neighbours against Israel, which is commemorated in Ps. lxxxii of the Vulgate. There is a link back with Haran here; for he was the father of Lot, while it is Lot's children, the Moabites and Ammonites, who are now, together with Assyria, threatening the Israelites. And, finally, we are told that 'Jerubbesheth is Hebrew.' Jerubbesheth was another name for Gideon, the great leader of Israel. It occurs only once in the whole Bible; and indeed, when Skelton wrote it was a comparative newcomer: we find it for the first time in the Venice Bible of 1519, and it was soon to disappear again from the Vulgate. As Parrot remarks, the name is Hebrew; and the current interpretation of it was 'judging the shameful (*iudicans igno-miniam*).'[10]

Now that we have the Bible in English we no longer read it: which sets us at a disadvantage immediately. Nor is the matter improved by the differences between Vulgate and Authorised spelling. But let us take heart. Parrot was obviously out to puzzle even the educated reader of his own age. Why else should he pick on these unfamiliar names for Job and Gideon? It is only by sheer spadework, then, that we are intended to dig out his meaning. Still, that is now over, and the pieces are in our hands. Let us see how they fit together.

The first two lines talk of two great heroes of old, Haran and Job, who behaved nobly even though one of them lived among the Chaldees and the other among the people of Uz. But their descendants, the children of Lot, have fallen away from this high standard; now they conspire with the Assyrians to attack Israel. And Gideon? Gideon, that judge of the shameful, is no foreigner, concludes Parrot – quite irrelevantly, it seems. It is only when we reach the first envoi of the poem that the mystery is solved for us. There, we find that Jerubbesheth undoubtedly stands for Wolsey.

The argument now reveals itself: it is a political analogy. In the good old days Israel was immune even to enemies from without. Her heroes could survive a whole lifetime among the heathen and preserve their virtue uncorrupted. But now it is a different story. The children of Lot call in the hated Assyrian; while Israel's worst foe of all is no alien but the very leader of her people, Wolsey – an excellent judge of what is shameful!

The mere mention of Jerubbesheth appears to scare Parrot. With a vile pun he takes refuge in mock self-reproach. Or seems to: for when we examine his words we note that he has broken into Flemish and, in the very next breath, referred to the town of Poperinghe in Flanders. Now, as we shall see, Skelton was writing towards the end of 1521 – at which time Wolsey was in Calais.

But for three weeks in August he had been closeted with the Emperor in nearby Bruges. In his very disclaimer, then, Parrot is hinting where we ought to look. Someone has been after the pears in Flanders!

But the neatest, and certainly the most shattering, thrust comes in a stanza that follows:

> *Ic dien* serveth for the exstrich fether;
> > *Ic dien* is the language of the land of Beme;
> In Afric tongue *byrsa* is a thong of lether;
> > In Palestina there is Ierusaleme.
> > *Colustrum* now for Parot, white bred and swete creme!
> Our Thomasen she doth trip, our Jenet she doth shail:
> Parrot hath a black beard and a fair grene tail.

On the face of it Parrot is still innocently showing off his poly-gluttony. He calls to mind the motto, 'I serve,' which, with the ostrich-plume, was at this time one of the royal crests. (It had not yet come to be reserved for the Prince of Wales.) *Ich dien*, he remarks, is German – the language they speak in Bohemia. And we may think there is nothing more to it than the naïve pun in 'serveth.' The next line has been criticised, on the score that a Greek scholar would have known βύρσα is Greek for a hide. But in this case, at least, Parrot is more than a step ahead of his critics. He did not rely, Parrot, exclusively on his dictionary; sometimes he read Vergil in the original, and *cum commento*.

Now, it had become the Renaissance fashion to print Vergil with extracts from five commentaries. And in 1487 Landino's edition notes, beside *Æneid* I. 367: 'DONATUS: *byrsa*: which means "hide" both in Greek . . . *and in Punic*.' This Donatus was a fifteen-century discovery; and it was not until 1535 that his commentary (where he reveals that in fact the Punic word for hide was *bursaft*) was printed in full. So one can hardly blame Parrot, in 1521, for assuming that *byrsa* was not only Greek, but 'Afric.' He was at least abreast of contemporary scholarship – which is more than can be said for his detractors.[11]

But there is a great deal more to the line than a mere parade of learning. For one thing it is intended to recall the origin of Carthage, as explained by Vergil in the passage where *byrsa* occurs. The city had been won by trickery. Dido had asked for as much land as an ox-hide would cover, and when this was granted she had cut the hide into strips and surrounded enough territory for a metropolis.

But for the Tudor there was a far more topical meaning to the word. The *burse* was the official container in which was carried the Chancellor's great seal. In Shakespeare's *Henry VIII* Wolsey's first entry is made 'with the Purse borne before him.' Can there be any doubt, then, that Parrot's *byrsa* too stands for the Cardinal? And there is still a further and vital reference to note. Parrot talks not of a hide, but of a 'thong of leather.' In part, it is true, he is thinking of Dido's wily action; but he has also a more modern text in mind. 'Of unbought hide men carveth broad thong,' says the *Proverbs of Hending*; and in our Introduction we heard Margaret Paston's dry comment: 'Men cut large thongs here of other men's leather.' That was in 1465; but if Dame Margaret had lived until 1521 Wolsey could have shown her what was really possible in the way of thong-carving. After starting life as a poor chaplain he was already the wealthiest man in England. . . . The contrast between the King, who is content to serve rather than rule, and his Cardinal-legate of a Chancellor, who has used Dido's cunning to enrich himself at the expense of all England, is devastating.[12]

And yet, what has Parrot actually said? He has played the commentator on a phrase of German and a term in Vergil: nothing more. Indeed, he has already lost interest and is crying out for *colostrum* – his favourite beestings – like the spoilt pet he is. While in the final couplet, rubbing our eyes, we find ourselves confronted with – the gaudy male, suddenly flaunting the pride of his perennial youth. Here the symbolism becomes wholly sexual. From his carven cage, he reminds us, Parrot sees the ladies in all their frailty; they trip and straddle in the queer dance of love while he looks on, bright-eyed, a smaller image of that spirit of Lust which is described in the *Court of Love*:

> Stood one in green, full large of brede and length,
> His beard as black as feathers of the crow.

And what is his brilliant tail but the dream of every old man from the time of Chaucer's Reeve:

For in our will there sticketh ever a nail
To have an hoar head and a greenë tail . . .[13]

For a deceiving moment, in fact, Parrot is merely the Green Lover.

§ 3. WHO IS PARROT?

In the closing stanzas of the poem proper Parrot appeals for
'liberty to speak.' For he is no vulgar fowl, no magpie or starling –

But Parot is mine own dere hart and my dere derling.

And in impressive accents he goes on:

> Parrot is a fair bird for a lady;
> God of His goodnes him framed and wrought;
> When Parrot is ded, he doth not putrefy;
> Yé, all thing mortal shall torn unto nought
> Except mannes soul, that Christ so dere bought,
> That never may die, nor never die shall:
> Make moch of Parrot, the popegay ryal.
>
> For that pereles Prince that Parrot did create,
> He made you of nothing by His majesty.
> Point well this problem that Parrot doth prate
> And remembre among, how Parrot and ye
> Shall lepe from this life, as mery as we be.
> Pomp, pride, honour, riches and worldly lust,
> Parrot saith plainly, shall tourn all to dust.[14]

Who is this popinjay royal so mysteriously exempt from decay,
the bird of Paradise with all languages at his command, who is at
once the Green Lover and the wise son of Deucalion, as well as a
wine-bibber, a chatterer of crazy nonsense and a gaudy minion
of the ladies? Most recent critics are satisfied to think him 'merely
Skelton.'[15] But (satire apart) allegory does not normally work in
these simple personal terms; and Parrot claims the status of
allegoria for his poem. A more pertinent suggestion is that he
stands for Anima, man's soul – which gains support from the odd
reading *she* for *he* (l. 217) in all the early prints.

But if we look closely, we see that Parrot is careful to distinguish himself from man's soul. The soul, he declares, will never die; whereas Parrot will die but not putrefy. In any case, no contemporary would have dreamt of identifying Anima with the popinjay of Paradise. It was a scholastic axiom that 'the soul, being spirit, cannot dwell in a dry place.' Ascribed to St. Augustine, the cliché was so familiar that one of Rabelais' topers makes use of it in the famous drinking scene. How, then, could Parrot be the Soul, dwelling as he must do exclusively *in sicco*?[16]

No; Parrot is neither Skelton nor the Soul. On his own showing he stands for something halfway between man's soul, which never dies at all, and his body, which not only dies, but rots. Surely there can be only one answer: *the poetic faculty*. Parrot represents that strange inspiration which descends upon a man and makes him utter that which will 'not putrefy.' Later ages would call it Imagination. Socrates too had it in mind when he sought to define the poet: the irrational enthusiasm which characterises the drunkard and the maniac as much as the prophet and the bard. And in Skelton's day it crops up in every discussion of poetry.

Now we see why Parrot is said to come from Paradise, and why he shows an eternal freshness and beauty even in death. Irresponsible as he seems when in wanton mood, he yet brings with him a breath of immortality. It is for this reason that Skelton bids us 'make much of Parrot, the popinjay royal.'

There is an epilogue to this solemn close. A strange series of apparently disjointed notes, rather like a leaf from the poet's notebook, it has so far gone unexplained – a queer excrescence on a queer poem. But in fact, when rightly understood, it clinches our interpretation of the allegory.

A mysterious lady here makes her appearance for the first time. Galathea by name, she addresses Parrot in these words:

> Speke, Parot, I pray you for Maryes sake,
> What mone he made when Pamphilus lost his make.[17]

A side-note informs us that she is thinking of a little work then familiar to everyone – so familiar, indeed, that it has given us the word 'pamphlet.' *Pamphilus de amore Galatheae* was the best, as it was the most popular, of the medieval imitations of Ovid. Its theme is almost exactly that of Richardson's *Pamela* – as seen from the standpoint of Mr. B——. The well-to-do young Pamphilus falls in love with the poor but respectable Galathea. Venus advises *ars et officium* – devotion tempered with cunning. In the end he lures his love to the house of the inevitable crone, where, to the shrill repetition of *Pamphile, tolle manus*! he makes the most of the occasion. The crone finds a happy way out in marriage, and all ends well. In England Pamphilus had an extraordinary popularity; all the same, its tone of Gallic banter was not one to commend itself to officialdom. Like the *Art of Love*, its use was strictly banned to the grammarian at Oxford.[18]

So Galathea is referring to herself when she begs Parrot to repeat Pamphilus' sweet moan at the loss of his mate. On the other hand, since there is no sign of this tragedy in the Latin poem, it is clear that Skelton must be using the name symbolically. This becomes patent when we read Parrot's unexpected version of the lament:

> *My proper Besse,*
> *My praty Besse,*
> > *Turn ons again to me,*
> *For slepest thou, Besse,*
> *Or wakest thou, Besse,*
> > *Mine hert hit is with thé.*

> My deisy delectabil,
> My primerose commendabil,
> My violet amiabil,
> My joy inexplicabil,
> > Now torn again to me.
> I wil be firm and stabil
> And to you serviceabil
> And also prophitabil,
> If ye be agreabil
> > To turn again to me.

> *My proper Besse,* etc.[19]

What earthly connexion can this homely English ditty have with Pamphilus and Galathea, one asks. It seems to be merely a bit more of Parrot's aimless gibberish; and indeed the problem has generally been given up as insoluble. But the Early Tudor reader would catch the point at once. It was a clear allusion to one of his favourite songs. A moralised ballad, of a type then popular, it began:

> '*Come over the burn, Besse,*
> *Thou little pretty Besse,*
>> *Come over the burn, Besse, to me!*'
> The burn is this world blind
> And Besse is mankind,
>> So proper I can none find as she;
> She dances and leaps,
> And Christ stands and clepes:
> 'Come over the burn, Besse, to me!'

We find it still being quoted in *King Lear*.[20]

Besse, then, is Mankind – and so, consequently, is Galathea. And all at once we remember the derivation of the name Pamphilus. Skelton's dictionary translated it for him as *totus amor:* the all-loving. Accordingly Pamphilus, like the singer in the ballad, can be no other than Christ, the God of Love. What the age would call a wanton trifle turns out to be pious allegory – Christ's lament over the fickleness of humanity!

Parrot is actually giving us an illustration of the poet in his most serious guise: the revealer of God's word. And it is obviously intended as a warning. Even when he seems at his most frivolous, we should never forget that his light words *may* contain a profound and holy truth. His 'cloudy figures' should not be allowed to deceive us. And the fact is underlined in a characteristic quotation from Martial: 'My pages are lewd but my life without spot.'

Incoherent as it is, therefore, our epilogue turns out to be much more closely linked with the poem than appears at first sight. It completes the revelation of Parrot's identity by showing him as the vehicle of religious truth. But, as we shall shortly demonstrate, even this does not exhaust the meaning of Galathea's sudden entry just before the curtain's fall.

§ 4. THE BACKGROUND TO *SPEAK, PARROT*

There is, fortunately, no longer any need to prove that *Speak, Parrot* was written late in 1521. Arrived at independently by Gordon, Nelson and myself, the evidence for this date has been amply set out elsewhere.[21] In brief, it is based upon certain figures which follow the envois to the poem. Varying from 30 October,

'33,' to about December, '34,' they are detailed enough to prove beyond a doubt that Skelton was referring to Wolsey's 1521 visit to Calais. And when we find a similar numeral used to date three, and perhaps four, other works of his,[22] it becomes obvious that we are dealing with Skelton's own private system of chronology. It began in October or November 1488 – when, we have suggested, Skelton first entered the Tudor service. But however it arose, we owe a great deal of information to this genial little idiosyncrasy of the poet's.

On the face of it, Wolsey's behaviour in 1521 should have won the hearty approval of that stout Francophobe, Skelton. Officially, the Cardinal arrived at Calais on 2 August as a peacemaker; his task being to reconcile Francis and Charles – now Holy Roman Emperor and at war with the French. But in fact, as everyone seemed to be aware, he was going there to hold off the French as long as possible before openly siding with Charles. 'And,' comments Brewer, 'there was not a man throughout the realm of England . . . who did not rejoice at the prospect.'[23] Why, then, should Skelton have protested so vigorously?

Indeed, it was at this moment that his caution finally deserted him and he spoke out 'true and plain.' Through the whole of the poem proper Skelton had managed, somehow, to keep his satire under control. Glancing back over it, we spy no single reference which could be used against him in a court of law – as he ends by pointing out, triumphantly. All along, he had been working under the safe shield of metaphor and allegory. But on 30 October something happened. It was on that day – dated with meticulous care – that he wrote an envoi to the poem, directed at Wolsey much more clearly than anything which had gone before. Speaking now *in propria persona*, Skelton asks Parrot to bid Jerubbesheth 'home to resort';

> For the cliffes of Scalop they rore wellaway
> And the sandes of Cefas being to waste and fade,
> For replicacion restles that he of late ther made.[24]

The allegoric pavice is beginning to wear thin. Calais may not be mentioned directly; but everyone knew his Bible well enough to recognise Cephas as another name for St. Peter – and Calais well enough to recall St. Peter's in the sandy flats just behind it.

It was no great step from that to the equation: scallop=seashell
=Scales or Escalles, the village on Cap Blanc-Nez a few miles
off.[25] There is still a modicum of camouflage; but, when we
remember the date at which the envoi was circulating, the target
is better defined than it seems. If *Lenvoy primere* were thrust under
Skelton's nose by an irate Cardinal, he would have a lot of explaining to do.

The second envoi throws off the screen almost entirely. It is
now 'seignor Zadok,' chief priest of Israel, who is being urged to
return. And Skelton continues:

> With porpose and grandepose he may fede him fat,
>   Though he pamper not his paunch with the grete seal:
> We have longed and loked long time for that,
>   Which causeth pore suters have many a hongry mele.

When Wolsey went to Calais he carried with him the Chancellor's
great seal – 'which,' remarks Hall, 'had not been seen before.' It
was a typical example of his by now insatiable appetite for power.
Its absence caused such confusion among the 'poor suitors,' who
found that nothing could be done for them in the English courts,
that Pace had to write and beg for its speedy return. But Wolsey
was obdurate. So, 'during the continuance of the Cardinal in
Calais all writs and patents were there by him sealed, and no
sheriffs chosen for lack of his presence.' Let him have his porpoise
and grampus, cries Skelton from England, so long as he lets us
have the seal![26]

The secret is out at last. Allegory has dwindled to metaphor,
and even the metaphor is translated into plain English. With his
mention of the poor suitors and their hunger for the great seal,
Skelton has abandoned his defences and is fighting in the open.
From now to the end of the poem his satiric cloak is a mere formality; it is worn in such a way as to reveal everything. But the
question remains. Why did Skelton choose to speak out at this
particular moment?

§ 5. GALATHEA

Some time after the first of December 1521, in another of his
tailpieces, the poet introduces Galathea once more. Again she
addresses Parrot:

I compas the conveyance unto the Capitall
Of ouer clerk Cleros – whither thider, and why not hither?
For Pass-a-pace-apace is gon to cach a mole
Over Scarpary *mala vi*, monsire Cy-and-slidder:
What sequel shall folow when pendugims mete together?

compas=ponder.   ouer=our.   whither=to what end, why?   *mala vi*=with ill hail.

Parrot responds with a hymn of hate against the man who is
'Franticness and Wilfulness and Brainless ensemble':

His wolves hede, wan, blo as lede, gapeth over the crown;
   Hit is to fere lest he wold were the garland on his pate,
   Paregal with all princes far passing his estate. . . .[27]

blo=livid.   to fere=to be feared.   were=wear.   paregal=equal.

There can be no doubt as to the events Galathea is referring to.
In the exchanges at Bruges the Emperor Charles had promised,
in return for England's support, to back Wolsey at the next papal
election. On 24 November England came out openly as an imperial ally – and on 2 December Pope Leo died of a chill. Here was
Charles's opportunity to keep his side of the bargain. Wolsey saw
the tiara actually within his grasp. Wild with excitement, he
plunged impetuously into action. He wrung letters of support
from Henry and sent them by special envoy to Rome.

His choice for this important mission was the mercurial and
dapper Pace. But with all his dandyism Pace was no fool: only the
previous April he had been appointed Greek Lecturer at Cambridge. Witty, music-loving, fanatically anti-French, he had
already spent a great part of his career in confidential missions of
this kind.[28]

A close friend of the schoolmaster Lily, Pace was not the kind of
person to endear himself to Skelton. This is evident enough in the
nicknames of our poem: they indicate a slippery individual who is
always vanishing on dubious errands. Nor is the present one any
exception. Pace is now off on the unsavoury job of mole-catching,
and the hunt is taking him over the Tuscan hills. What kind of bird
a *pendugim* was is not certain: Dyce suggests, very plausibly, the
penguin. A group of them might well be likened to the solemn
conclave of cardinals which was now meeting to elect a new
pope. The mention of Tuscany, and still more of the Roman

Capitol, in conjunction with the date, make it certain that the papal conclave is in question.[29]

But who is 'our clerk Cleros'? It is generally agreed that the name must be Greek, and that it stands for John Clerk, the English Ambassador at Rome. But what does Galathea say about him? 'I ponder,' she begins, 'his *conveyance unto* the Capitol.' The motion towards is unmistakable. Yet John Clerk had been in Rome since the previous April: how, then, could he convey himself or be conveyed thither in December? No, tempting as it seems, this theory must be rejected.

The true solution appears when we examine the movements of Pass-a-pace-apace. Pace arrived at Ghent on 22 December. On the 24th he had a long interview with the Venetian Ambassador – an old friend of his. Among other things he wanted a passport for one of his attendants, who was going on to Rome ahead of him. Poor Pace, in fact, had fallen ill at the very outset of his journey; and, knowing that he could never make his usal speed now, he had decided to send on his confidential servant – *Thomas Clerk*. But all his precautions were useless. Long before Clerk, travelling post as he was, had got to Rome, the Cardinals on 9 January had elected the Emperor's old tutor Pope Adrian VI. And, despite Charles's repeated promises, his Ambassador had made no attempt to put forward Wolsey's name in the conclave.[30]

But this disappointment was still in the future. When Skelton wrote his comment, at the end of December 1521, the news had obviously just reached England that Thomas Clerk was speeding on ahead of Pace with the royal message. So the 'garland' might yet be seen incongruously crowning the wolf's head that now gaped lividly behind the English throne. There is no need for us to ask who that is: already Wolsey has been described as Lycaon, who was turned into a wolf for his evil ways. His name – often Latinised as *Wolvesæus* – gave an ideal basis for the pun.[31]

Our original query is still unanswered, however. Was it mere personal hatred that exploded, at the end of 1521, into this astonishing diatribe? Partly, we cannot doubt; there is no reason to question either the depth or the sincerity of the poet's anger. Long before it had been driven home to Sir Thomas More, Skelton saw in Wolsey 'the evil genius of Henry and of England.'[32] But I do not think that this was the sole cause of the change-over, in

Speak, Parrot, from covert satire to open abuse. That is why we pinned down the spot where it occurs. For it took place, be it noticed, *just after the first entry of the mysterious Galathea.*

Now, we have already identified this lady as a personification of Mankind. But there is a further point to bear in mind. The true allegory is capable of more than one interpretation. In its full development it can be read on various levels. Thus we find Bernard André composing 'a notable exposition of Vergil's *Eclogues* according to the four interpretations.'[33] The Tudor reader was trained to poetic ambiguity. He was in no way distressed by the effort, so painful for us, of conceiving Spenser's Duessa as not only a wicked lady in a romance, but as the abstract Falsehood and the contemporary Queen of Scots at one and the same time. And in *Speak, Parrot* Skelton was, I believe, taking a similar liberty.

Let us look again at the epilogue where Galathea makes her entrance. She begs Parrot to sing for her a lover's lament. Parrot does so – in the form of a little song to Besse. A religious meaning has been proposed for this, and I do not now wish to question its validity in the slightest. The point is, this does not exclude a 'historical' interpretation as well. And I believe Skelton hit on the name Besse with a smile of satisfaction; for it was the name not only of Mankind in the ballad, but – *of his patroness, Elizabeth Countess of Surrey*! Galathea, I am convinced, also represents the lively and headstrong girl who became second wife to the Earl of Surrey.

There was nothing undignified, as we may tend to feel, in such a procedure. The *Song of Lady Bessy* had already graced the contraction by applying it to the Queen of Henry VII; and the very ballad used by Skelton was shortly to be adapted to the praise of Good Queen Bess herself.[34] While for the amorous note, as between patroness and poet, Skelton was drawing on the entire tradition of courtly love. His model, Lemaire de Belges, indeed, had carried it a good deal further than he. Meanwhile, our theory accounts for much that was hitherto baffling about the poem. It explains, for example, why Parrot stresses so incessantly his position *vis-à-vis* the ladies. This is emphasised over and over again. Parrot is sold to ladies great of estate, with maidens full merrily to deck his cage for him. He learns with ladies, and goes with them to school; he is meet to dwell among ladies; he is a fair bird for a lady. . . . All this, it might be argued, was merely to conceal his satire. I do not think so. On the contrary, I believe it had a basis in literal fact – the fact that about this time Skelton became an intimate of the Countess of Surrey.

The very clumsiness of the device is also explained, if not excused, on this hypothesis. From any other point of view, Galathea is a bad mistake. She comes in too late to contribute anything to the poem itself; and her main rôle is to egg Skelton on to speak his mind about Wolsey. Otherwise, she only succeeds in wrecking the structure of the poem, which after her appearance trails on in an endless series of afterthoughts, hopelessly unbalancing the work as a whole. But, conceived as a real person, her irruption becomes at least comprehensible.

If our conjecture is valid, we have still to account for the Countess's unladylike spurring of her protégé into such open invective. What was it that induced Galathea to play the Fury in this remorseless way, with her –

Now Parot, my swete bird, speke out yet ons again,
Set aside all sophims and speke now trew and plain?[35]

CHAPTER TWELVE

WAR AND PEACE

Earl of Surrey: I'll startle you
Worse than the sacring bell, when the brown wench
Lay kissing in your arms, Lord Cardinal!

SHAKESPEARE: *Henry VIII.*

§ 1. *VIEUX RÉGIME*

AT THE death of Henry VII there was one duke left in England. The decimation of the old feudal baronage set going in the Wars of the Roses had been quietly completed by the first Tudor King. Only his method was less that of violence than the more profitable one of confiscation. Henry left the survivors more or less in peace: merely ensuring that they did not have the power to give him any trouble. The whole of his policy, indeed, is typified in his treatment of the Howards.[1]

Time had been when a Duke of Norfolk could blandly support his claim to an estate with the armed might of three thousand retainers. But that epoch, Henry had decided, was over. The same Duke's son celebrated the Tudor's Coronation in the Tower; and when he came out four years later, Henry kept him on the northern marches for a decade, far from any temptation to stir up faction, however innocently, at Court. Neither his title nor his estates were restored to him. He remained Earl of Surrey till he was seventy, when Flodden compelled Henry VIII, in common decency, to reward him at last with the family dukedom. But all through his life Thomas Howard I stood crippled in the most effective way – through his pocket.

It was in this atmosphere of proud but penniless grandeur that Thomas, his heir, was brought up. Although, in 1495, he had been permitted to marry Anne Plantagenet with great ceremonial in Westminster Abbey, the daughter of Edward IV had little to bring him but her royal blood; at her death, in the winter of 1512, he found himself as poor as he had started.

But Thomas was of different metal from his father. The latter appeared to have resigned himself to the new Tudor ways: not so the son. Young Thomas refused to acquiesce in the disappearance

of the Howard glory. Small, lean and dark, there was a smoulder-
ing fire of pride in that compact body that boded ill for his
opponents. It showed even through the courtly polish of his normal
demeanour. When he was nearing sixty – still without a grey
hair to his head – a Venetian saw him and recorded his verdict:
'He is prudent, liberal, affable and astute; associates with everybody, has great experience in the administration of the kingdom,
discusses affairs admirably. . . .' The sting comes in the final words:
' . . . aspires to greater elevation.' A man of more ambition than
scruple, Thomas Howard II.

His first concern was the restoration of the family finances. A
Howard was not bred to the pinching ways of the average City
burgess; and young Thomas, as his wife could testify, 'was always
a great player.'[2] When to this weakness was added the necessity
of cutting a suitable figure at the Octavian Court, it is hardly
surprising that on his first wife's death Lord Thomas found it
advisable to think seriously, since he could not earn one, of marrying into a fortune. It was indeed his only resource. But where his
father had looked towards the well-lined gentry of East Anglia, the
son turned instinctively in the direction of the great Duke of
Buckingham. Not only (then) the sole duke, but the richest man
in England, Buckingham had a number of marriageable daughters. What more eligible match for a Howard, even if he were
penniless and older than their father?

So at Shrovetide 1513 Lord Thomas was a guest at the stately
castle of Thornbury, covertly sizing up the Stafford sisters in the
intervals of riding over the Duke's three parks and assisting him
at his favourite sports of horse-breaking and relic-visiting.[3]

Almost at once Thomas's choice fell on Elizabeth. Barely
nineteen to his forty, she was so much more sprightly and intelligent than the others that it was hardly a question of choosing
at all. But there was a snag. Girl as she was, Elizabeth was already
bespoken. In her own blunt phrase, written twenty-four years
later, the Duke 'had bought my lord of Westmorland for me.' This
was little Ralph Neville, later the fourth Earl. In Thomas's eyes
it was of far less moment that this was also a love-match – that
indeed, according to Elizabeth, 'he and I had loved together
two year.' Possibly Elizabeth was exaggerating; it was a way she
had. And there is something to be said for Thomas's scorn of a
passion which began when the boy was scarcely twelve and the

girl seventeen. All the same, the romantically inclined will be pleased to note that, after the eventual wreck of her marriage, Ralph Neville was the only man who stood by his boyhood sweetheart when all her family – even her own children – turned their faces against her.[4]

However, as we have more than once had occasion to observe, Tudor love-affairs had nothing to do with marriage. For Lord Thomas the only obstacle was her father's contract with the Nevilles. The rest was mere childish folly. So, in his plausible way, he set to work on Buckingham. What arguments he used we do not know; but they ended in his carrying off the desolate girl, together with a dowry that would to-day be nearly £50,000, plus a goodly share of the Stafford wardrobe and jewellery, and an assured income for his bride of 500 marks or, in modern money, £10,000 a year. It seemed an excellent bargain – until he settled down to live with a wife who hated him.

§ 2. OLD NOBLE AND NEW PRIEST

From the first, Wolsey had sensed in the Howard clan his keenest menace. They stood for everything that he lacked – race, tradition, a feudal exclusiveness; and in addition they had an arrogance of blood that matched his own haughty self-confidence. If he was to rise in the Tudor Court, it could only be by breaking the long-established domination of the Howards.

Actually, the old man proved unexpectedly compliant. After his one abortive stand in 1512, when he rode away from Court in a huff, he gave little further trouble. By temperament simple, unreflecting and loyal, he had already accepted the Tudors, and when Wolsey became their chief representative, Norfolk sighed and accepted that too. His own politics were the naïve Francophobia of the average Englishman. No doubt that is why he behaved so badly at Mary's marriage to Louis XII. Otherwise, from the moment Wolsey became a cardinal and his official superior, no sign of opposition came from the tired old Duke. So long as Wolsey's policy remained anti-French, indeed, he was moderately content; and the Venetian Envoy was even able to report him as 'very intimate with the cardinal.' After all, they had both gone to the same school at Ipswich.[5]

It was a different matter with the son. On 31 May of this same year, Surrey's voice had been loud enough in the 'great snarling' that broke out in the King's Council to cause his expulsion. Was it now or later that, 'when the cardinal took upon him to check the earl, he had like to have thrust his dagger into the cardinal'? At any rate it was, quite literally, war to the knife between Wolsey and Surrey – as the former was well aware. The Howard contempt was not a thing to disregard because the head of the house was ready to dissemble it.[6]

Wolsey's counter-attack was made, typically, from the flank. Shortly after this, rumours began to reach the King of disaffection among his nobility. When the 'great personages' in question spoke of coming to Court, Henry had asked them, in a roundabout way, 'to bring with them a very small company.' An obscure undated note from King to Cardinal refers to the Dukes of Suffolk and Buckingham, three earls and 'others which you think suspect.'[7] Surrey's name is markedly absent: the Cardinal was far too clever to put him in the forefront of his complaint.

Besides, he had a better way of dealing with that high-handed militarist. This was to send him overseas. Kildare had been fomenting more trouble in Ireland; there was urgent need in Dublin for a man who was not afraid to use force. The Earl of Surrey seemed an eminently suitable choice. He left England in May 1520, and remained safely out of the kingdom until Wolsey had struck his blow at the baronial opposition.

His father-in-law was Wolsey's target. Of all the great nobles, Buckingham was the nearest in blood to the throne. He was enormously rich, highly overbearing, and far from intelligent. If he could be lured to his destruction, that should be a salutary lesson to his fellow peers. The plan was not easy. Buckingham had at least the brains to realise his situation as a possible pretender. Latterly he had stayed away from Court a good deal, busying himself with his beloved Thornbury. Even in the Court jousts he made a point of asking to fight on Henry's side and not against him.[8] But his temper was as notorious as his unfathomable contempt for Wolsey. Once, when Wolsey ventured to dip his hands in the basin that Buckingham was holding for the King, the irate Duke let the water splash over into his shoes.

That eighth deadly sin, as Skelton calls it, of peevishness was to bring about his doom.

Despite his vast possessions, the Duke was not a generous

employer. Two or three of his servants bore him a grudge; bribery did the rest. For the Duke was not only petulant, but pious; and he had come under the influence of a prophet – a not uncommon feature of Tudor religion. This worthy (on Buckingham's own admission) had foretold the events of 1513, and had then gone on to criticise the King for not fulfilling his father's will. It might even mean that his issue would not prosper, hinted the Prior darkly. Then came the vague forecast that some of Buckingham's blood would prove great men: followed by a demand for money.

It all sounds supremely foolish and harmless. But to the King – as Wolsey knew very well – it was gunpowder. Henry still had no male heir, and it was beginning to look as though he never would. To trespass on that ground was fatal. Moreover, Henry was human; and at the back of his mind there still rankled that distant memory of 1510, when Buckingham had trounced him like a schoolboy for running after his sister.

The Duke's fate, indeed, was sealed before the trial began. It was known that the King believed him guilty; and who would dare go against the royal decision? Surrey might have; but then Surrey was in distant Ireland. By a crowning irony it was his father, the Duke of Norfolk, who was high steward at the trial. Tears burst out of the old man's eyes as he pronounced sentence. The condemned man was the least moved of them all. A lesser man than Wolsey, his last words were by so much the prouder: 'An he had not offended no more unto God than he had done to the Crown, he should die as true man as ever was in the world.' On 17 May 1521 he was brought to Tower Hill and his head struck off with an axe. The full barbarity of the sentence had, as was customary, been remitted by the King's grace.

§ 3. POET OF THE HOWARDS

Skelton's sympathies, it has long been evident, were entirely feudal. He had room neither for the new learning nor for the new men who embodied it. It was natural, therefore, for him to gravitate towards one of the great noble houses. They could give him flattery, patronage, hospitality, a room of his own; while he could place his pen at the service of all they represented, and give it the finality and grace of art.

There were many ways by which he might have made the acquaintance of the Howard family. It is not impossible, even, that he started life in their livery. But in any case, during his residence at Diss he could hardly have escaped riding over to pay his respects at Kenninghall. In this former hunting-lodge of the Mowbrays lived old Surrey (as he was then) among a swarm of his vassals and kinsmen – for assiduous marriage had linked the Howards to half the East Anglian gentry. Very probably it was at Kenninghall that Skelton first met the Wyndhams and their bewitching daughter, Jane. And he had not yet wholly deserted his nearby parish when, at Easter 1513, Lord Thomas brought home his wealthy Stafford bride.

Did Skelton remember her as a baby? Her father had been a ward of the Lady Margaret's; he must have brought her along, sometimes, for the old lady to dandle and stuff with comfits. But now she was grown up – and into that most irresistible of creatures, a loveless girl-wife.

After 1514 she was the Countess of Surrey; but this brought her a short-lived satisfaction. Her husband had married her frankly for her money. Even with that, however, the couple led a restless and impoverished life. They seem to have had no permanent home of their own. In the intervals of begetting children and attending at Court – where Surrey spent most of his time, gaming and idling expensively – Elizabeth was hurried round from one to another of her father-in-law's many mansions.[9] All the aristocracy lived much the same uprooted life, but at least they had somewhere to call home.

The girl did not lack spirit, however. Before long the Surrey family life had degenerated into perpetual bickering, which rose sometimes to a royal frenzy. Years afterwards, an embittered old woman, Elizabeth claimed that about the end of 1519, when she had suffered two nights and a day in travail with her daughter Mary, her husband dragged her 'out of her bed by the hair of the head about the house and with [his] dagger gave her a wound in the head.' Surrey, who reports the story, laughs it off as pure hysteria. 'She had the scar in her head,' he avers, 'fifteen months before she was delivered of my said daughter, and the same was cut by a surgeon of London for a swelling she had in her head of drawing of two teeth!'[10] It sounds possible. But it is no doubt equally true that, like a great many other fine Tudor gentlemen, Surrey saw nothing wrong with a little wife-beating. And from what we hear later of Elizabeth's 'wild language,' she is not likely to have submitted tamely to such notions of marital discipline.

In this atmosphere it was small relief to hear, in 1520, that Surrey had been appointed Lord Deputy of Ireland. Naturally, he took his family with him, arriving at Ringsend on 23 May. But Elizabeth must have found the cramped Dublin garrison even less endurable than a daughter-in-law's quarters in Norfolk. Soon, to the threat of the wild Irish without the pale was added the terror of plague within; and on 3 August the new Lieutenant wrote to Wolsey begging leave to send his wife and children at least as far as Wales, where they could stay 'near the seaside till this death cease.' No reply has survived; but we may fairly guess that permission was granted, for the Countess was later to refer to a time when her husband was absent from her for more than a twelvemonth. In no other year was Surrey away for more than ten or twelve weeks. And as he returned from Ireland just before the Christmas of 1521, we may conclude that the Countess had preceded him somewhere about September 1520 – and had, presumably, found good reason for not going back.[11]

Where was Elizabeth during this grass widowhood of hers? Part of the time she must have spent at Court, attending the Queen. In the letter already quoted she claims with pride that, unlike her husband, she 'hath lived always like a good woman: as it was not unknown when I was daily waiter in the court sixteen years together, when he had been from me more than a year on the king's wars.' The arithmetic is somewhat feminine, but its purport is hardly in doubt. The rest of her year must have been passed at one or other of Norfolk's country houses.

In either place, had she not done so before, she might have made Skelton's acquaintance. He was still Orator Royal; and in addition, one faint clue suggests that he was also installed in the literary circle of the Norfolks. His *Garland* contains the statement:

> Of my lady's grace at the contemplacion,
> Out of French into English prose,
> Of mannes life the Peregrinacion
> He did translate, enterpret and disclose.

He is talking of that 'enormous gloomy poem' written by Deguile-ville, the *Pélérinage de la vie humaine*. But who was my lady's grace, at whose request Skelton had undertaken this redoubtable labour?

Brie suggested the Countess of Surrey; but she had not yet won the right to be addressed as 'her grace' – a title then confined to royalty, dukes and archbishops. Dyce thought the Lady Margaret was intended, and most critics have agreed with him. But surely, used *tout court* in a poem written for the Countess of Surrey, it is much more likely to mean her mother-in-law, the pious Duchess of Norfolk. There is nothing singular in her wishing to possess Deguileville in English: his monkish pessimism was still fashionable reading for ladies, and above all for one of my Lady Agnes' devout inclinations.[12]

At all events, Skelton unquestionably had a way with women. Perhaps it was his cloth that gave them confidence; perhaps it was what they spied, or thought they spied, beneath it. Whatever it was, in London he had persuaded the Lady Margaret to entrust her grandson to him; in Norfolk it had been Lady Wyndham and Jane. Nor should we forget, at the other end of the scale, Long Meg and Elinor Rumming. And now, as he approached his sixtieth birthday, came the rash and appealing Elizabeth.

She must have been a ready victim. On his side, Skelton could offer her the seductive homage her husband so conspicuously failed to provide. Unreal as it was, the courtly love of a poet for his patroness gave a strange satisfaction to the mind starved of normal affection. Its very formality saved it from becoming more than a delightful day-dream; while within that formality a genuine human relationship could blossom unchecked.

In other words, Skelton and the Countess got on famously. The old poet was witty, gallant, and well known if a trifle *démodé*; what was more important, he shared all her prejudices. If there was one thing Elizabeth cherished all her life, it was her faith in blue blood. Chapuys noted how strictly she 'stood by rank and antiquity of race.' And the loathing she felt for her husband's mistress was all the greater because, in her own words, she was 'but a churl's daughter and of no gentle blood.' That she was writing this to Cromwell, a churl's son, did not enter her head; for Elizabeth was not distinguished for cool reflection. On the contrary. What brother Henry called her 'sensual and wilful mind' worked purely in terms of passion.[13] Nothing could control her when she was in one of her black rages. Evidently, this haughty and impetuous creature had much in common with Skelton. How well they would understand one another, linked as they were by the mysterious bond of temperament!

Elizabeth, it would seem, was home in time to see the swift trial and execution of her father. Her feelings may be imagined. There is no doubt that, in common with everyone else, she looked on Wolsey as Buckingham's murderer. (Indeed, the Cardinal more or less admitted the fact to the French Ambassador that same year.) [14] This mortal insult to her blood could not go unavenged. And so *Speak, Parrot* came into being. It was the Countess, of course, who kept urging Skelton to add to it, to sharpen his attack again and yet again, until even the 'general satire' of its close became an invective of unparalleled personalities directed against a single man. The balance of the poem was ruined completely; but how could Skelton protest? He could only salve his artist's conscience by inserting the name of his fair temptress. Galathea – holding out her Vergilian apple of discord – is Skelton's apology for this misshapen offspring of the marriage between Art and Politics. [15]

§ 4. COLIN CLOUT COMES TO TOWN

By the time the last stanzas of *Speak, Parrot* were being written Surrey himself was back in England, breathing fire (we may be sure) at having been got out of the way so cunningly. [16] On this topic he and his wife were in full agreement – united, if not in love, then in hatred. And now they were both pressing Skelton to continue his campaign.

But the Howards were not his only allies. Among Skelton's friends in the Palace was a modest clerk of the kitchen, by name William Thynne. But Thynne was none of your ordinary royal domestics. In his spare time he was also by way of being something of an antiquarian. His grand passion was the literature of his native land – above all, the serene and sunny genius of Dan Chaucer. For years he had been busy collecting every MS. of the poet he could lay hands on; and in 1532 his labours were crowned by the appearance of the sumptuous *Workes of Geffray Chaucer newly printed, with dyuers workes which were neuer in print before.* Skelton, alas! did not live to see this triumph of *pietas*; but he must have wrangled long hours with his scholarly friend over the poet they both worshipped, in their different ways, so devoutly. Moreover, they had another weakness in common – a complete and thorough detestation of the great Cardinal. And, if we can trust his son's memory, much of Skelton's next satire against Wolsey was actually written under Thynne's hospitable roof.[17]

In Francis Thynne's account the story begins much later – only just before Wolsey's fall. By this time Master William's qualities had won the recognition they deserved. He was now chief clerk of the kitchen and on excellent terms with the King, who had let several profitable sinecures come his way. His life-work too was well on the way to completion, and Henry was deeply intrigued by it. With his usual high-handed enthusiasm, he demanded to be kept *au courant*. Accordingly, one day William showed him a story he meant to include among the *Canterbury Tales*:

> This tale when king Henry VIII had read, he called my father unto him, saying:
>
> 'William Thynne! I doubt this will not be allowed; for I suspect the bishops will call thee in question for it.'
>
> To whom my father, being in great favour with his prince (as many yet living can testify), said:
>
> 'If your grace be not offended, I hope to be protected by you.'
>
> Whereupon the king bid him go his way and fear not.
>
> All which notwithstanding, my father was called in question by the bishops, and heaved at by cardinal Wolsey – his old enemy for many causes, but mostly for that my father had furthered Skelton to publish his *Colin Clout* against the cardinal, the most part of which book was compiled in my father's house at Erith in Kent. . . .[18]

Written three-quarters of a century later, the son's version is naturally peppered with inaccuracies. To mention one only, Thynne senior did not rent his house in Erith until 1531 – two years after Skelton's death.[19] But errors of detail do not invalidate the statement as a whole, which is definite and convincing enough. Our interest, however, is in the tail of the story. And I see no reason to doubt that Thynne – who was later to have more than a smack of Luther's sack – hated and despised the worldly Cardinal as generously as Skelton himself. What more natural, then, than that in 1522 he should have encouraged him to write his next satire against Wolsey, and given him the run of his study for the purpose? Where this took place is not clear. Not at Erith, it is obvious. Nor, apparently, was it before 1526, when he became chief clerk, that he was granted 'an official lodging at

Greenwich.' Stow records that he was buried in the Church of Allhallows, Barking: which suggests that his real home lay some-where near the Tower.[20] The exact spot, however, is immaterial; what matters is the clear family tradition. William Thynne 'had furthered Skelton to publish his *Colin Clout* against the card-inal, the most part of which book was compiled at' his house, wherever that may have been.

A mere handful of educated readers was all that could be expected for *Speak, Parrot*. Apart from the satire, its appeal was extremely limited; and where the satire became most visible – in the envois – sheer caution would confine it to a tiny group of those in the know. But having once spoken out, Skelton could not go back to learned obfuscation. After all, the prime object of a satire is to be read. And the nobility were far from being the only people in England who hated Wolsey. All over the kingdom tales were being whispered of his pride, his plate and his women, his gorgeous robes and fabulous meats and the palaces he was never tired of building. Much of the rumour was rank gossip; but it showed what people were thinking. Couldn't Skelton take advantage of this? What was to prevent his writing a really *popular* Wolsey satire – one that the man in the street could grasp, one that would spread from mouth to mouth in booth and tavern and hayfield, making articulate what so many people were already feeling in a dim kind of way, and – perhaps – raising it to a universal roar that would blast the Cardinal clean off his lofty but isolated perch? And what more suitable medium than his own rapid Skeltonic?

With Thynne and the Howards to egg him on, Skelton was not long in producing what was wanted. Had he been asked to describe *Colin Clout*, its author would probably have called it a pastoral – though anything less like our conventional idea of the genre it would be hard to imagine. Technically, however, Skelton would be right. His new poem was a dramatic monologue delivered by a simple countryman. And here again, a device prompted by mere human caution is responsible for the work's æsthetic success. In his creation of the naïve yokel Colin –

> Thus I, Colin Clout,
> As I go about

And wandring as I walk,
I here the people talk – [21]

Colin, with his disarming 'men say,' and his shocked asides,
Skelton has given a triumphant objectivity to his complaint.
Moreover, this unsubtle countryman sees, or appears to see, things
in the round. As he rambles on, the real nature of England's
malady is laid bare: a barbarous nobility, unlettered and hence
unfit for power, and a worldly Church with the brains to rule the
country but not, unfortunately, itself. There is genuine insight
in this 'rustic' view of Early Tudor politics. No wonder Spenser
picked on Colin, rather than one of Barclay's realistic puppets,
when he wished to restore dignity to the pastoral.

There is no particular order in Colin's complaints. Ten Brink
thought he spied a certain 'concentric' form about them; but if this
means anything more than a constant return to the point, I have
failed to detect it. And indeed, as that point happens to be
Wolsey, a certain degree of irrelevance is more or less inevitable.
A detailed examination of the poem, then, would throw little
light on its true nature. There is more to be gained by con-
centrating on a few significant passages.

It is the prelates who are really at fault. After enumerating some
of the charges he hears brought against them – greed, neglect,
ambition – Colin notes how all this is endangering the very
existence of the Church. True, he admits with fine irony, some of
them – 'almost two or three' – are wise and learned clerks. But
even these –

                  are loth to mell
        And loth to hang the bell
        About the cattes neck
        For drede to have a check.
        They are fain to play deuz deck,
        They ar made for the beck.
        Howbeit they are good men,
        Moch herted like an hen. . . .

mell=meddle.   deuz deck=low (in gaming).   beck=nod of command.   moch
                        =much.

How much stronger than our 'chicken-hearted' is the laconic
simile of Colin! At the same time he does not enlighten us as to the
identity of the cat that needs belling.

From this point on Colin slips, with the inconsequence of the ballad, into the second person. Henceforth the poem becomes a kind of open letter to the prelates. But its generalities are deceptive. For example, the next complaint sounds as wide as it is well-worn:

> For some say ye hunt in parkes
> And hawk on hobby larkes[22]

until we remember that Wolsey lived openly with a Mistress Lark, and had had two children by her. Her brother was now Master of Trinity Hall, Cambridge, and had been instrumental in the Duke of Buckingham's betrayal.[23]

This, then, is Skelton's technique in *Colin Clout*: a series of general charges which might be, and often were, applicable to many of the bishops – but of which Wolsey was the prime exemplar. And he could not have chosen a more effective method. In this way the Cardinal's personal shortcomings are given perspective; we see them in relation to society. It is not the vice of a single prelate, or even a group of them, that counts. It is the new secularism, and its repercussions from top to bottom of the Church. For instance: The parish priests ordained by such prelates are, fatally, illiterate fools. And what can be expected of such vagabonds, on whose lips a collect sounds 'like sawdust or dry chips'? Naturally, they spend most of their time at the tavern, with their wenches. And why not, when they see even in the mansions of their superiors a 'wife' or a pretty housemaid?

But then precisely the same thing is going on at a higher level. How are the bishops themselves selected?

> Over this, the foresaid lay
> Report how the pope may
> A holy anker call
> Out of the stony wall
> And him a bishop make,
> If he on him dare take
> To kepe so hard a rule
> To ride upon a mule
> With gold all betrapped,
> In purple and paul belapped;
> Some hatted and some capped,
> Richely and warm bewrapped

(God wot to their great paines)
In rotchettes of fine Raines
White as mares' milk,
Their tabertes of fine silk,
Their stirops of mixt gold begared;
There may no cost be spared.
Their moyles gold doth eat,
Their neighbours die for meat.[24]

lay=laity. anker=anchorite. paul=pall. rotchettes, etc.=rochets of Rennes
cloth. tabertes=tabards. begared=adorned. moyles=mules.

With such luxury as the criterion for the episcopal bench, is it to
be wondered at that the lesser orders are corrupt? The detail of
the ironic vision, of course, is drawn from the spectacle of the
Cardinal-legate in procession. Wolsey, says Polydore, was the
first 'among all priests, bishops and cardinals that ever wore silk
for his uppermost vestment.' And Polydore's conclusion chimes
well with what Colin had heard from the laity: 'Yet was it not
alone; for as divers other priests imitated him, some envy was
raised on the whole clergy.'[25]

It is now, perhaps, easier to understand the solemnity with
which Colin went on to draw the moral of all this. It is the oldest
moral in the world – that pride shall have a fall:

For Tholomé told me
The son somtime to be
In Ariete
Ascendent a degré
Whan Scorpion descending,
Was so then pretending
A fatal fall for one
That shall sit in a trone
And rule all thinges alone.
Your teth whet on this bone
Amongest you everychone
And let Colin Clout have none
Maner of cause to mone. . . .
Sory therefore am I,
But trouth can never lie.[26]

Tholomé=Ptolemy. son=sun. *In Ariete*=in Aries, the sign of the Ram. every-
chone=everyone. mone=moan.

The fact that history was on Skelton's side later gave this passage an almost scriptural value. It became known as Skelton's Prophecy; and, in the days before Sunday-paper astrology, was copied and recopied by men with a keener interest in politics than poetry. The moral I would draw from it is a good deal more modest. To me it sounds very much like the peroration to the first part of *Colin Clout*. It is highly probable that, as with *Speak, Parrot*, sections of the poem were handed round for circulation as soon as they were completed. And on this warning note, we may guess, the opening instalment of *Colin Clout* came to an end.[27]

Its success cannot be doubted. Who could resist this blunt and pithy résumé of the Church's predicament since Wolsey had reached its head? There must have been appeals in plenty for a continuation of the satire. And Part Two was duly begun:

> My pen now will I sharp
> And wrest up my harp
> With sharp twinking trebelles
> Again' all such rebelles
> That labour to confound
> And bring the Church to the ground.
>
> wrest=tune.   trebelles=trebles.

Colin is still a devout son of the Church. He is appalled by the charges brought against it. Men are now openly criticising its very dogmas. In every alehouse they attack the sacraments and chop logic over such problems as predestination, recidivation and hypostasis. In 1517 Martin Luther had nailed up his theses to the church door of Wittenberg; and by 1522 his doctrines had infected many of Colin's countrymen. Everywhere, laments the bewildered rustic, new and heretical sects are springing up. They cry out against the wealth of the Church, its greed and shameless pluralism, and the way the priests –

> can nat kepe their wives
> From them for their lives.[28]

Did Skelton's mouth twist a shade wryly, one wonders, as he penned these veracious lines?

COLIN CLOUT COMES TO TOWN

But for it all, Colin continues, they lay the fault at the bishop's door. Because now –

> prelacy is sold and bought
> And come up of nought;
> And where the prelates be
> Come of low degré
> And set in majesté
> And spiritual dignité,[29]

there is an end to the Christian virtues. Here we have it – the nub of the whole tirade! Follows a brilliant statement of the political struggle then under way between Nobility and New Men.

But Skelton finds it more and more difficult to keep to his diplomatic plural. Try as he may, the detail insists on taking a personal turn. When Colin talks of the towered and turreted palaces erected by the prelates, what reader could fail to catch the reference to Hampton Court, with its thousand rooms, its acres of window glass and its –

> Aras of rich aray
> Fresh as flowrs in May,
> With dame Diana naked,
> How lusty Venus quaked
> And how Cupid shaked
> His dart and bent his bow
> For to shote a crow
> At her tirly-tirlow. . . .[30]

Logically, he could claim, his position was unassailable. Were not the Triumphs of Petrarch, which he is here describing, among the most popular of all motifs for tapestry? Bishop Ruthal, for one, had a set of them – which came into Wolsey's hands after his death in 1523, to the confusion of the commentators. But Wolsey had at least two other sets of Triumphs;[31] and it was *his* mania for hangings that attracted all the comment at the time. 'One has to traverse eight rooms,' wrote the Venetian Ambassador, 'before one reaches his audience chamber, and they are all hung with tapestry, *which is changed once a week*.'[32] Millionaire as he was, the Bishop of Durham could not compete with grandeur on that mammoth scale.

The final remarks, however, allow of no ambiguity. What alternative could be read into the comment:

> It is a besy thing
> For one man to rule a king
> Alone, and make rekening
> To govern over all
> And rule a realm royal
> By one mannes verrey wit?

Or for the observation that no one is now able to approach the King except through 'your president';

> Nor to speke to him secretly,
> Openly nor privily
> Without this president be by
> Or elles his substitute
> Whom he will depute?
> Neither erle ne duke
> Permitted? by saint Luke
> And by swete saint Mark,
> This is a wonderous wark!

Once again Skelton has given himself away – and this time much more seriously than in *Speak, Parrot*. It is doubtful whether the Parrot envois ever got much farther than the Howard circle. But *Colin Clout* was a very different kettle of fish. Here was a poem that could do more damage than a thousand sermons. In its seductive and memorable rhythms were enshrined the Plain Man's view of Wolsey; and plain men all over the country were beginning to repeat them to each other. Whether Skelton actually tried to get his poem set up in type, like the Scottish *Ballad*, we cannot be sure. It sounds like it, at least:

> And so, it semeth, they play,
> Which hate to be corrected
> Whan they be infected,
> Nor will suffre this boke
> By hoke ne by croke
> Printed for to be. . . .³³

216

Perhaps, optimistically, he did take along the first part of his poem to the booksellers – Fawkes, it may be, or Pynson. But already the novel problem of the Press was exercising the Church. Only the previous May there had been a grand holocaust of Lutheran books at St. Paul's. It would be natural, then, for the text of this anti-clerical satire, if submitted for printing, to come into Wolsey's hands first. At any rate, there can be small doubt that before it was completed the two men met face to face. Was Skelton summoned 'afore my lord cardinal into his gallery' at York Place, where these dread interviews usually occurred?[34] Wolsey's rages were already a legend.

Yes, quite obviously, by the time *Colin Clout* reached its candid close, imprisonment for its author was more than a threat; if Wolsey's minions once laid hands on him it was a certainty. How Skelton must have blessed his foresight in getting that clause omitted from his lease! For the last words of the poem were unmistakably penned, not in Thynne's study, but in his own room within Westminster sanctuary:

> The forecastel of my ship
> Shall glide and smothely slip
> Out of the waves wode
> Of the stormy flode,
> Shote anker and lie at rode
> And sail nat far abrode
> Till the cost be clere. . . .[35]

wode=mad.　Shote anker=shoot anchor.　rode=roads.

The period of armed neutrality was over. Henceforth it was to be the immense legal might of the Cardinal *versus* the poet's quill. The odds, however, were not quite as heavy as they sounded. So long as Skelton stayed within the Abbey precinct, Wolsey could do nothing, Chancellor and Legate though he was. And a cool confidence in the impregnability of his refuge breathes through Colin's farewell to the reader.

§ 5. *WHY COME YE NOT TO COURT?*

It is possible that there was a deeper reason for the poet's unexampled self-assurance. Did he glimpse, a second time, the Cardinal's imminent fall?

Certainly, the autumn of 1522 found Wolsey's popularity at a

lower ebb than it had ever been before. He himself, in all probability, was baffled by the mounting signs of discontent. They merely
confirmed him in his scorn for public opinion; for was he not now
riding the Englishman's pet hobby-horse – hatred of France?
But for all his political flair Wolsey never grasped that elementary
truth, that a people may be touched anywhere but in its pocket.
As Hall observes, this was 'the only thing that draweth the hearts
of English men from their kings and princes.' Honest xenophobia
is as easy as it is inexpensive; and the Englishman has always been
an adept at it. But in May 1522 Wolsey found himself committed
to his second Continental war in nine years – with a treasury now
practically empty. This time the whole burden of financing it
fell upon the people of England. And, with equal honesty and even
more vigour, they objected.

To begin with, £20,000 – well over half a million to-day – was
borrowed from the city of London in June. But all too soon it was
discovered to be but a slight preliminary to what was coming. On
20 August Wolsey sent for the Mayor and Aldermen once more.
Now he demanded a further tenth of the city's treasure. This was
staggering. 'For God's sake,' cried one of the fathers, 'remember
this, that rich merchants in ware be bare of money!' But there was
no arguing with the Cardinal. Meanwhile a royal commission was
going round each shire to evaluate men's goods. Officially it was
a muster roll, to provide a just basis for the arming and equipment
of the country. On the basis of this innocent assessment, a tenth
was rigorously demanded, to be paid at once. No less than
£352,231 were obtained within the next twelve months. [36]

It is true that, as the loyal Hall reminds us, no one was assessed
under the value of £5 (now £150). But the rest of the country
was united in opposition to the unwanted war. Glad as they were
to see Surrey's army descend to its locust work in the north of
France, they strongly disliked the notion of impoverishing themselves for the privilege. And as time went by things got steadily
worse. Within the next three years Wolsey had to face a hostile
Parliament and even, in East Anglia, open rebellion against what
turned out to be 'perhaps the most violent financial exaction in
English history.' [37]

It was under the first flush of this reaction that Skelton's last
Wolsey satire was written. Popular support is explicit in his very
signature:

> Hęc vates ille
> De quo loquuntur mille
> (This the bard wrote
> Whom thousands quote.)

There is no longer any shadow of pretence; the poem is an open
assault upon the Cardinal and all his works. The *persona*, whether
peasant or parrot, is frankly removed, to let free a spate of purely
Skeltonic vituperation. Evidently, *Why Come Ye Not To Court?*
could only have been written from the safety of sanctuary – and
at a time when it looked as though the great tyrant had over-
reached himself at last.

Even the semblance of formal unity is abandoned. It is frank
journalism, scribbled down in the heat and excitement of the
moment. Skelton is answering the oldest and most modern of
questions: 'What newes, what newes?' Nor is he ashamed to mark
the end of his separate articles:

> But now upon this story
> I will no further rime
> Till another time,
>> Till another time, etc.[38]

Like the envois of *Speak, Parrot* or the sections of *Colin Clout*, the
parts of this poetic pamphlet were obviously sent round as they
were written, hot from the desk. Fortunately, there is no difficulty
about its date. Skelton tells us that it was finished in the thirty-
fourth year of his royal service; and nothing in the poem will be
found to place it later than 17 November 1522.[39]

Loosely strung though it is, however, *Why Come Ye Not To Court?*
has a unity, a unity of subject. For everything that has gone wrong
during this summer and autumn of 1522 Skelton blames one man.
No more of Zadoks and Jerubbesheths; it is openly 'the cardinal'
now. We are told how he bullies the Council in the Star Chamber;
how he ignores the Lenten fasts; how his pride is so touchy that he
has ordered the closing of that long-established Southwark
brothel, the Cardinal's Hat. It is his fault that the Scots are now
making fools of us in the north, signing agreements with Lord
Dacres, while Roos and Northumberland sit by and do nothing.
In London he tyrannises over the lawyers in Chancery as he does

over the lords in Council. Even the King, who trusts him so, is unhappy about it all.

It is almost frightening, this complete and simple candour. For all the caution he now displays, Skelton might be literally possessed, he is so utterly indifferent to the consequences of what he is saying. Henry is treated as coolly as though he were already lying beside his father in Westminster Abbey. For Skelton, this time, is determined to tell the whole truth. He has been asked why he no longer comes to Court. Well, this is why. . . .

The poem, indeed, is far from being the sheer Billingsgate it is sometimes thought. For one thing, it contains Skelton's most reasoned criticism of his hostility to Wolsey. After recounting some of his worst excesses he goes on:

> Now yet all this might be
> Suffred and taken in gre,
> If that that he wrought
> To any good end were brought;
> But all he bringeth to nought,
> By God that me dere bought![40]
> in gre=good-humouredly.   dere=dearly.

It is the essential *nihilism* of all this activity that he seizes on. And in this Skelton has the entire support of our closest modern student of the Cardinal's career. Professor Pollard sums up his policy as nothing more than 'a brilliant fiasco.'[41] Nor is Skelton's explanation, couched though it is in the ethical jargon of his day, fundamentally different from that of the modern historian:

> He is so ambicious,
> So shamles and so vicious
> And so supersticious
> And so moch oblivious
> From whens that he came
> That he falleth into *acidiam,*
> Which trewly to express
> Is a forgetfulness
> Or wilful blindness. . . .[42]

Ambition, claims the poet, has led Wolsey into the deadly sin of accidie, or wilful sloth in his duty to God. Professor Pollard sees in

him the 'characteristics of an age of self-made men, marked by
what modern psychology calls an "inferiority complex." '⁴³
Jargon for jargon, there is little to choose between the two
verdicts. Both see the Cardinal's weakness as essentially one of
class-consciousness. The external splendour and the love of
domination, with the amazing poverty of their results, reveal a
man struggling to forget his origins. For years the most powerful
man in Europe, Wolsey produced *nothing* but a palace or two and a
college – and these he left to be completed by others. In foreign
policy, in religious reform, in law and education, his vast influence
was almost entirely sterile. First and last, Wolsey's object was his
own authority. Perhaps never before has a statesman frittered
away such opportunities merely in order to make more. Consequently, when his ambition finally destroyed him, it destroyed
all he had fought for. Even Wolsey's religion, like his state, was in
the last analysis himself.

§ 6. DEFEAT WITH HONOUR

It is much less easy to understand what happened next. Early in
November 1522 Skelton brought his Wolsey satire to a close with
a wild shower of Latin mud. Wolsey was a wolf of the sea, a most
vicious bear, a butcher's ox, Britain's heifer of injustice, her golden
calf, her Oreb, Zeeb and Zalmunna; he was a thistle, a cruel
Asaph, an accursed Dathan, a flattering Achitophel and a stony-
hearted Goliath. . . . Early in January 1523 the same poet was
innocently dedicating the *Garland of Laurel* to His Most Serene and
Royal Majesty – together with my Lord Cardinal, most honoured
Legate *a latere*, etc.!⁴⁴

It is the most astonishing change of front our literature has to
show. So much so, that many critics refuse to believe their eyes and
have devised a number of ingenious suppositions to explain it all
away. The later dedications must be false; they were either
invented by the printers, or else tacked on to the wrong poems.
Such hypotheses do the greatest credit to their authors' faith in
Skelton: unfortunately, they have lost their only real support.
For Bale's categorical statement, that Skelton died in Westminster
'during his captivity,' we now know to be pure invention. It was
an inference, natural but mistaken, from the fact that Skelton
happened to live, and hence died, in sanctuary.⁴⁵

No, alas! there can be no doubt about it. Every one of Skelton's poems which we can definitely date after 1522 contains a public compliment to the Cardinal. What could have taken place, in the brief months between November and January, to induce this truculent and bitter opponent of Wolsey to change his tune with such pathetic completeness?

It will help, I think, if we recall a few of the facts. Actually, Skelton's *open* hostility to the Cardinal lasted a surprisingly short time. Even if we include the *Speak, Parrot* envois (which I believe were known only to a minute group), the three satires which could be taken as genuinely libellous were all written within a single year. And if we exclude *Parrot* the time is even shorter. The end of *Colin Clout*, and all of *Why Come Ye Not To Court?*, must have been composed in a very few weeks. What is more, their outspokenness renders it morally certain that they were written in hiding. Skelton no longer came to Court because he had retired to sanctuary; nor had he any intention of sailing far abroad, as he puts it, until the coast was clear.

On the other hand, his earlier Wolsey satires – *Against Venomous Tongues*, *Magnificence*, and the body of *Speak, Parrot* – contained nothing to which the Cardinal could lawfully take exception. And the moment we pause to consider, we realise how vitally necessary this caution was. Some writers talk as though Skelton was in no real danger from Wolsey. An avowed lover of letters, the Cardinal would have merely smiled, as we do, at the poet's angry lunges. Nothing could be further from the truth. In fact, the Cardinal was famed for the shortness of his temper: his dignity was too recent to permit of question. And when he did lose control of himself, Wolsey was a very nasty spectacle indeed. Not even ambassadors were safe. He confined the Imperial Envoy to his quarters, and threatened the Papal Nuncio, after a violent shaking, with the rack. Polydore Vergil, Sir Robert Sheffield, Richard Pace followed each other to the Tower; poor Pace, indeed, was driven out of his mind by his illtreatment. The least an offending poet might expect was a term of imprisonment. Court favour had not saved Cornish when he wrote a satire against Empson; and Wolsey was immensely more powerful than Empson had ever been.

It may be argued – it has been recently, in the case of Falstaff – that a few weeks in the Tower or the Fleet were no great indignity or hardship.[46] That is as may be. The real trouble was, one never knew how far the great man's displeasure would carry him. Only the previous reign five men had been executed for dispersing invectives against King and Council;[47] and Skelton could still remember the wretched end of Collingbourne, in 1484, over a two-line epigram. Meanwhile, somewhere between the gallows and the Fleet lay the grisly shadows of thumbscrew, rack and pillory. Indeed, the penalties devised by our ancestors were almost inexhaustible: the loss of a hand, or one's ears, was a normal consequence of political gossip. And over all there loomed, sharply, the dreadful fate of Buckingham.

It was no mere quip, then, when Skelton pulled himself up, in his last satire, with the words:

> I could say somewhat,
> But speke ye no more of that,
> For drede of the red hat
> Take peper in the nose;
> For than thine heed of go's,
> Of by the hard arse![48]

For drede of=for fear lest. Take, etc.=take offence. than . . . go's=then thy head goes off. Of=off. hard=very.

This was more than metaphor; it might very well become the starkest of realities.

Unfortunately, the border-line between covert and open satire is by no means easy to draw. In both *Speak, Parrot* and *Colin Clout* we noted a gradual process of unveiling which was no doubt imperceptible to the poet himself. Skelton probably did not realise exactly when he had given himself away. To have escaped (as he seems to have done halfway through *Colin Clout*) with only a reprimand was the greatest of good luck. But his exposure put him in a dilemma. Henceforth he had either to give up the campaign altogether, or go on with it in voluntary imprisonment.

That he chose the latter course says much for his personal courage. The risk was a fearful one. Nor was it improved by his treatment of the King's sacred person. Henry would hardly enjoy being told that he was 'governed by this mad coot' – even when it was charitably explained as the result of witchcraft. Let those who criticise Skelton for what followed first exercise their imagination on the poet's fate if he had come within Wolsey's grasp in November 1522.

Fortunately for him, he did not. Not even Wolsey dared violate the sanctity of Westminster. And so matters reached an impasse. Skelton's poems spread like heresy over the countryside, while the poet himself took good care not to stray beyond the wall of the Abbey precinct.

But, it was obvious, such a situation could not last. For one thing, the country was at war; and such propaganda as Skelton's was not making it any easier for the royal commissioners to raise funds for it. As a member of the Council, Abbot Islip knew this perfectly well. So too did Lord Admiral Surrey. Before long Skelton's patrons must have realised that they had let loose something uncomfortably like the winds of Æolus. We can only guess at the comings and goings, the earnest arguments laid before the poet and his replies, alternately suave and fractious, as he sat warm by his inexpugnable fireside. So long as he was prepared to spend the rest of his life there, Skelton had the whip-hand; there was no doubt about it. And why shouldn't he? As prisons go, sanctuary was the most spacious and pleasant imaginable. Decidedly, he would only abandon it *upon terms.* . . .

Those terms must have been a bitter pill to the Cardinal. He was accustomed to dictating, not receiving them. And from this wretched gadfly of a poet, of all people! But in this case there was, all too obviously, no alternative. . . . He had, first, to agree to forget all that Skelton had already written against him. Moreover, the next suitable prebend that fell vacant was to go to the poet. (Perfectly legal, this. Not being a cure of souls, an extra prebend would not involve Skelton in the sin of pluralism.) In return, Skelton promised to call a halt in his campaign of abuse. Instead, he would use his pen, as an Orator Royal should, to support any cause that truly represented the national interest. Such, it is clear from what ensued, was the tenor of their treaty.

Tradition has preserved for us the scene that took place when Skelton issued forth in triumph from his refuge. Anecdote though it is, its essence sounds as near to the truth as makes no matter. We must, of course, assume that the 'imprisonment' it mentions was the poet's self-imposed confinement:

> On a time Skelton did meet with certain friends of his at Charing Cross, after that he was in prison at my lord Cardinal's commandment. And his friend said:

'I am glad you be abroad among your friends, for you have been long pent in.'

Skelton said:

'By the mass, I am glad I am out indeed, for I have been pent in, like a roach or fish, at Westminster in prison.'

The cardinal hearing of these words, sent for him again. Skelton kneeling of his knees before him, after long communication to Skelton had, Skelton desired the cardinal to grant him a boon.

'Thou shalt have none,' said the cardinal.

Th' assistance desired that he might have it granted, for, they thought, 'it should be some merry pastime that he will show your grace.'

'Say on, thou hoar head!' said the cardinal to Skelton.

'I pray your grace to let me lie down and wallow, for I can kneel no longer!''[49]

It changes the flavour of the story, no doubt, if we attribute Skelton's assurance less to his faith in a sally of wit than to a previous gentlemen's agreement. But once again let us recall what was at stake. We have only to think back to the blasphemous cringing of Polydore in the Tower, or on to the grovelling of Edward, later Baron North, father of the great translator of Plutarch. In January 1525 North was released from prison, where he had been committed for writing against Wolsey. But it was not before he had licked the dust in such verses as:

> Now being in prison I am not able,
>   Sith that quietness from me is separate,
> Plainly to show his virtues innumerable . . .

i.e. Wolsey's; of whom he proceeds to write a eulogy to the acrostic: 'God preserve Thomas lord legate and cardynal!'[50]

Skelton never sank to these depths. On the contrary, his truce was a dignified acceptance of the inevitable. Perhaps he *had* gambled on the Cardinal's fall and been mistaken. Very well. He accepted his failure; but, as we shall see, it was without any abandonment of his real independence. No; Skelton's was an honourable surrender against overwhelming odds. And the *Merry Tales* suggest that he came out with all flags flying.

Book Five

COURTIER

CHAPTER THIRTEEN

A GROUP OF NOBLE DAMES

Remember your epiphanies on green oval leaves, deeply deep;
copies to be sent if you died to all the great libraries of the
world, including Alexandria?

JOYCE: *Ulysses.*

§ 1. A YORKSHIRE CHRISTMAS

LITTLE OVER a month later, Skelton was breathing
the free air of his ancestral north. The Christmas of 1522
saw him one of the house-party given by his newest patroness, the Countess of Surrey, in the fine old castle of Sheriff Hutton
a few miles beyond York. Built of local stone on a slight eminence,
Sheriff Hutton was as nobly planned within as it was without.
The approaching traveller was struck by its great gatehouse,
flanked by a tower at either end, which did away with all necessity
for a moat; while if he passed beneath it he was bound to confess,
with Leland a year or two later, that 'the stately stair up to
the hall is very magnificent, and so is the hall itself, and all the
residue of the house: in so much that I saw no house in the north
so like a princely lodgings.' The old Earl of Surrey had made it
his headquarters all through the 'nineties, while he was guarding
the northern marches; and Henry VII had granted him its use
for life. (This had not prevented Henry VIII from offering it, in
1522, to the Earl of Shrewsbury on his appointment to the same
post; but this seems not to have been accepted.) So when the time
came to find accommodation for the Countess during the winter, her
father-in-law was able to spare her, if she was prepared to brave
the climate, this well-preserved residence in the Yorkshire wolds.[1]

It was a real holiday for the aging poet. The last days of autumn,
while he had been negotiating an honourable surrender from his
house in Westminster, had proved a considerable strain; and now,
in sharp, damp December, it was a glorious release to be away

from it all, among the timeless oaks of Galtress Forest, surrounded
by the flattering attentions of the Countess's ladies-in-waiting.
The Earl was still at Court, discussing the strategy of Henry's
campaigns in the following spring. There was nothing to disturb
the idyll. Winter had not yet shown its white claws. For the first
time in at least a year, Skelton felt that he was able to relax. For
all his age, he had put up a good fight. Wolsey was not likely to
forget his last devastating broadside! No; if the Cardinal was still
on his throne it was not Skelton's fault. But there it was. The
French war had to go on: everyone assured him of that. On the
whole, Skelton felt the soothing consciousness of a man who has
given of his best. Now he could turn to other things.

> Thus stode I in the frithy forest of Galtres,
>   Ensowked with silt of the miry wose, . . .²

As he squelched over the low 'moorish ground' that, in winter,
turned most of the Forest into a quagmire, Skelton felt the
centuries slide away. This was Chaucer's England; an England of
winding leafless rides down which the deer had been chased from
time immemorial.

Chaucer's England! The thought took him back to pleasant
evenings with William Thynne, when they had forgotten Wolsey
in the fresh simplicity of the *House of Fame*, or the spring sweetness
of the *Prologue* to the *Legend of Good Women*. Both poems had been
much in Skelton's mind these last few days. It was the thirty-first
of December. He was not getting any younger; and the truce with
Wolsey made it a good time for mental stock-taking. On this eve
of the New Year 1523 he was inspired to a summing-up of his
career, a Skeltonic *apologia*.

Chaucer had left his vision of the temple of Fame unfinished. A
good theme: looking back on what he himself had written, Skelton
felt he too had some title to a place in Fame's roll. The Countess
certainly thought so. Hadn't she set all her ladies to work embroidering that sumptuous laurel wreath for his New Year's gift?
And all through the quarrel with Wolsey she had stood by him
valiantly. Just like Queen Alcestis in the *Prologue* to the *Legend*.
(Did Skelton know the tradition that she was really Chaucer's
patroness, the Fair Maid of Kent?) Perhaps he could bring the
two themes into one poem – a graceful dream-allegory combining

his gratitude to Lady Besse with a grand defence of his life's work as a poet – just hinting at his recent pledge to write no more against the Cardinal. That might be the key-note: peace and goodwill. He would show them that he was not merely a satirist. Naturally, it would have to be in rhyme-royal again, to underline the change. His, last venture into formal verse! Something fairly ambitious was indicated. . . .

It began, as every good vision should, with the astrological date:

> Arecting my sight toward the zodiak
>   The signes twelve for to behold afar,
> When Mars retrogradant, reversed his bak,
>   Lord of the yere in his orbicular,
>   Put up his sword, for he coud make no war,
> And whan Lucina plenarly did shine,
> Scorpion ascending degrees twice nine. . . .

For anyone who cared to work it out, this gave the time within a matter of minutes. Even to-day it can be reduced with certainty to the beginning of January 1523. In that year Mars began to re-trograde on 13 January.[3] A pardonable anticipation; for Skelton was no doubt thinking of the martial Earl of Surrey, who also, in this winter season, could make no war. But other details bring it nearer. The moon was full – 'shone plenarly' – on the second of that month; while at the end of the poem Skelton sees Janus making his almanac for the new year:

> Good luk this new yere, the old yere is past![4]

The action of the poem, then, must be imagined as taking place on New Year's Eve – the last day of 1522. In Skelton's most aureate manner it tells how the poet, leaning against an oak-stump in Galtress Forest and brooding on the mutability of things, falls into a trance, in which he sees a noble pavilion where Dame Pallas is enthroned. The Queen of Fame is complaining to her that Skelton is 'wondrous slack,' especially in his duty to the ladies. Pallas defends him at some length. But Fame remains deferently obstinate. Pallas then bids her summon her throng of poets to see if Skelton is among them. The timely strains of Orpheus having rapt Skelton's tree-stump away in a forest dance, he is. Gower, Chaucer and Lydgate escort him before Pallas, who sends him to the great temple of Fame. They arrive; the palace is described, and the motley gathering. His English friends now leave him in charge of Lady Occupation, Fame's registrar. He is taken round the vast rampart to the gate Anglia, where a carved leopard displays an obscure device in Latin. Outside, the cheats and rascals clamouring for admission are raked by the palace cannon.

Then a mist rises, and somehow the poet finds himself in a walled garden where, on a splendid laurel-tree in the centre, a phœnix is busily making its pyre of olive branches. Around it Dryads and Muses are dancing, led by Flora. The poet's feelings are suddenly jarred by the sight of a hostile fiddler, but he relieves them in a short Latin satire. He is then led up, by a winding stair, to the Countess of Surrey's chamber. She sets her gentlewomen to weaving him a laurel crown; for, she declares, he has always honoured her sex – 'counterfeits,' of course, excepted. To Occupation's prompting Skelton replies with his well-known group of lyrics to the various ladies present. He returns proudly with his garland to the Hall of Fame, again escorted by the three English poets. All admire the new coronal, except Fame herself, who coldly requests his credentials. Occupation then recites the long list of his writings. When his poem on the laurel is reached, the whole assembly is rocked with tremendous cries of *triumpha!* The uproar wakes the poet from his trance – just in time to welcome in the New Year.

§ 2. THE MEANING OF THE VISION

How far this extraordinary poem 'comes off' will depend very much on what the reader is expecting. As an allegory, it has one obvious weakness. To introduce the Countess of Surrey among the mythical characters who make up the rest of the cast is not exactly consistent art. But purity of genre was never Skelton's leading characteristic. Besides, when he lived allegory was almost at its last gasp. The reason he chose it for the *Garland* was less from conviction than from a desire to emphasise his novel respectability. Allegory was, in the phrase of Mr. C. S. Lewis, the 'dominant form' of his day. Being an extremely competent writer, he managed to create out of it a very pretty poem; but like Pope's Homer its interest lies rather in its divergencies from the official model.

As we have hinted above, one at least of the *Garland's* functions was to reveal tactfully to his public Skelton's sudden change from political satirist to courtly troubadour. From this standpoint the key to the poem will be found in the 'herber' to which he was so strangely transported. The garden itself is wholly in the tradition of dream-allegory, with its carolling birds, its sanded alleys, turfed seats, and the silvery fish of its conduit. What is new is the spectacle in the centre of it:

> Where I saw growing a goodly laurel tre,
>   Enverdured with leves continually grene.
> Above in the top a bird of Araby
>   Men call a phenix; her winges betwene
>   She bet up a fire, with the sparkes full kene,
> With branches and boughes of the swete olive,
> Whos flagrant flower was chefe preservative
>
> Ageinst all infeccions with cancour enflamed,
>   Ageinst all baratous broisiours of old;
> It passed all bawmes that ever were named
>   Or gummes of Saby, so derely that be sold. . . . [5]

bet=beat.   flagrant=fragrant.   cancour=canker.   baratous broisiours=bruises of contention.   bawnes=balms.   of Saby=Sabæan.

There is nothing particularly abstruse about the symbolism. Then, as now, the laurel stood for poetry, the phœnix for immortality, and the olive for peace. Skelton is suggesting that a poet's immortality depends upon a timely use of the olive branch. An odd sentiment – made even odder by the strange emphasis upon the last symbol. Not only do we get a commendation of the olive's healing power, but no less than two sidenotes suddenly appear at this point, each referring to the olive and its transcendent virtue. The thing makes sense only if we remember that in *Ware the Hawk!* Skelton had dubbed *himself* the phœnix of England. It is, in fact, a disguised personal statement. If he is to survive as a poet, Skelton implies, it can only be by cultivating the arts of peace.

In this picturesque but obscure fashion Skelton tacitly abjures any further assault upon the Cardinal.

But we have still to deal with the broader symbolism of the poem. What did Skelton mean by the Palace of Fame and the delectable garden? Have they any other than a literal *significacio?* It has been claimed, and with reason, that they have. Dr.

Nelson argues that the gate Anglia, with its fierce leopard above and the mob of rascally suitors pressing towards it, stands for the Court of Henry VIII. The slippery rampart and the sudden gun-fire show the dangers that lie in wait for the aspirant to its pleasures. As for the garden, that is specifically located in the grounds of the Countess of Surrey. It is in fact nothing else than the Countess's household, of which Skelton was now a member.[6]

So far I have no fault to find with the interpretation. What I cannot agree with is the assumption that Skelton's transfer from Court to Countess came *after* the writing of *Why Come Ye Not To Court?*[7] The only possible evidence for this in the poem is the description of the garden as 'a *new* comfort of sorowes escaped.' Actually, in Skelton's day the word *new* did not always connote novelty; it could mean merely 'fresh' or 'elegant.' But even temporally it affords an unreliable mode of measurement. Everything depends on your initial unit. And from the point of view of a man's lifetime, two or three years might well be comprehended under the word.

But even more decisive against Nelson's theory is the incident which forms the poem's climax. I cannot see the Countess embroidering her garland for Skelton except by way of reward. Reward for what? For entering her household? Even in the case of a prominent poet it sounds an extravagant sort of welcome. As for the reason given by the Countess herself, that we have already dismissed as fantastic: the last thing Skelton had been distinguished for was *Frauendienst*. But the laurel would be a natural and fitting token for a man who had just conducted a vain but gallant offensive against Wolsey. In this, then, as in all the rest of the poem, the innocent Chaucerian manner is an elaborate farce. The Countess is really thanking the poet for political services rendered.

Had she, in her turn, anything to do with the peace negotiations that followed *Why Come Ye Not To Court?* The general trend of the poem suggests strongly that she had. It is a pity we know so little of her movements during this particular period. One thing we do know, however. Lady Besse not only had a strong sense of loyalty towards her servants, high or low, but she was an adept, when necessary, at the gentle art of flattery. Later we find her urging Cromwell, again and again, on behalf of a 'very honest man' who had been the family brewer and was now unemployed. And barely two years after the *Garland* she was writing in the most honeyed tones to the great Wolsey himself. He had apparently been of some service, at her request, to a Manningtree clothier that she patronised; and Elizabeth (now Duchess of Norfolk) hastens to thank him for his 'abundant goodness' not only in this, but also in 'all my other suits and causes.' She cannot find words to express her gratitude; but 'in my hearty good will am and shall be ready to do anything that shall stand with your pleasure; humbly beseeching you so to accept me and to continue your special good grace towards me, the trust whereof at this day is to my singular pleasure and comfort.' Only after this considerable dose of flummery does she feel that she can get on to her real point, which is to beg for her husband's return from the north. The letter then closes with more sugared compliment and the gift of 'a couple of does.' [8]

Such language, it is true, was a convention of the age. But the Cardinal's taste for it was as unbounded as all his other appetites. Even More, accustomed as he was to the foibles of the great, was struck by its openness. So we should by no means reject the possibility that the Countess, too, had put her evident gift to work in persuading Wolsey to come to terms with 'Skelton, my clerk.' [9]

The poet's own attitude, however, was much less complaisant. He was prepared to cover up, after a fashion, his earlier indiscretions. It is also true that he dedicated a copy of the poem jointly to King and Cardinal; that he prayed the latter 'to be mindful of the prebend which he promised me erewhile'; and declared himself to be hovering between hope and fear. But there is a marked absence of flattery in the forthright words; while in the English verses that follow (though no one appears to have noticed it) there is even something suspiciously like a threat:

> 'Twene hope and drede
> My life I lede,
> But of my spede
>   Small sikernes.
> Howbeit, I rede
> Both word and dede
> Should be agre'd
>   In noblenes,
>
> Or els, etc. [10]

spede=success.   sikernes=certainty.

232

OLD ENTANGLEMENTS

For a man who is supposed to have capitulated, there is a remarkable note of independence about these final words. They hark back to the confidence of Skelton's first Wolsey poem, *Against Venomous Tongues*. There, Skelton had insisted that no man was truly noble who would take offence at his remarks. And here, after begging the Cardinal not to forget his promise of a prebend – a *promise*, mark you – he adds the reminder that a true nobleman always keeps his word. If he doesn't . . .

Adressed to the most notorious parvenu in England, that unfinished clause brandishes over Wolsey's head the obloquy of all right-thinking people. Hardly, one would say, the gesture of a sycophant.

§ 3. OLD ENTANGLEMENTS

'Fine ladies,' remarks Froude in his dry way, 'have had an attraction for men of genius from Athanasius's time. . . .'[11] He is talking of Erasmus; and indeed there is an interesting parallel between the great humanist's relations with the youthful lady of Vere, whom her husband 'ill-treated and occasionally beat,' and Skelton's with the high-spirited and equally neglected wife of the Earl of Surrey. Skelton, it is true, was twice Erasmus's age; but the attraction was not noticeably different for that. There was the same consoling screen of religion, and the same spirit of semi-platonic gallantry at work behind it. Only Skelton had the advantage of a well-defined tradition which had governed the exchanges between poet and patroness for centuries past. And now, freed at last from the political obsessions of the past twelvemonth, he was able to give it full rein.

At Sheriff Hutton, in fact, Skelton came as near as the age allowed to the simple troubadour of the Middle Ages. And no one can deny that he played his part with considerable gusto. To the general reader, I think it is true to say, Skelton is still known mainly as the author of the *Garland* lyrics. That he was now in the neighbourhood of sixty-three only adds to their triumphant success – except that we now see it as due rather to a lifetime of art than to the romantic effervescence of youth.

Even here, however, there is no complete and magical transformation. When we examine the lyrics we realise that (as the *Garland* has already warned us) the original Skelton has not changed his spots. As a matter of fact, so far from revealing a simple-minded commender of female charms, the lyrics betray the follower of Juvenal at his most devastating.

We have already indicated that the *Garland* had another motive besides the political. It was partly a result of *Elinor Rumming*. That poem must have caused something of a flutter among the ladies at Sheriff Hutton. It was not the sort of thing a troubadour produces. And the eleven lyrics which now came dutifully from Skelton's 'dreadful trembling fist' were clearly intended to wipe out this offence and restore him to the position claimed for him by the Countess – librarian of all ladies.

And most of them do just this. The songs to Margery Wentworth and Isabel Knight, Margaret Hussey and Isabel Pennell are delightful examples of the poet as a payer of courtly compliment. Two of the ladies, however, get special treatment. One of them was Margaret Tilney – who, having married into one of the oldest knightly families in England, which had provided two wives for the present Duke of Norfolk, should obviously have been accorded particular respect. And so, to all appearances, she is. With marked reverence Skelton begins:

> I you assure
>   Ful wel I know
> My besy cure
>   To you I owe,
>   Humbly and low
> Commending me
> To your bounté.[12]
>> besy cure=busy care.

But on proceeding we find that Lady Tilney is gracefully compared to only two women of antiquity, Canace and Phædra – *both of whom were guilty of incest!*

Now let us avoid jumping to conclusions. In fact, as Dyce pointed out, even the most sinful of classical lovers were apt to be treated with respect by medieval and Early Tudor alike. He quotes, happily, the following lines from Feylde:

> Phedra and Theseus,
> Progne and Thereus,
> Pasyphe and Taurus

> (Who liketh to prove),
> Canace and Machareus,
> Galathea and Pamphilus
> Were never more dolorous,
> And all for true love

where, out of five examples of true love, two were incestuous (and the very ones in question) while one concerns Pasiphæ's lust for a bull.[13] The naïve convention, then, did undoubtedly exist. And if Lady Tilney objected to her poem, Skelton had any number of precedents to shelter behind. For all that, it appears to me more than suspicious that the poet – who was certainly familiar with the stories of Canace and Phædra – should have picked out these two *and no others* as likenesses for Margaret Tilney. In fact, I believe it to have been a sly and quite deliberate dig.

And the reason appears the moment we investigate Lady Tilney's antecedents. When Skelton addressed her, she was the wife of Sir Philip Tilney of Shelley, Norfolk – a brother of the reigning Duchess of Norfolk. But her maiden name was Brews. Margaret, in fact, seems to have been no other than a sister-in-law of Jane Scrope – the charming girl whose sparrow had been so signally lamented by the poet almost twenty years before.[14]

There can be no doubt as to what has happened. The long apology for *Philip Sparrow*, a little later in the poem, makes that all too clear. Jane was not at Sheriff Hutton herself, to speak her mind about it. But her sister-in-law was. And Lady Tilney, we may be sure, was highly displeased at the liberties Skelton had taken with the present Mrs. Brews. *Philip Sparrow* had already tarnished the family name; and now *Elinor Rumming* on top of it – the Brewses publicly linked with the gross ale-wife of Leatherhead! . . . Doubtless the topic gave rise to some plain speaking on her part.

Enough was said, at least, to warrant Skelton's inserting into the *Garland* his elaborate 'explanation' of the affair – though one doubts whether its tone was repentant enough to satisfy the indignant Margaret:

> It is too late for blame:
> The less, then, her ill name!

True, this bluntness was wrapped in the decent obscurity of Latin. But at the same time Skelton quietly took his revenge in the lyric. Such anxiety over a sister's fair fame, he implies, was positively incestuous!

Even more interesting, from the biographical point of view, is the little poem to Mistress Gertrude Statham. Here an unusual relationship is avowed from the start:

> Though ye wer hard-herted
> And I with you thwarted
> With wordes that smarted,
>   Yet now doutles ye give me cause
>   To write of you this goodly clause. . . .[15]

On the face of it this might very well refer to a recent quarrel; now – since Gertrude has contributed to the Countess's garland – graciously overlooked by the poet. But in fact (as we noted in our first chapter) it is highly probable that we have here our only reference to an incident which went back to the days when Skelton was still a green student at Cambridge.

Earlier in the *Garland* Skelton describes how he is shown round the peaceful garden where the Countess has her residence. All at once he is struck with a dismay which he is oddly reluctant to explain. But before his stumbling preamble is over, Occupation has gathered the cause of his agitation:

> Now what ye mene I trow I conject:
>   Gog give you good yere, ye make me to smile!

she breaks in; 'it's all on account of that "blunderer . . . yonder that playeth diddle-diddle!" ' At this point Skelton inserts an obscure Latin satire on 'an adversary of the poet's.' So far as one can render it it goes:

A 'tuppenny-ha'penny groom' at first sight, then a mere lackey:
Hunting the gnat, he is good at that, with eye leering sideways –
Look at him snatching, catching, clutching flies on the wing now!
Whatsoever Mercury brings, or Jupiter, or the
Frigid Saturn, the Sun, or Mars, or Venus, or chill Moon,
If you should chance to give it words or set it in writing,
Soon he's all asweat with the secret guilt in his entrails;
Bursting in flames, he flies to stir up this man and that man,

Spurring them on to fight; but the fires he lights are all vain, though
Silently his lips move, 'so that Codrus may blow up with envy.'°

It is not hard to detect a human being under the cloudy phrases –
many of them no doubt quotations, like the scraps of Persius and
Vergil at the beginning and end. Occupation has an allegorical
name for him, Envious Rancour. For Skelton he is that unpleasant
type of scandal-monger who, lacking the courage to justify his
gossip, gets other people to do his dirty work for him:

> He will set men a-feighting, and sit himself still
> And smerk, like a smithy cur at sperkes of steil,

Occupation puts it vividly.[16]

Fortunately, the poet thought fit to conceal the identity of his
foe under a screen that is easy to penetrate. The row of figures
which follows his satire soon resolve themselves into the name
ROGERUS STATHUM.[17]

Now, even without further evidence, it seems fair to surmise that
this Roger was some connexion of Mistress Gertrude's. And when
we learn that a Roger Stathum had married Gertrude Anstey of
Stow cum Quy, Cambs, in the distant days of 1482, we are surely
entitled to regard it as more than a coincidence. People married
young in those days. If Skelton was then a youth of twenty-two,
Roger was probably no older, while his wife was perhaps several
years their junior. Is there anything inherently unlikely in their
being still alive at the end of 1522 – both, now, in the service of the
Countess of Surrey? The names can hardly be called common;
and their union so rare that the possibility of another case may,
I think, be dismissed out of hand. Personally, I have little doubt
that Skelton was writing of Mr. and Mrs. Statham of Stow.

From this point, unfortunately, we are reduced to pure specula-
tion. It may be, of course, that Skelton had never set eyes on the
couple before he entered the Surrey household. Perhaps it was a
casual tiff with Mrs. Statham over some domestic triviality that
drew upon him the 'envious rancour' of her husband. But it is at
least equally possible that, in upbraiding the old lady as 'hard-
hearted,' Skelton had in mind those long-past days when, as a
lively scholar of arts, he had first made her acquaintance at Stow
or the neighbouring Cambridge.

That the poet should, in his last decade, have run into the very woman who as a girl had set his pulse aflutter with desire – it is a fascinating thought. Was it by any chance that oldest of stories, the love of the *povre escolier* for the dazzling heiress? Gertrude was certainly what would then be called a 'fortune' and now, more vulgarly, a 'catch'; for the Ansteys were among the best families in the county. But on that very account their daughters were not to be disposed of lightly. And so we have the inevitable sequel – the coming of the eligible suitor, Roger Statham, the long-drawn-out negotiations, and his final acceptance by the head of the family, Gertrude's brother Anthony. On the day of the wedding, 22 July 1482, the childless Anthony made his will 'and gave to the said Roger and Gertrude all the manor lands &c. that John Anstey his father by his will gave to him and his heirs.' While who knows what passion, rage, despair gripped in turn the heart of a young poet from the University near by?[18]

A biographer's fancy, perhaps; it is hard to renounce the excuse for a romance – above all one on such richly conventional lines. But in that case, what are we to make of the following passage in the lyric that Skelton composed for Mrs. Statham, now in her late fifties:

> I will that ye shall be
> In all beningnité
> Like to dame Pasiphé,
>> For now doutles ye give me cause
>> To write of you this goodly clause,
>
> *Maistres Geretrude,*
> *With womanhode endu'd,*
> *With virtu well renu'd.*[19]

For the future, Skelton wishes his virtuous Gertrude a 'benignity' that will approach the taurine cravings of Pasiphæ! It is his only wish for her – and once again, with Dyce, we may quote Feylde in his defence. Only this time we may be pardoned for feeling that that defence is wearing a trifle thin.

§ 4. GARDEN WEEDS

There is no further sign of Skelton's adherence to the house of Howard. Of course, that means little in so ill-documented a period.

It is entirely possible that the poet spent the rest of his life as a retainer of the Countess. We simply do not know. In any case it is obvious that his duties would be largely nominal. From the first he must have been free to come and go as he pleased: how else could he have written 'a great part' of *Colin Clout* at the house of his friend Thynne? So we must picture him as Lady Besse's favourite poet, with a place at her table whenever he chose to drop in. It is pleasant to think that, now and then, he may have looked over the shoulder of the little Henry Howard as he frowned over his Vergil, and perhaps given him a tip or two in versification. But of this, too, the records are silent. So far as we know them, Skelton's only poems after the *Garland* were dedicated, dutifully, to Cardinal Wolsey. We must remember, of course, that Skelton was still Orator Royal. Whatever his position in the Surrey household, his first loyalty was to the King; and, having reluctantly recognised Wolsey as the King's chief minister, the rest followed. But of that more hereafter.

Meanwhile, the Howard ménage was going, domestically, to pieces. From the beginning, as we saw, it was doomed to failure. Elizabeth was far too positive a person to sink into the Griselda her husband had envisaged. Soon, their home life became a battle of wills; and the incessant tug-of-war brought out the worst qualities in both of them.

Under Thomas's charm lay the heartless egotism of a thoroughly selfish man of the world. He was perhaps no more of a lecher than most of his fellow courtiers. Even his invitation to Cromwell may have been half in joke: though it is a little startling to hear a Lord High Treasurer announce to the King's Vicar-general that if the latter 'lust not to dally with his wife he hath a young woman with pretty proper tetins. . . .'[20] But his liaison with Besse Holland was no joke; and it involved the most brutal humiliation for his wife. Proud, lonely, and fanatically chaste, she found almost her entire household openly on the side of the reigning mistress – a creature, she exclaims bitterly, who was 'but washer of my nursery eight years.' It was an impossible situation. For nearly seven years it dragged on, amid scenes of increasing wildness. Then, early in 1534, it came to a head.

We have only the Duchess's version (she was Duchess of Norfolk now) of what happened. Her letters were written four years later – with, no doubt, her customary exaggeration. She had ended by trying to dismiss all the Holland coterie from her service. They had not only refused to go, but, when she became violent, 'bound me and pinnacled me and sat on my breast till I spit blood, which I have been worse for ever since.' There was the final shattering scene, when her husband 'came riding all night' – in his fury at this insult to Miss Holland's supporters – 'and locked me up in a chamber.' He then carried off all her jewels and wardrobe, leaving her nothing but a pension of £50 a quarter (now about £6,000 a year) – which, seeing that it came from her own fortune, she rightly regarded as niggardly.

From this time on they lived apart. The Duchess spent her time appealing for justice to all her acquaintances, Cromwell in particular. To the Duke's proposals for a divorce she turned a deaf ear. She would never give him *that* satisfaction, at least: had she not herself 'lived like a good woman' through all his many absences? At the age of forty she had become a nagging old woman, feared by her relatives and deserted by her own children. Her brother refused to have her in his house: her 'wild language,' he declared feelingly, 'might undo me and all mine!' Everyone looked upon her as half crazy; and perhaps, by this time, she was. Only the Earl of Westmorland, whom she had once so nearly married, had a kind word to say for her.

To this cautionary tale of a Tudor marriage the careers of her husband and son make a fitting epilogue. There are few more unedifying pages of history than Norfolk's manœuvres to gain power. At Wolsey's fall he seemed at last on the verge of triumph. But by this time Henry knew where to look for real service. It was the low-born Cromwell who succeeded that man of the people, Wolsey. To the end of his life Norfolk cringed and intrigued in vain. Henry preferred unscrupulous nobodies; they were more single-minded than Norfolk and the men of 'good estimation and nobility' he was constantly putting forward. Norfolk's only reward was the hatred of his fellow councillors.

In the end came the attainder of himself and his son, the poet-Earl. And the most bitter witness against the latter was his own sister, the Duchess of Richmond. Largely on her evidence, Surrey was condemned, and beheaded on Tower Hill in 1547. The only thing that saved the father of this precious brood was the sudden death of King Henry himself.[21]

CHAPTER FOURTEEN

THE REFORMATION LOOMS

It is necessary that all tho that have charge of the flock of
Christ endeavour themself to gainstand these pernicious heresies: wherein doubtless the most reverend father in God, my
lord legate, hath now meritoriously travailed, and so intend-
eth to persever and to continue, to the full extirpation of the
same.

FISHER: *Sermon concerning Certain
Heretics which then were abjured, 1526.*

§ 1. THE NEW ALIGNMENT

LESS THAN seven more years were now left to our poet.
One hopes they were pleasant ones – and, indeed, there is
some ground for believing that they were. At last he was
beginning to reap the fruits of his vigorous and unorthodox
career. Everywhere men were talking about the witty poet-parson;
telling story after story of his clever bouts with authority, both
at Diss and in the royal palace. It was in 1525 that the merry
tale of his quarrel with Bishop Nick reached the distinction of
print. The Skelton Legend was starting to blossom; and Skelton
was man of the Renaissance enough to enjoy its agreeable shade.

But apart from what other men said about him, the poet might
justifiably feel a certain sense of triumph. He had emerged from his
battle against Wolsey with honour unscathed: it was a moral if
not a material victory. And this inner security of his is evident in
the few scraps of information that derive from these later years.
While he had given up his campaign of invective, he did not regard
that as a promise to close his mouth altogether. In the very next
April he felt free to utter an epigram, if an innocent one, on the
Cardinal's latest outrage.[1]

It was quite compatible with this that he should have dedicated
his next long poem to the Cardinal. For this concerned a matter on
which they were entirely at one: the war against the Scots.[2]
Albany, Regent of Scotland, had marched a powerful army
down to the Tweed and then, for some reason which has never
been explained, retreated after a single brief assault on Wark

Castle. The English indulged in an orgy of self-congratulation, and foremost among them was the Orator Royal.

Poor as the poem is, in comparison with his other works, there can have been few which he wrote with greater pleasure. And when he dedicated it to my Lord Cardinal's right noble grace, it was as a reward for honest work that he ended:

> Go, litel quair, apace
>   In most humble wise
> Before his noble grace
>   That caused me to devise
>   This litel enterprise,
> And him most lowly pray
>   In his mind to comprise
> Those wordes his grace did say
> Of an ammas gray.

> *Je foy enterment en sa bone grace.*

The grey amice refers of course to the prebend already promised him, almost a year ago, by Wolsey. We need not comment on the fact that, so far as we know, the Cardinal's noble word failed to correspond with his deed. Skelton has already done that for us; and, knowing his Wolsey, in advance![3]

§ 2. A FUNERAL AND A TOMB

In 1524 the old Duke of Norfolk, who had retired to Framlingham the year before, died there at the advanced age of eighty. The whole country lamented his passing, and no less than nine hundred people gathered to pay homage to the great soldier.

The Duke had expressed a wish to be buried at Thetford. Roughly halfway along the route was Diss; and 'a mile without the town of Diss the corpse was met with all the procession of the town & so brought always to the church of the town, which, with the choir and porch, was hanged with black cloth and garnished with scutcheons.' Here a dirge was sung, vigil was kept all night about the body, and between six and seven next morning 'was a solemn mass sung by his chapel.' After this the procession reformed and continued its stately progress to Thetford.[4]

Obviously, if it were humanly possible, Skelton must have been present at these obsequies of the national hero and his own liege lord. Though his duties were now performed by deputy, he was still Rector of Diss; and, united as he was to the Howards, it would have been an insult for him not to attend. So we may imagine the poet heading the choir and congregation as they went to meet the cortége, and escorting it proudly to his sabled church. One wonders which of the distinguished mourners found a bed for the night at his parsonage – and whether their needs were ministered to by the same good lady as had once embroiled Skelton with his bishop.

Tradition also links the poet, if not with the funeral, with the sepulchre of his greatest enemy. Since the story appears in the pages of Elis Gruffydd as well as in the *Merry Tales*, we may quote the less familiar version of the former. It is only, perhaps, an anecdote, but it does seem to catch the spirit of Skelton's later dealings with Wolsey:

> During this time the cardinal of England had set some of the best craftsmen to be found in the whole of Christendom at work on brass and marble to make a great carved tomb in which to lay his carcase to rot after his death. As he was riding from his palace to the monastery of Westminster he happened to meet Skelton the poet, who followed him to the place where these men were working. After the cardinal had inspected the work from all sides and had perceived the poet he said:
> 'Sir Skelton, what do you think of this work?'
> The poet praised it as he well could, but after a long talk he asked the cardinal on whose tomb he was spending all that money. The cardinal replied that it was for his own body. The poet replied mockingly:
> 'If you take my advice you will take possession of it while you are in life and health, for fear your executors should not take the trouble to put you in when your soul and body part!'
> These words angered the cardinal and he took them as a joke, but they came true.[5]

In locating the scene at Westminster, both our sources are mistaken. Henry VIII had presented Wolsey with the unfinished mausoleum in Windsor Chapel, abandoned by his father in favour of the Abbey. So it was at Windsor that, in the words of

Herbert, 'Wolsey had begun a monument for himself . . . which one Benedetto, a statuary of Florence, took in hand 1524. and continued till 1529.' Nevertheless, Skelton was right: the Cardinal never used his magnificent cenotaph. After his disgrace and death, Henry decided to convert it for his own use; but the King was no luckier than the Cardinal. For years the monument lay neglected in a palace lumber-room, until finally it was transferred to St. Paul's, decked with a huge gilt coronet, and employed to cover the mortal remains of – Lord Nelson![6]

§ 3. HOLY CHURCH IN PERIL

Another anecdote comes in aptly here, for it reminds us that something had now replaced Wolsey at the head of Skelton's numerous hates. This was the rising menace of heresy.

The tale itself is late and doubtful; all the same, it is worth retelling. It concerns Skelton's relations with Stephen Gardiner, soon to become a bishop and Henry's most ardent supporter in his battle with the old Church. There is nothing impossible in their friendship. Young though he was, Gardiner had in 1524 become a lecturer at Cambridge, and 'about the same time was made tutor to a son of the duke of Norfolk' – and Skelton's patroness, Lady Besse.[7] It would be natural for the old tutor and the young to be on familiar terms. And, the times being what they were, their talk must have turned often on those dogmas which were now being so bitterly assailed. Chief of these was transubstantiation. Was Christ really present in the sacrament, and if so, in what sense? One of the arguments was expressed in the tag, *Crede et manducasti* (Believe and thou hast eaten Him).

Gardiner had, it seems, made great play with this aspect of the problem. A little later, however, he had cause to regret his loud emphasis on Belief. For, having lent Skelton his palfrey to ride away on, he failed to get it back. On enquiring the reason, all he got by way of answer was a Latin jingle to this effect:

Thy saw which did ease us
Re the body of Jesus
   (Believe thou hast eaten: thou must have)
Now solveth my care
Re thy borrowed mare:
   Believe that thou hast it: thou dost have![0]

Unfortunately, another tradition fathers the rhyme on Erasmus, who had neglected to return a nag of Sir Thomas More's.[8] Such is the fate of any successful quip.

It may seem curious that a blasphemy should be evinced as a proof of Skelton's theological 'soundness.' But in general it is the believer rather than the sceptic who jokes about his religion. And in this particular case the heretic is represented by Gardiner. All unwittingly, of course; there was no stouter conservative, doctrinally, than the future Bishop of Winchester. But if our story is true it shows him slipping into the Lutheran heresy that Faith is all that counts. Skelton's answer was a neat practical reminder of its dangers. What is more to the point, it was a thoroughly orthodox sally.

There is no need, here, to go into the complex details of this doctrinal struggle. They have been told many times over. There was nothing very novel about its nature. Heretics had always been a problem; and no one doubted – least of all the heretics themselves – that the Church in power had the right to discourage its opponents by every means up to the stake. Outside the wise pages of Rabelais – who is careful always to swear 'jusqu'au feu *exclusive*' – toleration was not a sixteenth-century virtue.

In the 'twenties, however, the Church in England was being threatened on all sides at once. Heresy had invaded Cambridge itself. And in the year 1527, just about the time when the Imperial mercenaries were swarming to the sack of Rome, two earnest young Cantab reformers, Thomas Bilney and Thomas Arthur, set off on a revivalist tour of London and East Anglia.

At a time like this it was asking for trouble. On 28 May the pair were reported, clapped in the Tower and left there while Wolsey led his brilliant embassy across the Channel. It was late in November before their case came up for hearing. As the weaker vessel, Arthur was the first to be dealt with, and he quickly recanted. But Bilney was less easily cowed. His judge, the gentle Tunstall, gave him every opportunity, but it was not until Saturday, 7 December, that he finally saw the wisdom of submission. He abjured in his turn, and Tunstall was able to deliver sentence.

With Arthur, he was to go next day before the procession at St. Paul's, bareheaded, with a faggot on his shoulder, and stand before the preacher throughout the sermon. After this public penance they were both to remain in prison until it pleased his grace the Cardinal to release them.[9]

§ 4. THE LAST POEM

There can be no doubt that Skelton's final satire is aimed at these two youngsters. The date of abjuration is there said to be the Feast of the Conception, i.e. 8 December.[10] It is curious, and a trifle pathetic, to watch the old poet loose the last barrage of his abuse, no longer against the worldly leader of his Church, but, at his request, against two of its youthful critics. Yet never had the Skeltonic rattled with such alliterative fury, such damning repetition, such multitudinous rhymes! One would guess he knew it to be his last satiric flight.

As an old scholar he begins by commiserating, in dutiful Latin, with Cambridge for having nourished this pair of changelings. This, with its side-note, is our chief evidence that Skelton's academic career began at the younger University.

The pamphlet itself – for that is what it is – falls into the inevitable three parts. First, a brief statement, in mixed prose and verse, of the case as Skelton sees it: a couple of foolish undergraduates whose first draught of learning has gone to their heads. Second, his reply – mostly in Skeltonics – to the young men's heretical beliefs, to wit, 'how it was idolatry to offer to images of our blessed Lady, or to pray and go on pilgrimages, or to make oblations to any images of saints in churches or elsewhere.' This forms the bulk of the poem. Third and last comes Skelton's Apology for Poetry – in its way as grand a defence as any the sixteenth century was to provide.

With Renaissance boldness Skelton claims that the true poet is God-inspired:

> By Whose inflammacion
> Of spiritual instigacion
> And divine inspiracion
> We are kindled in such facion
> With hete of the Holy Gost,
> Which is God of mightes most,
> That He our pen doth lede
> And maketh in us such spede
> That forthwith we must nede
> With pen and ink procede. . . .[11]

It is on these high grounds that he claims the right, as a poet, to meddle now in matters theological. But, he insists, the argument also holds good for that poem of affection *Philip Sparrow*, for the grave instruction of *Magnificence*, and – though this is tactfully unstressed – for the correction of *Why Come Ye Not To Court?*

Do not blame *me*, says the poet as he finally lays down his pen; it is God's goad that has pricked me on. And there can be no doubt that he believed every word he said.

§ 5. THE LAST PATRON

The *Replication* is prefaced by a long Latin dedication. Literally translated, it runs:

> To the most honourable, most exalted, and far the most reverend father in Christ and the Lord, my lord Thomas, on the title of St. Cecily[12] priest of the Holy Roman Church, most worthy cardinal and legate of the apostolic see, most illustrious legate *a latere*, &c., Skelton laureate, orator royal, declares most humble allegiance with all the reverence proper to so great and noble a prince of prelates, most equitable dispenser of all justice, and most excellent patron of the present little treatise, in whose most auspicious command, as it were the seal *or* wine-press of glorious immortality, this little screed is to be congratulated.°

Now, this sort of thing sticks readily in the modern gizzard. Both the custom and formalities of patronage have died so completely that we find it hard to see them in perspective. The task is not rendered easier by the absence, in English, of a superlative case. But in fact Wolsey was 'the most reverend father in God' that the English Church could boast. He was not only Cardinal-Archbishop, but, for the first time in a century, an English 'legate of the side.' Throughout history there has rarely been such a prince of prelates; and in addition he was, as Chancellor, master of equity and dispenser of all justice in the realm. In a word, Skelton's dedication contained nothing that would sound, to contemporary ears, even fulsome. Surely to write at such a command *was* something he could be congratulated upon? Otherwise, he is careful to offer the Cardinal no reverence that was not 'proper to' his extraordinary rank.

What we need for comparison, in fact, is not the enforced independence of the modern poet, untempted by a patron, but the situation of Polydore Vergil in 1515. Beside Polydore's 'most reverend lord my God' Skelton's superlatives pale into their true historical propriety.

When all this is said, there remains the sigh of regret. From our discreet distance, it still seems a pity that Wolsey's boldest enemy should have been jockeyed into supplying him with even the conventional terms of respect. If only he had kept out of it altogether! At the same time, it is quite unjust to damn the old satirist as a time-server. In the *Replication*, as in the *Duke of Albany*, Skelton is writing from entire and whole-hearted conviction. That his patron should now be Wolsey was unfortunate, perhaps, but inevitable. For Skelton was responding, like every other literate clergyman, to Holy Church's cry for aid.[13]

It is noteworthy that this time he was *not* writing hard on the heels of the event:

> And yet some men say
> How ye are this day
> And be now, as ill, . . .
> As ye were before. . . .[14]

This cannot refer to Arthur, who was sufficiently scared to disappear from history after his one sharp lesson. But not so 'little Bilney.' His spirit was as fine, in its way, as that of his antagonist, Sir Thomas More. After his return to Cambridge, he was soon caught preaching again; inevitably he was found, tried and burned at Norwich in 1531.

Nevertheless, all this did not happen immediately. After their sentence the two young men were taken back to the Tower; and, if we may trust Latimer's memory, it was 'a whole year' before Bilney was seen once more at Cambridge.[15] Either, then, the poem was written twelve months after the abjuration, or – which seems more probable – Latimer was including the earlier imprisonment in his reckoning. This would imply that Bilney's release occurred in May or June 1528.

Actually, such a date fits in neatly with certain other events of that year. The Church had been thoroughly alarmed by Bilney's obstinacy. With his accustomed vigour, Wolsey decided to mobilise new resources to meet the peril. In March 1528 Sir Thomas More was licensed to keep and read Lutheran books in order to refute them. The first result was his *Dialogue against Heresies* – a good half of which is devoted to answering Bilney. And, as Skelton himself informs us, it was Wolsey who ordered the poet to turn his peculiar talents against Bilney in 1528.

The cleverness of the plan is patent. More's legal brain – the finest of his day – was to cope with the problem from its theological side. But something more was needed; a more popular method had to be found. And what could be better than the one invented, tried and perfected by Skelton Laureate? Of its efficacy the Cardinal was himself only too painfully aware. Thus, while the lucid prose of More exposed the heretics' errors of reasoning, the Skeltonic would harass them with a ridicule that was even more damning. For nothing kills a cause so surely as laughter.

Skelton's new rôle as the Church's apologist brings him back, almost at once, into history. On 4 May 1528, in the chapel of Norwich Inn near Charing Cross, another trial for heresy was proceeding. The mild and worried Tunstall was confronted with yet another black sheep from his unruly flock. This time it was a serious-minded fuller of Colchester, Thomas Bowgas by name.

The trial did not take long. No martyr – he is not even mentioned by the all-inclusive Foxe – the terrified Bowgas agreed to abjure his heresies; and the Bishop absolved him on condition that he bore his penitential faggot next Sunday at Hythe, near Colchester. The case was closed. But among the witnesses, on that Monday in early May, the clerk of the court recorded two gentlemen. One was Marmaduke Tunstall, a relation and ward of the Bishop's. The other was *magister* Skelton.[16]

His identity can no longer be doubted. Who but the poet could have been present as an official spectator at this ecclesiastical trial? Plainly, he was there in his new capacity as defender of the faith, seeking fresh material for his poetic journalism. Poet, priest and publicist: one wonders if ever, before or since, his Church has known these functions quite so remarkably combined.

§ 6. JOHN SKELTON, GENTLEMAN

One thing may strike the reader as even more curious, and that is the poet's official description as *generosus*. Long ago we noted

Skelton's avoidance of the challenge uttered by Garnish on the score of his 'knavery.' If Skelton had claims to gentle birth, we remarked, he could hardly have failed to produce them. Instead, he drew attention to his laurel and his royal tutorship. To the modern ear, this sounds like evasion, and not very skilful evasion at that. But was Skelton really capable of such clumsiness?

The idea of the gentleman, it has been frequently claimed, is a notion peculiarly English. What is less often realised is the origin of this peculiarity. It may be expressed in a word: in England, and in England alone, the term was *bivalent* – not only morally, but socially. Even in the fifteenth century, when it makes its first appearance, *generosus* was applied to two quite distinct types of person. First and foremost, it described the man of ancestry who was not yet a knight. The name arose, as Sir George Sitwell has observed, in an attempt to distinguish the common criminal from the ruffian who was driven to crime by the accident of birth – the penniless younger son, forbidden by custom to justify his existence in the way of honest labour.[17]

But in England this well-born rapscallion was equated, officially, with quite another social type. This was the gentleman by profession. 'Students of law, for example, were gentlemen of the Inns of Court. . . . Similarly certain offices carried with them the status and title of gentleman. The four chief personal officers of the Lord Mayor . . . ranked as *generosi* and enjoyed the title of Master, or even Esquire. The same distinctions were, of course, closely followed in the royal service. . . .' The important thing to notice is that this distinction cut clean across the other. It was even possible for members of the same family to be legally recognised as of different social grades. Professor Reed aptly cites the example of Skelton's fellow dramatist, John Heywood. John's elder brother was a yeoman; he himself was, 'by virtue of his office at court,' a gentleman; and his younger brother, as an eminent lawyer, was actually an esquire.

We can now understand why, when Garnish jeered at Skelton for a knave, he promptly flourished back his university degree and his office at Court. 'Whoso abideth in the university,' Harrison was shortly to declare, shall be able to buy his coat of arms and 'be reputed for a gentleman ever after.'[18] His very title of 'master' was the same as that given to the man of birth. But in addition, Skelton had a status in the royal household which must have ranked him officially among its *generosi*. It was no blustering evasion, then, that made the poet cry:

> What eileth thé, rebaud, on me to rave?
> A king to me myn habit gave:
> At Oxforth the université
> Avanced I was to that degré;
> By hole consent of their senate
> I was made poet laureate.

He was, quite literally, presenting his credentials as a gentleman. And they were no more and no less valid than those of the gentleman-usher who faced him across the royal hall.

CHAPTER FIFTEEN

DEATH OF AN ERA

All, all, of a piece throughout:
  Thy Chase had a Beast in view;
Thy Wars brought nothing about;
  Thy Lovers were all untrue.
'Tis well an Old Age is out,
  And time to begin a New.

DRYDEN: *The Secular Masque.*

§ I. THE KING'S GREAT MATTER

IRONICALLY, IT was Wolsey who first put into Henry's mind the idea of questioning the validity of his marriage. Or so, at least, Catherine believed; and a good many other people thought the same. The Cardinal's motive was merely to replace a Spanish alliance with a French one. He was little aware that his tiny diplomatic seed of doubt, once planted, would grow into the jungle of the next seven years.

It all started very quietly, on 17 May 1527, with Wolsey summoning the King before him to justify his living with his brother's widow. It should have terminated just as quietly, with Wolsey declaring the marriage void and obtaining confirmation later from the Pope. That was what the Duke of Suffolk had done, with entire success. No one had allowed for the lofty resistance of Catherine herself; nor for the capture of Rome by her uncle, which put the Pope in his power. But these, together with Henry's passion for the elusive Anne Boleyn, ended by leading England, much to its own astonishment, into Protestantism.

After two years of legal quibbling, the legatine court met at Blackfriars on 21 June 1529. It was the day Shakespeare, with his unerring eye for effect, chose to dramatise in *Henry VIII*. Ignoring procedure, Catherine knelt before the King and made her grand, futile appeal. She had never consummated her marriage with Arthur; the question of validity, therefore, did not arise. But as she spoke she saw that Henry had made up his mind. So, instead of returning to her seat, she 'took her way straight out of the house.'

It was her last public appearance. Even as she knelt at Henry's feet the army of Francis I was being annihilated at Landriano. There was no longer any hope of a decision from Pope Clement. But when Campeggio stood up in Blackfriars and again adjourned the court, the Duke of Suffolk expressed the new 'temporal' view. With a mighty slap on the table, he broke out:

'By the mass, now I see that the old-said saw is true, that there was never legate nor cardinal that did good in England!' [1]

§ 2. SKELTON'S DEATH

It is useless to ask what Skelton's attitude could have been in this 'great matter' of the King's. Up to now he had managed to remain an erring, perhaps, but faithful son of his Church *and* servant of Henry's. Like everyone else, he must have been dismayed at the sudden threat to their harmony presented by the 'divorce.' What, one wonders, did he think of his patron's niece, Mistress Anne, who was now all-powerful at Court? Did he adopt the schoolmaster's view – that his pupil had fallen a victim to 'the filthy contagion of vice'? Or did he feel, like most of Henry's subjects, that the stability of the kingdom was the deciding factor?

We shall never know. For on the very day when his 'peerless pomegranate,' Queen Catherine, pleaded before the King at Blackfriars, Skelton was lying on his deathbed in nearby Westminster.

The cause of death is unknown. At seventy he was old enough for it to have been natural, of course. But perhaps his departure was hastened by that scourge of the period, the sweating sickness. Du Bellay had seen its horrifying ravages only the previous year. 'One has a little pain in the head and the heart,' he noted, 'suddenly a sweat breaks out, and a doctor is useless; for whether you wrap yourself up much or little, in four hours, and sometimes in two or three, you are dispatched without languishing.' There are no signs of such a severe epidemic in 1529, it is true. But on 3 July – less than a fortnight after Skelton's death – du Bellay describes Wolsey as 'hidden at Hampton Court, because he knew nowhere else to go. He has fortified his gallery and his garden. Only four or five are allowed to see him.' This strict retreat has been explained as due to another outbreak of the disease. If this is so, it might also explain why our poet died, to all appearances, too suddenly to make his will.[2]

About the date of his death, at least, there can be no question. 'He gave up the ghost,' Braynewode informed Bale, 'on 21 June 1529.' The poet, he added, was buried before the high altar of St. Margaret's, Westminster, with the inscription on alabaster:

IOANNES SKELTONVS VATES PIERIVS HIC SITVS EST[3]

It was his last and briefest boast: 'Here lies John Skelton, Pierian bard.' Both stone and inscription have disappeared long since.

But his passing did not go entirely unnoticed. In their accounts, the churchwardens of St. Margaret's record the ceremony that attended it. Four[4] tapers were set about his corpse; four torches were carried in procession; and the church bells tolled their solemn message longer (with one exception) than they were to do for anyone else that year. It was a funeral, neither modest nor sumptuous, such as might reasonably mark the death of a royal orator.

One other item yields us a glimpse into Skelton's life as a resident of England's second capital. A special knell was rung for him by 'Our Lady' Brotherhood. This was the parish gild of the Assumption, to which belonged many of those who were attached to the neighbouring Palace. Among its members we find a Duchess of Bedford, an Earl of Dartmouth, a lord privy seal and several gentlemen of the Chapel, as well as chandlers, monks, barbers and lesser fry. Literature too had its representatives. An early list includes the translator of Cato, Benedict Burgh, the printer Caxton, and his successor, Wynkyn de Worde. Skelton's name is nowhere visible; but there can be no doubt that he was a brother. It is pleasant to see our fierce old fighter engaged in the more social activities of his beloved Westminster.[5]

Several months later, on 10 November, the Rector of St. Margaret's obtained permission to administer his estate. This was William Mote, S.T.B.; whose learning, at least, is testified by the neat Italian hand in which he signed his church accounts in 1528. Another month, and he was to become Vicar of St. Bride's, Fleet Street – whose parsonage beside the Thames had been occupied in turn by Empson and Wolsey. One hopes that their grim shadows did not blind him to the needs of Skelton's 'widow' and children. Their state was desperate, for the law of his Church strictly forbade a priest to bequeath anything to his mistress. [6]

§ 3. WOLSEY'S FALL

In the moment of his death, at least, Skelton was fortunate. Only a month or two earlier, the German princes had made their protest against the edict of Speyer which gave the name Protestantism to the world. In the following autumn the Parliament met that was, before it ended, to establish the Reformation in England. The thing itself Skelton knew and abominated; but he was spared the pain of seeing his royal master give it his official blessing.

But in avoiding so much that was bitter, he also lost one sight that would have delighted him beyond measure. He missed the dramatic fall of Cardinal Wolsey. As long ago as 1522 he had prophesied it; but when he turned his face to the wall in 1529 the Cardinal was, to all appearances, as high on Fortune's wheel as ever. Nevertheless, it would not be long before he could whisper to Colin Clout, 'Dead shepherd, now I find thy saw of might!'

His actual downfall came about almost by chance. Degraded to his archbishopric, he had yet been spared imprisonment or the rage of Parliament. But as he rode north, planning a splendidly humble entry into his Cathedral of York, 'in the vamps of our hosen,' news reached Henry that Clement had just issued a new brief about his marriage. Whatever it said, the King had no intention of risking its promulgation in the conservative north. As for evidence against the ex-Cardinal, he had written letters to Francis, to Charles, to the Pope in person. None were openly treacherous, but the situation was too dangerous for clemency.

On 22 November 1530, Wolsey was met by an escort headed by Sir William Kingston, Constable of the Tower. Quickly he cut short the official's stammering rhetoric. 'I know,' he exclaimed, 'what is provided for me.' Perhaps he did. The party reached no further than Leicester Abbey. There Wolsey made his last confession. Eventually the sick man's tongue began to fail him; the Abbot was hurriedly called in to administer extreme unction; 'and incontinent the clock struck eight, at which time he gave up the ghost. . . .' [7]

So passed the last of the great princes of the English Church. And his whole age is lit up in the verdicts that were passed upon his death. 'Here,' wrote Cavendish, 'is the end and fall of pride and arrogancy of such men, exalted by fortune to honours and high dignities.' This was Skelton's judgment too; the medieval sentence upon the New Men whose leaping individualism threatened to disrupt the closed circle of the common weal. But Henry drew another moral; and it pointed forward as clearly as Cavendish's pointed back. 'Three,' he concluded, 'may keep counsel, if two be away; and if I thought that my cap knew my counsel, I would cast it into the fire and burn it.' [8]

Society and the Self. It was in the clash of these ideologies that modern England was born.

NOTES

ABBREVIATIONS TO THE NOTES

CHEL   *Cambridge History of English Literature.*
CPR   *Calendar of Patent Rolls.*
CS   Camden Series.
CSP   *Calendar of State Papers.*
CUP   Cambridge University Press.
DNB   *Dictionary of National Biography.*
EETS   Early English Text Society.
EHR   *English Historical Review.*
EL   Everyman Library.
ESEA   Essays and Studies of the English Association.
ESt   *Englische Studien.*
LP   *Letters and Papers* (esp. of Henry VIII).
MLN   *Modern Language Notes* (of America).
MLR   *Modern Language Review.*
N & Q   *Notes and Queries.*
OED   *Oxford English Dictionary.*
OUP   Oxford University Press.
P.C.C.   Prerogative Court of Canterbury.
PMLA   *Publications of the Modern Language Association* (of America).
P.R.O.   Public Record Office.
RES   *Review of English Studies.*
RS   Rolls Series.
SP   *State Papers.*
Stud. Phil. *Studies in Philology.*
TLS   *Times Literary Supplement.*
VCH   *Victoria County History.*
W.A.M.   Westminster Abbey Muniments.

Dyce   Alexander Dyce, *Poetical Works of John Skelton*, 1843.
Gordon   Ian A. Gordon, *John Skelton, Poet Laureate*, Melbourne and OUP 1943.
Nelson   William Nelson, *John Skelton, Laureate*, Columbia U.P. 1939.
    Except where otherwise expressed, the place of publication of books cited is London.

INTRODUCTION

1. J. Gairdner, *Paston Letters*, 1904, IV. no. 604.
2. *Ibid.* IV. no. 619n.; nos. 589ff.; John Smyth of Nibley, *The Berkeley MSS* (ed. Sir J. Maclean), Gloucester 1883-5, II. 101ff.
3. He died in 1519: see Eileen Power, *Medieval People*, Pelican ed., p. 158.
4. H. G. Wright, *Tales from the Decameron*, EETS 205 (1937); *Fulgens and Lucres* II. 754-6; *Gentleness and Nobility* 1121-4 (ed. K. W. Cameron, Raleigh (N. C.) 1941).
5. A. Smythe-Palmer, *Ideal of a Gentleman*, n.d., *passim*; cf. Burckhardt, *Civilisation of the Renaissance in Italy*, 1944, pp. 218ff.
6. G. Baskerville, *English Monks and the Suppression*, p. 285, n. 2.
7. See especially Nelson, Chap. I.
8. For details see my (unpublished) dissertation, 'The humanism of John Skelton,' Cambridge 1938; and the introd. to the forthcoming EETS ed. of Skelton's *Diodorus* by Professor F. M. Salter and the writer.
9. Pynson print (Huntington Library, California), sig. A.4.
10. With the possible exception of the recently discovered fragment of *Good Order*, which has a ref. to the 'new founde land': see Frost and Nash, ' "Good Order": a morality fragment,' *Stud. Phil.* XLI (1944), p. 490.
11. A convenient recent account is in J. W. H. Atkins, *Medieval Literary Criticism*, CUP 1943. For the *Poetria noua* of Geoffrey see E. Faral, *Les arts poétiques du XIIᵉ et du XIIIᵉ siècle* (Bibl. de l'Ecole des Hauts Etudes, fasc. 238), Paris 1924, pp. 194ff.
12. MS. C.C.C. Camb. 357. An edition is being prepared for EETS (see above, n.8).
13. Fol. 215ᵛ.
14. Fols. 231-31ᵛ. Cf. Poggio: 'Semelem Iupiter ob pulchritudinem in forma hominis cognouit.' (In a paper which unfortunately reached me too late for discussion ('John Skelton's contribution to the English language,' *Trans. Roy. Soc. Canada*, 1945, pp. 119-217), Professor Salter has collected no less than 816 words from the *Diodorus* alone which precede the earliest mention in *OED*. A further 640 are gathered from his poems. When every allowance has been made for the inaccuracy of *OED* these remain astonishing totals.)
15. *Garland* 22-3. In the latter line all texts have *mose*; but 'myry wose' occurs in *Diodorus*, fols. 11, 24ᵛ; in 9 (as 'wosy myre'); while fol. 27 has 'sylt & fatte wose.' This is surely decisive.
16. *Poetria noua* 281, 595: quoted in *Garland* 1521, *Speak, Parrot* 51 (gloss).

17. Ll. 113-23; cf. *Poetria noua* 375ff.
18. *Poetria noua* 562ff.
19. *Philip Sparrow* 988ff.
20. It is true that Hafiz had already offered to barter Bokhara and Samarkand for the mole on the cheek of his Turkish maid of Shiraz. But Skelton's Persian was, we may safely guess, rudimentary. For Gascoigne's 'Praise of the fair Bridges . . . on her having a scar in her forehead,' see Percy, *Reliques*, EL, II. 16.
21. Ll. 1184-93.
22. *Poetria noua* 594-5.

CHAPTER ONE

1. See the writer's 'Skelton: a genealogical study,' *RES* XI (1935), pp. 1-15. For conjectural parents see R. L. Ramsay, *Skelton's Magnyfycence*, EETS, E. S. 98 (1906), pp. cxxv-viii; Gordon, pp. 12-13; Dyce, I. xxvi. W. Hamilton (*N & Q*, 4 February 1893) says that the poet was born at Norwich in 1461; unfortunately he does not state his source. For other Norfolk Skeltons see Blomefield, *Hist. Norfolk*, ed. 1805, IV. 89; C. L. Kingsford, *Prejudice and Promise in 15th. Cent. England*, pp. 59-60; *CPR Ed. IV-Rich. III*, 150; Nelson, pp. 59-60; Gordon, p. 11. An Emma Skelton, widow of Beccles, died there in 1531, but her will (Ipswich Dist. Prob. Reg., Bk. XI, fol. 56) shows no connexion with the poet. It is perhaps just worth noting that in *Speak, Parrot* the bird declares he is no 'churlish chough' (209). As Nelson has remarked, Wolsey's crest included a chough; but the bird also appears in the arms of various branches of the *Cumberland* Skeltons, though it does not seem to have survived the migration south. (Burke, *General Armory*, 1884, *sub. nom.*) Nevertheless, Wordsworth was 'certain of having read somewhere . . . that Skelton was born at Branthwaite Hall, in the County of Cumberland' (Grosart, *Prose Works of Wordsworth*, III. 334).
2. Hall's *Chronicle*, ed. 1809, p. 380.
3. *Against Garnish* IV. 63.
4. *Replication*, gloss to l. 1 of *Eulogium*: 'Cantabrigia Skeltonidi laureato primam mammam erudicionis pientissime propinauit.' For Cambridge in Skelton's day see Rashdall, *Universities of Europe*, OUP 1895; J. B. Mullinger, *University of Cambridge . . . to 1535*, CUP 1873.
5. *Colin Clout* 550-2.
6. Trans. Mullinger, *op. cit.*, p. 427.
7. *Garland* 1412ff.
8. *Ibid.* 1038-40.
9. See App. I(J), and below, Chap. XIII, § 3. This important item was first discovered by Professor F. M. Salter.

10. For Ruckshaw see T. A. Walker, *Biog. Register of Peterhouse Men, Part I*, CUP 1927, pp. 56-7; J. and J. A. Venn, *Alumni Cantab., Part I*, CUP 1922-7, III. 495. His will is quoted in *Testamenta Eboracensia*, IV. 231, with a few additional facts.

11. Venn and Venn, IV. 83. He was prebendary of Southwell 1488-1500; and is almost certainly the 'Mag. Skelton' mentioned by Walker (*op. cit.*, p. 101) as perendinating at the college in 1503-4. The Computus Roll of 1503-4 also records that 'M. Skelton' owed 8 shillings 'de implementis & amerciamentis,' and Walker tells us that William owed the college 80 (*sic*) shillings for farming implements in 1493-4.

12. See Venn and Venn; *DNB; CPR Hen. VII, passim*. The date of his death (1499) and of his degrees renders unlikely Nelson's suggestion that he was a fellow student of Skelton's.

13. For Suckling and Fisher see A. H. Lloyd, *Early Hist. of Christ's Coll. Camb.*, CUP 1934; cf. also *DNB* and Venn and Venn.

14. Nelson, p. 71, first suggested the acquaintance between Fisher and Skelton, to which I now subscribe despite my earlier hazard (*PMLA* LIII, 605) that Skelton attacked Fisher in *Speak, Parrot*.

15. Lloyd, *op. cit.*, pp. 391-2.

16. Culley and Furnivall, *Caxton's Eneydos*, EETS, E. S. 57 (1890), pp. 3-4.

17. For the conflicting views see, e.g., Warton, *Hist. Eng. Poetry*, ed. 1870, pp. 401ff.; Mullinger, *op. cit.*, p. 540; H. C. Maxwell-Lyte, *Hist. Univ. of Oxford to 1530*, 1886, pp. 235-7; C. E. Mallet, *Hist. Univ. of Oxford*, 1924, I. 182; Strickland Gibson, *Statuta antiq. Vniu. Oxon.*, OUP 1931, p. lxxxv, n. 8; E. K. Broadus, *The Laureateship*, OUP 1921; Burckhardt, *Renaissance in Italy*, 1944, pp. 123-4; Nelson, pp. 40-7.

18. *Garland* 324, 397.

19. Gibson, *op. cit.*, p. lxxxviii; Boase, *Reg. Univ. Ox.*, I. 298.

20. See Boase, Warton, *loc. cit.*

21. Gibson, p. lxxxv. I do not understand why Nelson (p. 44) denies that the rod and birch were presented at Cambridge: the ceremony was identical at both universities (G. G. Coulton, *Social Life in Britain*, p. 55).

22. It explains, e.g., the curious case of Maurice Birchenshaw, student of *rhetoric* in 1511 (Boase, I. 298). On 8 December he supplicates that 'his 14 years' study in *grammar and rhetoric* may suffice for his admission to inform and teach in the same faculty. This is granted on condition that he compose 100 verses on the nobility of the university.' The 6 February following, now terming himself bachelor of

grammar, he further supplicates for a dispensation to read any book on the art of poetry except Ovid's *Art of Love* and Pamphilus. Now these two books were specifically banned to all masters of *grammar* (*Mun. Acad. Ox.,* RS, p. 441). Surely, then, what we have here is a comparative beginner in the rhetorical course who is granted his grammar degree only, as yet. There is no question of his being qualified for the laurel – though the circumstances suggest that he will not remain satisfied with his grammar degree. Actually, we know that he didn't: see Foster, *Alumni Oxon., sub nom.;* A. F. Pollard, *Wolsey,* p. 308.

23. Ed. Mead, EETS, 173 (1928), l. 658. For the superiority of rhetoric to grammar see Rashdall, I. 242. In Guarino's school at Ferrara rhetoric followed grammar as 'the last and most advanced course' (Weiss, *Humanism in England,* p. 85).

24. *Garland* 1184-5. For a comedy as an academic test see Boase, *loc cit.* (Richard Smyth).

25. *Against Garnish* IV. 80-4.

26. *Calliope; Against Garnish* IV. 137ff.

27. See Nelson, pp. 161-5, and below, Chap. XI, § 4.

28. For the king's whereabouts in 1488 see Gladys Temperley, *Henry VII,* pp. 412-13; for his presenting of degrees at Cambridge, Nelson, p. 14.

CHAPTER TWO

1. For the reign of Henry VII I have drawn on W. Busch, *Eng. under the Tudors,* Vol. I, 1895; J. Gairdner, *Henry VII,* ed. 1913; Gladys Temperley, *Henry VII,* 1917; F. A. Mumby, *Youth of Henry VIII,* 1913; K. Pickthorn, *Henry VII,* CUP 1934; Hall's *Chronicle,* ed. 1809; the *Great Chronicle of London;* Bacon; and other authorities, quoted as they occur.

2. Polydore Vergil, qu. Thornley, *England under the Yorkists,* p. 134.

3. Qu. Thornley, *op. cit.,* p. 117. A good account of Henry's orators will be found in Nelson, Chap. I. Cf. also *DNB* and the records of the period.

4. Blythe is described as King's Chaplain in 1488 (*CPR Hen. VII,* I. 237).

5. For André see Rymer, *Foedera,* XII. 317; Gairdner, *Memorials . . . of Henry VII,* RS, p. ix.

6. For the details of this outbreak see Hall, p. 443; Bacon, pp. 502-4; G. Brenan, *Hist. of House of Percy,* ed. Lindsay, 1902, I. 129-32.

7. Northumberland Elegy 8, 14, 127-8, 144, 142.

8. *Ibid.* 69-77; cf. 90-6.

9. *Why Came Ye Not* 286-7.

NOTES

10. See my 'Robert Gaguin and the English Poets,' *MLR* XXXII (1937), pp. 430-4 (with a trans. of André and a text of Gaguin, Carmeliano and Gigli); cf. also Nelson, pp. 25-6.

11. See App. I(A.3).

12. This was first pointed out by Nelson, p. 63 n, citing H. de Jongh, *L'ancienne faculté de théologie de Louvain*, Louvain 1911, pp. 73-4. A course in rhetoric at Louvain had existed since at least 1448 (N. Vernulaeus, *Academia Lovaniensis*, Louvain 1667, p. 64), and in 1476 was extended to days when no other lectures were on, so that all students might attend (J. Molanus, *Hist. Lovaniensium*, ed. de Ram, Brussels 1861, II. 942). Francesco de Crema drew his first salary on 1 December 1492 (de Jongh, *loc. cit.*).

13. H. de Voecht, 'Excerpts from the register of Louvain Univ., 1485-1527,' *EHR* XXXVII (1922), p. 91. This list, however, is incomplete.

14. Allen, *Opus epist. Erasmi*, I. 204.

15. See App. I(A.1).

16. *The Rose Both White and Red*, fols. 67-9ᵛ of Treas. of Receipt Misc. Bk. E. 36/228, which contains (i) a 1518 list of jousting equipment for the king and his supporters, (ii) 'A booke of the Kinges Revell stuff being in the charge of Iohn ffarlyon̄ lately deceased. whiche is now commytted vnto one Brigges. . . .'

17. For the Chapel Royal see C. W. Wallace, *Evolution of Eng. Drama up to Shakespeare*, Berlin 1912, pp. 12-13, 28-9.

18. Cornish's connexion with Westminster was first noted by Nelson, p. 121.

19. Jervis Wegg, *Richard Pace*, 1932, p. 129.

20. For Pen see the forthcoming EETS ed. of Skelton's *Diodorus* by Edwards and Salter.

21. Full details of this dispute are given by A. H. Lloyd, *Early Hist. of Christ's Coll., Camb.*, pp. 230ff.

22. See App. I(A.2).

23. For contemporary Fleet Street see Kingsford, *Prejudice and Promise*, p. 133 and map; Stow, *Survey of London*, EL, p. 349. The watertower was built in 1478.

24 For Westminster see F. O. Mann, *Deloney's Works*, OUP 1912, p. 536. For Jane Shore, *DNB* and Percy, *Reliques*, EL II. 88-91.

25. Refs. to Long Meg are collected by Mann, *op. cit.*, pp. 531ff. See also Dyce, I. lxxxi-v.

26. *Garland* 1241-7.

27. Villon, *Testament* 1783; P. Champion, *Rondeaux, balades et autres pièces joyeuses du XVᵉ siècle*, p. 18.

28. MS. Royal, App. 58, fol. 6ᵛ.

29. H. A. Harben, *Dictionary of London*, 1918, s.v.

30. MS. Trin. Coll. Camb. R 3. 17, fly-leaf 1. The handwriting of the poem, which is evidently a rough draft, is totally unlike Skelton's. Cf. L. J. Lloyd, 'A Note on Skelton,' *RES* 1929, pp. 302-6 (who, however, wrongly gives 'in extasie' for the last line).

31. For Reed see J. Foster, *Alumni Oxon.*, *sub nom.*; for Arthur's education see André in *Memorials . . . of Henry VII*, p. 413, and Nelson, pp. 15, 75.

32. F. M. Salter, 'Skelton's *Speculum principis*,' *Spec.* IX (1934). But cf. Nelson, *loc. cit.*

33. See *LP Rich. III-Hen. VII*, RS, I. p. 389.

34. Lord Herbert of Cherbury, *Hist. of Eng. under Henry VIII*, ed. 1870, p. 109. Herbert's authority is Paolo Sarpi; see his *Istoria del Concilio Tridentino* (*Opere*, Bari, III (1935), p. 26): '. . . Enrico VIII re d'Inghilterra, il qual non essendo nato primo primogenito regio, era stato destinato dal padre per arcivescovo di Cantorberi, e però nella puerizia fatto attendere alle lettere.'

35. See respectively *CSP Span.* I., pp. 163, 178; J. E. B. Mayor, *Eng. Works of Fisher*, EETS, E. S. 27 (1876), pp. 301, 292; C. H. Cooper, *Memoir of Margaret, Countess of Richmond and Derby*, CUP 1874, p. 52; D. and S. Lysons, *Magna Britannia*, 1813, I (i), p. 59. (The relevant lines of the epitaph are: 'Principibus puerum primis eduxit ab annis/ Richmundae Comitissa. . . .')

36. Cooper, *op. cit.*, p. 67.

37. See respectively Hardyng's *Chronicle*, ed. Ellis, 1812, p. i, n. (l. 2 reads: 'to scole at . . .'); J. E. Neale, *Queen Elizabeth*, 1945, p. 23; P. L. Carver, *Palsgrave's Acolastus*, EETS 202 (1937), pp. xxiii-vi; *Against Garnish* IV. 95.

38. Henry Parker, Lord Morley, in H. G. Wright, *46 Tales from Boccaccio*, EETS 214 (1943), pp. xi-xii; cf. Fisher, ed. Mayor, p. 308.

39. So *DNB*; Cooper makes it *c.* 1502 (p. 75).

40. Lord Morley (Wright, *loc cit.*).

41. See App. I(B).

42 Cf. Medwall (A. W. Reed, *Early Tudor Drama*, p. 102); and Colet (Seebohm, *Oxford Reformers*, EL, p. 327).

43. *Garland* 1182, 1175, 1176, 1173, 1177, 1174, 1172, 1191, 1174 gloss, 1180.

44. MS. Royal 19 C. VIII.

45. *Garland* 1181; F. Brie, 'Zwei verlorene Dichtungen von J. Skelton,' *Archiv f. . . . Neü. Sprach.* 1919, pp. 226-8; Ovid, *Ars amat.*, 1. 5-8.

46. Despatch qu. Mumby, *Youth of Henry VIII*, p. 50. It is obvious that Eltham was the prince's home: nearly all the refs. locate him there.

47. Hone was allotted two servants as schoolmaster to Princess Mary (J. G. Nichols, *Chronicle of Calais*, CS, 1846, p. 65); Palsgrave three, as schoolmaster – and councillor – to Henry Fitzroy (Carver, *op. cit.*, pp. xxiii-vi). The latter's salary was £13 6s. 8d.

48. For the Cornish rebellion see Bacon and the *Great Chronicle*.

49. *Great Chronicle*, p. 274.

50. *Garland* 1224-6, with gloss: 'Notat bellum Cornubiense, quod in campestribus et in patencioribus vastisque solitudinibus prope Grenewich gestum est.'

51. P.R.O. MS. E101/414/16: unpaginated account of John Heron, Treasurer of Exchequer. (In the following February the same reward is granted twice to 'my lorde prince [i.e. Arthur's] poete.')

52. *Great Chronicle*, p. 286.

53. E. Gordon Duff, *15th Cent. English Books*, OUP 1917, no. 372.

54. *Bouge of Court*, 34-5.

55. *Ibid.* 204-10, 231-8.

56. *Ibid.* 526-32.

57. *Ibid.* 537-9.

58. See App. I(C.2).

59. See *Palsgrave's Acolastus*, pp. xxiiiff.; W. S. Childe-Pemberton, *Elizabeth Blount and Henry VIII*, 1913, pp. 158ff.

CHAPTER THREE

1. Allen, *Opus epist. Erasmi*, I. 118. (F. M. Nichols' trans.).

2. See W. Nelson, 'Thomas More, Grammarian and Orator,' *PMLA* LVIII (1943), pp. 341-5.

3. Allen, I. 1 (p. 6), 104; cf. IV, p. xxi.

4. MS. Egerton 1651, fols. 6ᵛ, 10. (On the last page Erasmus began to rewrite the poem, but after three lines decided, with an 'ut habet*ur*,' to leave it as it was). See App. I(D).

5. Trans. by Preserved Smith, *Erasmus*, New York 1923, p. 62.

6. This is rightly emphasised by Nelson, pp. 72-3.

7. Allen, *loc. cit.* (Nichols' trans.).

8. For the attribution to Pico see Dyce, ed. Boston (Mass.) 1856, I. lxvii. The song was copied 'from an MS. . . . consisting of *Hymni*, &c., by Picus Mirandula.' The mistake was probably due to the fact that Pico's *Hymni heroici* were addressed to various *coelites* (saints), while Erasmus's MS. begins with poems to Michael, Gabriel and Raphael. For Skelton's references to Erasmus see *Speak, Parrot* 48-9, 158-9.

9. For Suffolk see especially Hall, *Chronicle*, p. 495, and *DNB*. A good

account is given in Chap. VIII of Charles Williams, *Henry VII*, 1937.

10. Mumby, *Youth of Henry VIII*, p.9.

11. Temperley, *Henry VII*, p. 210.

12. See App. I(A.2); and on the negotiations, A. H. Lloyd, *op. cit.*

13. I take it that the 2*d.* paid for fire and drink would not cover more than a gallon of the best ale (1¼*d.* in 1519, according to Whittinton's *Vulgaria*, EETS, p. 57) or a pint of sweet wine (at 8*d.* a gallon, *ibid.*). And the latter would not go far among three. For the Countess's relations with Cambridge town see C. H. Cooper, *Memoir*, pp. 46-7, 80.

14. For this false alarm see *CSP Span.* I, pp. 254-5. For Henry's treasurer and fool see P.R.O. MS. E101/415/3, 23 December 17 Hen. VII, and Nicolas, *Privy Purse Expenses of Elizabeth of York*, p. 2.

15. See App. I(E.1). This item was first noted by Nelson, *op. cit.*, pp. 77-8, 242. I agree with both his identifications and his emendation.

16. P.R.O. MS. E101/415/3, end of vol.: 'memorandum that sir peter Greves is bounded in an obligacion in xl li. to geve his attendaunce from hensforth in doyng his office as clerk of the kinges closet as he hertofore hath don.' (But in any case £40 or £100 seem to have been the regular penalties demanded by the Court of Requests at this period: see P.R.O. Ct. of Req. Misc. Bk. II, *passim*). For Churchyard's lines see Dyce, I. lxxviii.

17. *Great Chronicle*, p. 296.

18. Skelton's holograph: MS. Addit. 26787. First printed by F. M. Salter, 'Skelton's *Speculum Principis*,' *Spec.* IX (1934), pp. 25-37.

19. On this curious phenomenon see K. Polheim, *Die lateinische Reimprosa*, Berlin 1925; C. S. Baldwin, *Medieval Rhetoric and Poetic*, New York 1928, pp. 252-4.

20. MS. Addit. 26787, fols. 10-10ᵛ. (This stanzaic form does not occur elsewhere.)

21. See Allen, *loc. cit.* above, note 3. For the tag see *Adagia* 2. 3. 53, where it is traced learnedly to Homer. For the Latin of succeeding quotations see App. IV.

22. MS. *cit.*, fol. 20.

23. Mumby, *Youth of Henry VIII*, p. 13.

24. Leland, *Collectanea*, 1770, IV. 258.

25. *Ibid.* V. 377.

26. See App. I(C.3).

27. P.R.O. MS. E101/415/3 (week ending 25 June '17 Hen. VII); Nicolas, *Privy Purse Exp. of Eliz.*, p. 28. This important point was first observed by Nelson, *op. cit.*, p. 75. He also remarks that Arthur's tutor is described in the latter as a 'Scottishman,' which implies that the Prince of Wales had once more changed his teacher.

NOTES

pp. 77–80

28. For Hone or Hoon(e) see *Grace Book B of Univ. of Camb.*, *Pt. I*, pp. 121-2, 222; *Grace Book Gamma*, p. 37; *LP* I. 2656.

29. G. Mattingly, *Catherine of Aragon*, ed. 1944, p. 153, quoting Fuensalida.

30. For Mountjoy see the dedic. to Erasmus's ed. of Livy (1554), I. sig. a4, where he says Mountjoy was made companion of Henry's studies while the Prince was still *adolescens*. As Erasmus was well aware, this term included the years between 15 and 30 (Varro) or 14 and 28 (Isidore of Seville): which makes rather unlikely the frequent assertion that Mountjoy superintended Henry's studies from 1499, when the boy was only eight. In 1529 Mountjoy gave his age as '52 or thereabout' (*LP* IV. 5774).

31. For Greves see *Materials for . . . Henry VII*, I. 25, 99; II. 359; *LP. Rich. III-Hen. VII*, II. 89; *CPR Hen VII*, I. 24, 255, 303; II. 136, 266; *LP* I(i). 37 (p. 14); II(ii). 3725; Blomefield, *Norfolk*, ed. 1805, I. 16-17; MS. Addit. 7099, fols. 84, etc. (The royal account-books contain frequent references.) For his slackness see above, note 16. For the Countess's renting of Diss see *LP* I(ii). 3313(6): the sum there owing from her for Diss and Hempnall in September 1508 (£100) was the same as the annual rent exacted from Lord Fitzwalter when these manors were restored to him in July 1509 (*LP* I(i). g.132(90)). As to the value of Greves' benefices, the *Valor ecclesiasticus* of Henry VIII (ed. 1810) gives £30 11s. 8d. for Buckby, £13 6s. 8d. for St. Michael's, York, and £14 13s. 1d. for Baroughdon. (In 1490 Greves exchanged the last for the free chapel of Thursby, Yorks, which I have failed to trace in the *Valor*. But I imagine he did not lose by the exchange.)

32. See App. I(E.2).

33. For William Guy (Prior, 1484-1505) see E. A. Webb, *Records of St. Bartholomew's, Smithfield*, OUP 1921, I. 220-2; *VCH London*, 1909, I. 480; *CPR Hen VII*, II. 428, 441. For Bray see *DNB*. (Nelson, followed by Gordon, makes the curious error of calling him second *husband* of the Lady Margaret.) For ladies in charge of prisoners see A. Abram, *Social England in the 15th Century*, p. 143. For the reading *janitoris* see Dyce, I. xxvi: the P.R.O. authorities, to whom I put my own interpretation, pointed out that 'it seems rather an informal way of alluding to' the Countess. But there was no courtesy wasted in these early minutes: cf. the bald reference to Sir Reginald Bray, and the 'kinges moder poete' of the account-book (see above, Chap. II, note 51). For the Chapel Royal party see Nicolas, *Privy Purse Exp. of Eliz.*, p. 23. For the Skelton reference see his Latin elegy on the Countess, l. 14: 'Dormit Micenas. . . .'

34. *Great Chronicle*, pp. 344-7. The attribution to Cornish was made by Stow. Nelson's suggestion (*op. cit.*, p. 121n.) that Stow had in mind the *Treatise between Truth and Enformation* must also be rejected, for that poem was avowedly composed 'in the Fleet' (MS. Royal 18 D. ii).

35. See App. I(F.1(a)).

36. *Cuncta licet cecidisse.*

CHAPTER FOUR

1. Not Langham, Essex, as Dyce thought (II. 369-70). For Thomas Spring see Barbara McClenaghan, *The Springs of Lavenham*, Ipswich 1924. He probably got to know Skelton when visiting his property near Diss.

2. G. Baskerville, *English Monks and the Suppression, passim.*

3. For Diss see Blomefield, *Norfolk*, ed. 1805, I. 16ff. I have also to thank Mr. Coningsby Gayford of Mere Manor and Mr. Cushing of Diss for much courteous information.

4. Ecton, *Valor ecclesiasticus temp. Hen. VIII*, 1810-, III. 300.

5. *Festial*, EETS, E. S. 96 (1905), p. 5.

6. See App. I(F.1(*a*)).

7. Cooper, *Memoir of the Lady Margaret*, pp. 97, 250.

8. See App. I(A.1).

9. P.R.O. MS. E36/214, fol. 57. For Fisher's oration see Mullinger, qu. above, p. 40. Gairdner, who originally attributed it to Blythe and is followed by Nelson, p. 70, silently corrected himself in his *Henry VII*, p. 4. (I have to thank Professor A. F. Pollard for this fact.)

10. For the Vicar see *Grace Book B of the Univ. of Camb.*, Pt. I, *passim*. He was employed by the university from 1488 to 1505-6, but his identity remains obscure. Professor Moule's list of vicars (I was informed by the Rev. A. B. Wright, Vicar in 1935) has no name between John Paxton (1454) and Robert Glanfield (1520).

11. Nelson, pp. 82-101.

12. *Replication*, verse, 1-8.

13. *Trental* 38-49.

14. *Skelton's Magnyfycence*, EETS, pp. lx-lxii.

15. *Garland* 1452-7.

16. *Ship of Fools*, ed. 1874, II. 331.

17. *Magnificence* 408.

18. Nelson (p. 105n.) first offered this explanation of the 'pretty gin' by which Skelton entered the locked church.

19. *Ware the Hawk!* 51-7.

20. *Ibid.* 145-8.

21. *Ibid.* 329-32.

22. Blomefield, I. 467. (Nelson, p. 104 n., suggested that the man might be a Smith, but apparently took the word *curate* to bear its modern meaning, since he proposed a John Smyth of Diss as the culprit.)

23. See App. I(F.1(*b*)).

24. In my identification of Skelton's Clarke with the will-writer (*TLS* 22 May 1937) I wrongly suggested that he was Sir John the soul priest; to be followed by Gordon, p. 120. But Nelson had already corrected this (p. 103n.), though he takes Sir John for a son of Skelton's victim.

25. H. Deimling, *Chester Plays*, EETS E.S. 62 (1892), p. 137, where it is quoted as a shepherd's delicacy.

26. *Materials for . . . Hen. VII*, I. 536.

27. *LP* I. 438(3 m. 24).

28. See respectively J. Hooper, 'Skelton Laureate,' *Gent. Mag.* 1897, pp. 297ff.; W. W. Capes, *Hist. of Eng. Church in 14th and 15th Cent.*, pp. 259-60.

29. See respectively F. Makower, *Constit. Hist. of Church of Eng.*, p. 402, n. 29; G. Baskerville, 'Elections to Convocation . . . under Bishop Hooper,' *EHR* XLIV, p. 6. (I have to thank Mrs. Paul Gotch for this last item.)

30. *Jests of Scogin* in W. C. Hazlitt, *Shakespeare's Jestbooks*, II. 78-80.

31. G. Baskerville, *English Monks*, pp. 261-6.

32. Bale, *Index Britanniae scriptorum*, OUP 1902, p. 68.

33. See App. II(1).

34. Qu. Baskerville, *op. cit.*, p. 138.

35. *Hundred Merry Tales*, ed. W. C. Hazlitt, 1887, no. xli; cf. the slightly earlier but mutilated text pr. Dyce, I. lxxiv-lxxv.

36. Hazlitt, *Shakespeare's Jestbooks*, II. 130-1. In this version the gift of birds (woodcocks this time) also appears, but nothing is made of it: the whole point of the tale concerns the tumble into the moat. In the *Merry Tales* the birds have become capons: see Dyce, I. lx-xi.

37. *LP* IV(iii). 6139.

38. On Nick see *DNB*. For his use of Hoxne see Norwich Institution Bk. XIV, *passim*. Nick's verdict on Skelton was probably much like the one he passed on the Rector of Badingham, *dominus* William Clerke, in 1511. On 12 November Johanna Bret of Stradebroke, widow, was ordered not to annoy the Rector; on 21st Clerke appeared in person and humbly submitted himself. The Bishop enjoined him not to consort with Johanna, and not to annoy, nor implead, nor cause to be impleaded any of the parish of Stradebroke. (His parishioners seem to have reacted very much like Skelton's!) By way of penalty he was to . give 20s. (£30 to-day) for the improvement of the Cathedral Church

of the Holy Trinity, Norwich. (*Ibid.*: abstract by the Rev. E. D. Stone in the Dioc. Registry, Norwich. Original not available).

39. See Dyce, I. lxi-ii.

40. See App. II(2).

41. On Skelton's apocryphal poem to his wife see F. Brie, *Skelton-studien*, pp. 21-5; L. J. Lloyd, *RES* 1929, pp. 302-6. I may add that another text of the poem, but without title, is set to music in MS. Royal, App.58, fol. 19ᵛ, ending: 'Quod doc*ter* Coper.'

42. *Colin Clout* 572-80.

43. See App. I(F.2(*a*)). First recorded by Nelson, pp. 113-14, 243.

44. See App. I(F.2(*b*)). I have to thank the Secretary of the Diocesan Registry, Norwich, for drawing my attention to this item. Cf. also Nelson, pp. 114-15.

CHAPTER FIVE

1. See App. I(G). Sir N. H. Nicolas, *Scrope and Grosvenor Controversy*, 1832, II. 60-1, describes the husband as Sir Richard Scrope, Knight, as also does Banks, *Dormant and Extinct Peerages*, 1883, s.v. *Scrope*. But cf. *Testamenta Eboracensia*, III. 297-9; G. P. Scrope, *Hist. of Castle Combe, Wilts.*, 1852, pp. 287-8; Stow, *Survey*, p. 305 – all of which refer to him as Richard Scrope, Esq. Stephen I assume to be the posthumous child mentioned in Richard's will, though, of course, he may have died earlier.

2. On the Wyndhams see *Paston Letters, passim*; Blomefield, *Norfolk*, VIII. 112-13.

3. See below, p. 2, and *Paston Letters*, II. 77.

4. Will of Sir Thomas Wyndham: see App. I(G.4). This double marriage misled the genealogist as early as 1563 (see *Visit. of Yorks 1563-4*, Harl. Soc. Pub. 16, 1881, pp. 279-80, where Eleanor's daughter is made wife of Sir *John* Wyndham).

5. His identity is oddly obscure. Dugdale, Burke and Gairdner call him vaguely Richard, Lord Scrope; Cokayne (*Compl. Peerage*, VII (1896), p. 307) makes him Sir Richard le Scrope, i.e. father of our Jane, and so does the *Visitation* cited in last note. But although in her own will, proved 15 May 1515 (Nicolas, *Testamenta Vetusta*, p. 530), Margaret leaves a jewelled St. Michael to 'the countess of Oxford, *my sister*,' there is no mention of her among all the detailed bequests of the Countess's mother, Eleanor Wyndham, senior, in 1505 (see below). Their exact relationship, though obviously a close one, I have failed to trace.

6. H. Ellis, *Three Bks. of Polydore Vergil's Hist.*, CS 1844, p. 188.

NOTES

7. *Great Chronicle*, pp. 318-19 – the only detailed account.

8. For the Austin Friars and Sir John see Stow, *Survey*, pp. 160-1 (where *Windam* is is misread *Windany*). For Richard's burial see his will (App. I(G.1)) and Stow, p. 305.

9. Nicolas, *Privy Purse Exp. of Eliz.*, p. 5 (4 April 1502).

10. For the Abbess see *VCH London*, I. 518-19.

11. For Carrow see E. Power, *Medieval Eng. Nunneries*, 1922; W. Rye, *Carrow Abbey . . . near Norwich*, Norwich 1889; also E. Power, *Medieval People*, Chap. III; Baskerville, *Eng. Monks*, Chap. VIII.

12. *Philip Sparrow* 651, 634-48, 614-27.

13. A. Jessop, *Visit. of Dioc. of Norwich*, CS 1888, p. 209 (1526).

14. *Philip Sparrow* 179-82.

15. *Reynard the Fox*, Chap. XVI.

16. Ovid, *Amores* 2. 6; Martial 1. 109; Statius, *Silv.* 2. 4.

17. Skelton's use of breviary and missal is discussed at length by Gordon, pp. 122ff.

18. Jessopp, *op. cit.*, pp. 17, 145. Of the two other Margeries in 1492 neither survived to 1514.

19. *Philip Sparrow* 128-37.

20. *Ibid.* 754-66.

21. I strongly suspect the final *s* to be a misprint of Kele's gravely perpetuated by all his successors, including myself!

22. *Ibid.* 1135-40.

23. J. O. Halliwell, *The most pleasant song of the Lady Bessy*, Percy Repr., 1847, p. 66.

24. *Philip Sparrow* 1123-5.

25. *Ibid.* 1104 (Dyce 1114). I quote the A. V. numbering: Vulg. is Ps. cxviii.

26. *Ibid.* 890-1, 986-7, 1019-20. The quots. are (A.V.) Ps. cxix. 17; lxiii. 3; cxix. 33; xlii. 1; cxix. 49; cxix. 125 (Vulg.: cxviii. 17; lxii. 4; cxviii. 33; xli. 2; cxviii. 49; cxviii. 125).

27. For this tradition see C. S. Lewis, *Allegory of Love*, OUP 1936.

28. Based on the frequency of rhyme-runs over four, parallelism of opening word, and alliteration. These give the following order for the Skeltonic poems: *Philip Sparrow, Ware the Hawk!, Elinor Rumming, Colin Clout, Why Come Ye Not, Duke of Albany, Replication*. Other tests confirm this order for the last four; but for *Elinor Rumming* see next chapter.

29. See App. I(G.2).

30. *Genealogist*, N.S. XI. 59 – though Copinger, *Manors of Suffolk*, VI. 113-18, says 7 December, and Blomefield, *Norfolk*, X. 186, says 1514.

31. *Paston Letters*, V. no. 898.

32. W. C. Metcalfe, *Visit. of Suff. in 1561, 1577 and 1612*, p. 117. The Scropes were already related to the Brewses through Jane's aunt, Anne Lady Scrope of East Harling, Norfolk. In her will (1498) she left a girdle to Jane's mother – 'syster Wyndham' – and a ring, etc., to her niece, Katherine Brewse (*Scrope and Grosv. Controv.*, II. 76-7). Katherine was Jane's mother-in-law and was born a Wingfield: hence the connexion with Lady Scrope, whose second husband had been Sir Robert Wingfield.

33. See App. I(G.3). It may save some future researcher if I point out that the Katherine Brewse of Kessingland whose will is calendared in F. A. Crisp, *Cal. of Wills at Ipswich, 1444-1600*, Bk. IX, fol. 48, is actually Katherine *Brewster* and not Thomas's mother.

34. *LP* I(i). pp. 38, 41; II(i). 1083; VI. 589 (2). It should be mentioned that 'mistres Brewis' does appear, together with her other sister, the Countess of Oxford, in another list of attendants on the Queen for the Field of Cloth of Gold (*Chronicles of Calais*, CS, p. 25). This must have been a preliminary draft, as neither is given in the *LP* version.

35. Nicolas, *Test. Vet.*, p. 674. Elizabeth had married William, Viscount Beaumont, on 24 April 1486. In the following year he lost his reason, and in 1495 was committed to the care of his old comrade-in-arms, the Earl of Oxford, at Wivenhoe (Essex). This was how, after his death in 1507, Elizabeth came to marry the Earl (Cokayne, *Compl. Peerage*, II. 63). As 'my olde lady of Oxford' she was in the habit of sending some of her cheeses to the King each November (Nicolas, *Privy Purse Exp. of Hen. VIII, 1530-2*, pp. 89, 173, 277).

CHAPTER SIX

1. J. P. Collier, *Household Bks. of John Duke of Norfolk and Thomas Earl of Surrey*, Roxb. Club 1844, pp. 466, 477, 481. The Skelton entries in the Reigate parish register (23 September 1561-21, February 1577/8) were kindly brought to my notice by W. Hooper, Esq., of Redhill. *VCH Surrey*, III. 294, notes that a John Skelton was assessed among the *lay* subsidies at Kingston in 1524-5.

2. First recorded by J. H. Harvey (*TLS* 26 October 1946) from Court Rolls of Pachenesham Manor, S. C. 6/15, County Hall, Kingston-upon-Thames.

3. *Elinor Rumming* 195-203.

4. MacCracken, *Minor Poems of Lydgate*, EETS 1934, II. 675.

5. *Chester Play of the Deluge* (J. Q. Adams, *Chief Pre-Shak. Dramas*), 229-32; Greene, *Early Eng. Carols*, 419 Aa, Ab, B.

6. Marcel Schwob, *Le Parnasse satyrique du quinzième siècle*, Paris 1905, no. LXVIII; cf. nos. VIII, LVII, LXII, etc.

NOTES

pp. 118–32

7. *Elinor Rumming* 34-47.
8. *Ibid.* 64-9.
9. *Ibid.* 80-4.
10. *Ibid.* 436-58.
11. *Early Tudor Poetry*, 1920, p. 217.
12. R. Hughes, *Poems of John Skelton*, 1924, p. xiv.
13. For Brie see note 28 to last chapter. My own attempts to check his figures make the resemblance between *Elinor Rumming* and *Colin Clout* even closer. For date of latter poem see Chap. XII, § 4.
14. *Garland* 1258-9, 1276-8.
15. *Ibid.* 412-13 (cf. 426-7, 440-1), 784-6, 1234-5.

CHAPTER SEVEN

1. Allen, *Opus epist. Erasmi*, I. 215 (Nichols' trans.).
2. *Rose both White and Red.* 36-9.
3. MS. Addit. 31922, fol. 28ᵛ (where last word is 'fend').
4. Hall, *Henry VIII*, ed. Whibley, I. 15, 13.
5. MS. Addit. 31922, fol. 71ᵛ.
6. *LP* I(i). 112.
7. See App. I(H).
8. When Skelton began to use his new title of *orator regius*: see below.
9. MS. Addit. 26787. Of the poems, although Salter doubts whether the first was written in 1494, this seems the only natural interpretation of the phrase: 'in sua puericia, quando erat insignitus Dux Eboraci.' That the other was a birthday gift I infer from: 'illi hanc ego phillida mitto,' which must be an echo of Vergil, *Ecl.* 3. 76: 'Phillida mitte mihi: meus est natalis, Iolla'. It is possible, indeed, that the whole MS. was given to Henry for his birthday.
10. Nelson, p. 117.
11. Polydóre Vergil, *Prouerbiorum libellus*, Venice 1498, sig. dᵛ-d ii(s.v. 'Sedere ad Eurotam'). The phrase does not seem to be in Erasmus's more famous *Adagia*.
12. See App. I(I.1).
13. The *Chronique de Rains* MS. is dated, by Skelton's private system, between November 1511 and 1512. As it is not signed *orator regius*, it must have been presented before May 1512: see my article in *PMLA* 1938, p. 601.
14. The patent is now missing but was seen by du Resnel, who says it was dated in the 5th year of Henry's reign (Dyce, I.xv). This commenced on 21 April 1512. The *terminus ante quem* is Skelton's use of *orator regius* after May: see my article cited above, pp. 601-3.
15. *Calliope* 15-20 (my italics).

272

16. Nelson, p. 123. Nelson, however, contends that Skelton used the term *orator* in the sense of 'diplomat,' and that he acted as royal secretary. His arguments are unconvincing: see text.

17. For the reign of Henry VIII I have drawn upon Hall; Lord Herbert of Cherbury, *England under Henry VIII*, ed. 1870; J. S. Brewer, *Reign of Henry VIII, 1509-30*, 1884; A. F. Pollard, *Henry VIII and Wolsey*; Mumby, *Youth of Henry VIII*; and G. Mattingly, *Catherine of Aragon*, ed. 1944.

18. *Against the Scots* 120; *First English Life of Henry V*, ed. Kingsford, OUP 1911 – who dates it 1513-14 (p. x).

19. Hall, ed. Whibley, I. 46, 51.

20. *CSP Ven.* II. 166.

21. W. Camden, *Reges, Reginae, Nobiles & alij in Ecclesia . . . West-monasterij sepulti*, 1600, who prefaces the texts with 'In tabula pensili' and 'In altera tabula pensili.'

22. Hall, I. 96.

23. *Ibid.* I. 72.

24. For quots. see *ibid.* I. 64-93.

25. *Ibid.* I. 113.

26. Carlo Sforza, *Living Thoughts of Machiavelli*, 1942, pp. 96-7.

27. R. B. Merriman, *Life and Letters of Thomas Cromwell*, OUP 1902, I. 39.

28. Nelson, pp. 124-33.

29. *Chorus . . . contra Gallos* 4.

30. *Induction* 392ff.; *1 Hen. VI*, 4. 2. 12-13.

31. Latimer's *Sermons*, EL, p. 179.

32. Mumby, pp. 203, 206-7 (cf. *LP* I(ii). 2162, 2200).

33. *Ibid.*, pp. 207-8 (cf. *LP* I(ii). 2226).

34. *CSP Ven.* II. nos. 331, 337 (qu. Nelson, p. 127).

35. The parallels are given at length in Nelson, pp. 129-33.

36. *Ballad* 37-40.

37. Not Pynson, as Nelson says (p. 127 n.).

38. Dyce, I. 190. The 'Regius' of the earlier prints, Lant and Kynge and Marche, I take to be an untimely correction.

39. Hall, I. 64; cf. *LP* I(ii). 2065.

40. *Survey*, EL, p. 267.

41. Herbert, p. 229.

42. Hall, I. 112-13.

43. *LP* I(ii). 4582. This is pointed out by Gordon, p. 172; who, however, does not appear to realise that it by no means ended the affair.

44. Hall, I. 118.

45. See App. I(F.3): first noted by Nelson, p. 118.

CHAPTER EIGHT

1. For the Garnish family see J. J. Muskett, *Suffolk Manorial Families*, Exeter 1894-1911, II. 265; W. P. Copinger, *Manors of Suffolk*, 1905-11, VII. 159-61 (for Roos Hall, with illus. 159); *DNB*, s.v. 'Garneys'; *LP passim*; and a useful summary in Helen Stearns, 'John Skelton and Christopher Garnesche,' *MLN* XLIII (1928), pp. 518-23.

2. *Against Garnish* III. 24ff.; *CPR Hen. VII*, II. 238-9, 351. As his sister and heiress she then inherited the property of Sir Gilbert Debenham.

3. *Paston Letters*, V. 901.

4. *LP* I(i). g. 257(24); g. 709(59). For the widow's identity see *ibid.* I (Addenda), I(i). 562(2); 746. Garnish was already married to her in Sept. 1514 (*ibid.* I(ii). g. 3324(32)). For Risley see Hall or Bacon, *passim.*

5. For Gibson's accounts see *LP* I(ii). 2349. For his connexion with the revels see Wallace, *Evol. of Eng. Drama*, p. 30.

6. Mumby, pp. 263ff.

7. Hall, I. 123-4.

8. Dyce, I. xxxi-ii. But cf. Leland, *Collectanea*, ed. Hearne, 1770, II. 704.

9. *LP* I(ii). 3348.

10. Hall, I. 124.

11. Brewer, I. 40-1; Mumby, pp. 291-3.

12. *LP* I(ii). p. 1539.

13. Brie, *Skelton-studien*, pp. 59-64, gives an impressive list of parallels.

14. See W. M. Mackenzie, *Poems of William Dunbar*, 1932, App. C.

15. *Flyting* 409.

16. Helen Stearns, *loc cit.*, n. 1.

17. III. 133-4.

18. Pollard, *Henry VIII*, p. 65.

19. Mumby, pp. 266-7.

20. III. 71-2.

21. I. 16; cf. Heywood, *Four PP* 46. Nothing is known about the shrine, to judge from a correspondence in *TLS*, 9, 16, 30 Aug. 1934. Since then, however, I have identified the 'catacumbas of Cayre' not with anything in Cairo, as Dyce thought, but with the famous mausoleum of Caria. It is Skelton's version of 'Caricum sepulchrum,' which he found in Erasmus's *Adagia* (4. 3. 3.) as a type of 'something sumptuous and magnificent.' But I have traced no direct connexion between Garnish and Cattawade.

22. The identification was first proposed by Gordon in *TLS*, 15 November 1934; but he appears to have been sufficiently convinced

by Nelson's criticism not to mention it in his book. Nelson (pp. 144-5) believes that the scribe was an unknown courtier also attacked by Barclay in his *Eclogues* under the name of Godfrey Gourmand (I. 838-48). But it seems more in accordance with Barclay's poetic habits to assume that he was merely making use of a traditional (or inventing a new) alliterative type-name. For Godfrey's waist see *Pastime* 3502.

23. Cf. e.g., the charge of syphilis in II. 8-9.

24. *Paston Letters*, IV. 532.

25. IV. 2.

26. Brewer, I. 218-19.

27. Hall, I. 177-8.

28. Dyce, I. xxxiii.

29. Merriman, *Life and Letters of Thos. Cromwell*, II. 367 (no. 60).

30. III. 137-41.

31. His identification followed on my discovery of the date of his death in Marshe (*TLS*, 22 May 1937), though then I mistakenly assumed that he came from Diss.

32. W.A.M. 32,348, 32,389, and especially 32,364, where occur the refs. to the chapel and 'my lord Prynce*s* housbold' (dated 1489-93).

33. *LP* I. g. 132(97), g. 2222 (Herts), p. 1538; II. 1056, 3239; III. g. 405(18). Care is needed to avoid confusion with other William Bedells, e.g. those in *LP* I. g. 357(41) and III. 3695; *ibid.* III. p. 1362; *Materials for . . . Hen. VII*, I. 445. For Rokeby see *DNB*, s. v. 'William Rokeby.' For the act of Apparel see Pollard, *Wolsey*, p. 52n.

34. H. Anstey, *Epist. acad. Oxon.*, OUP 1898, II. 653-4 (my trans.; first noted by Nelson, p. 119). For the Roys mentioned in the letter see Anstey, II. 635-6; *LP* II. 1075. Roys' own will (pr. 1 June 1527, PCC: 20 Porch) reads, of course, as innocently as Bedell's; and he seems to have had no difficulty in persuading a don – John Morris, Doctor of Degrees – to act as executor.

35. For these and the other refs. see App. I(I.3).

36. See *Castle of Perseverance* (Adams, *Chief Pre-Shak.* Dramas), ll. 196-9.

CHAPTER NINE

1. A. F. Pollard's excellent *Wolsey*, 1929, serves to correct the eulogies of Brewer and Bishop Creighton (*Cardinal Wolsey*, 1898). See also Cavendish's *Life*, ed. Singer, 1827, and Pollard's sketch in *Encyc. Brit.*

2. Brewer's denial (I. 61) that Polydore Vergil has this story is strange in view of the latter's description of the father as 'probum *at lanium*' (*Historia*, Basle 1555, p. 633).

3. Herbert (p. 461) was first to notice that Wolsey was 'at what price

soever' a supporter of Rome; and his judgment has since been amply documented by Pollard.

4. Pollard, *Henry VIII*, p. 70.

5. Elis Gruffydd's Chronicle, MS. Mostyn (Nat. Lib. Wales) 158, fol. 410 (I owe both ref. and trans. to the kindness of Professor Bryn Davies). Possibly, however, this incident is merely a garbled version of the stripping of the King's party staged by Henry himself in 1511 (see *Great Chronicle of London*, 1938, p. 374). Gruffydd's name for it, *y lladrad malpai* (The Sham Thieving) would fit either.

6. G. Mattingly, *Catherine of Aragon*, p. 123.

7. Polydore Vergil, *Historia*, p. 632.

8. Pollard, *Wolsey*, pp. 23 n., 55.

9. *Ibid.*, pp. 56-7, with refs.: to which add Brewer, I. 271-2. Quots. are from Cavendish, pp. 91-2.

10. *LP* II(i). 1222.

11. *Skelton's Magnyfycence*, EETS, p. cxviii.

12. Ll. 22-3. (Dyce's numbering is ruined by his inclusion, following Marshe, of the Latin glosses in the text.)

13. Ll. 16-19.

14. Ll. 35-41.

15. Cavendish, pp. 149-50. (Cf. Hall, II. 99, on Wolsey's reception at Montreuil: 'and al the Canapies were set with *TC* for Thomas Cardinal, and so were all his servauntes cotes.') Unfortunately, the very detailed account of the 1515 ceremony which Fiddes reproduced from the heralds' office (*Life of Wolsey*, 2nd ed., 1726, p. 201) gives no description of liveries.

16. Pollard, *Wolsey*, p. 327.

17. Cavendish, p. 96.

18. Elyot, *Governor*, EL, p. 130.

19. A second difficulty is one of dating. The poem's title begins: 'Skelton Laureate, *oratoris regis tertius*, against venemous tongues. ...' Dyce's *versus* for *tertius* hardly fits in with the English. Another possibility is *orator regis tertius* – 'third orator royal'; the other two being perhaps André and Gigli? But it seems highly unlike Skelton to proclaim himself third in anything. On the whole, the most reasonable emendation seems to be *tertio* (*sc. anno*): which would make the poem written 'in the 3rd year of the Orator Royal' – on the analogy of Anno Domini.

But Skelton became orator about May 1512. The third year of his oratorship, then, ended in May 1515 – some months before Wolsey became Cardinal. On the other hand, Skelton already had a private calendar, dating from his entry into the Tudor service. This began between 30 October and 17 November. If he fitted his new title into the old chronology, this would bring us down to as late as 17 November 1515. Which just fits our case.

CHAPTER TEN

1. For a short summary see F. S. Boas, *Introd. to Tudor Drama*, OUP 1933.

2. *Garland* 1184: the gloss is an adaptation of Psalm xxxvi. 1 (Vulg.: xxxv. 2).

3. *Ibid.* 1177; Frost and Nash in *Stud. Phil.* XLI (1944), pp. 483ff.

4. By Professor Pollard, *Wolsey*, p. 101n.

5. See J. Ritson, *Bibliographia poetica*, 1802, p. 106; H. E. D. Blakiston, 'Thomas Warton and Machyn's Diary,' *EHR* XI (1896), pp. 282-300; R. L. Ramsay, *Skelton's Magnyfycence*, EETS, p. xixn.

6. Ramsay, *op. cit.*, pp. xxii-v, first dated the play with precision, and is only doubtful where he suggests it was probably written before the Treaty of Noyon in August 1516.

7. *CSP Ven.* II. no. 788. This was Chieregati's report to Mantua as late as 16 October 1516. For these events see Pollard, *Wolsey*, pp. 99-118, and *Henry VIII*, pp. 85-98; also Brewer, I. Chaps. IV-VI.

8. *Magnificence* 282, 346-61.

9. My discussion of the play hardly does more than summarise the exhaustive treatment of Ramsay, *op. cit.*, Introd.

10. *Criterion*, January 1932, p. 318.

11. Qu. Pollard, *Wolsey*, p. 304.

12. *Magnificence* 1239-50, 483-4. On the whole subject see Ramsay, cxii-vi.

13. For the Earl see *DNB*; E. B. de Fonblanque, *Annals of House of Percy*, 1887, I. Chap. VIII; G. Brenan, *Hist. of House of Percy*, ed. Lindsay, 1902, I. Chap. VI.

14. *Magnificence* 1726-34.

15. Brewer, I. 106-7.

16. A. Froude, *Henry VIII*, EL, I. 228.

17. See *LP* II. 215, 970; *DNB*; Brewer, I. 264–6; Gairdner, *Hist. of Eng. Church in 16th cent.*, pp. 64–5.

18. Qu. Pollard, *Wolsey*, p. 114.

19. For sanctuary see M. E. C. Walcott, *Westmin. Memorials*, 1849, pp. 80ff. A. P. Stanley, *Hist. Memls. of Westmin. Abbey*, 1882, pp. 346ff.; Stow, *Survey*, pp. 418-19.

20. See I. D. Thornley, 'The Destruction of Sanctuary,' in *Tudor Studies*, ed. Seton-Watson, 1924, pp. 182-207; W. S. Holdsworth, *Hist. Eng. Law*, ed. 1935. III. 305.

21. See Pollard, *Wolsey*, pp. 116, 179.

22. *Historia*, ed. 1570, p. 657.

23. John Newebery (see *Materials for . . . Hen. VII*, II. 392).

24. See App. I(I. 2): first noted by Westlake in *TLS*, 27 October 1921.

25. H. F. Westlake, *Westminster Abbey*, 1923, II. 424, 426.

26. *Opusculum Roberti Whittintoni. . .* , Wynkyn de Worde: 22 April 1519.

27. Cf. Beatrice White, *Vulgaria*, EETS, p. xxx (and n.); and the book itself, with its emphasis on court etiquette. Whittinton was not yet, it is true, official schoolmaster to the henchmen, though he became so later: the post was held by Francis Philip, executed for treason in 1523 (Hall, *Chronicle*, ed. 1809, p. 673). But he was probably Philip's assistant.

28. Holdsworth, *loc. cit.*, maintains that clerks (of whom Skelton, of course, was one) were unable to take sanctuary; they must, 'as the church had successfully insisted in the 13th century, be handed over to the ecclesiastical courts.' But this account does not even distinguish between the general right of sanctuary and the much more comprehensive privilege held by Westminster. The Westminster charter, as rendered by Stow (*Survey*, p. 411), covers any person, 'of what condition or estate soever.'

29. R. Keilwey, *Reports*, 1688, fols. 190-2; Pollard, *Wolsey*, p. 53n. In 1532 there were still 49 persons registered in the sanctuary of Westminster, their offences ranging from murder, church-breaking and debt to the robbing of hen-roosts (*LP* V. 1124).

CHAPTER ELEVEN

1. For the details quoted see P. Hamelius, *Mandeville's Travels*, EETS, Chap. 34 (p. 200); Dante, *Purgatorio*, 28. 97-102, 121-6; Bartholomæus Anglus, *De . . . proprietatibus*, Frankfort 1601, lib. 15, cap. 112 (pp. 682-3); M. M. Lascelles, 'Alexander and the Earthly Paradise,' *Medium Aevum* V (1936).

2. Neckam, *De naturis rerum*, ed. Wright, RS, cap. 36 (p. 87); cf. Vincent of Beauvais, *Speculum*, Duaci 1624, 2. 15. 168. I have failed to trace a 'scientific' account which gives Paradise as the bird's habitat, but cf. Lydgate, *The Cock hath Low Shoon* 91; and *Parliament of Birds* (ed. Hazlitt, *Early Pop. Poetry*, 1866, III. 169).

3. *De gen. deorum*, Basle 1532, 4. 49.

4. See Aristotle, *De animal.*, 8. 12, and Vincentius, *loc. cit.*; *Othello* 2. 3; Neckam, *loc. cit.*; A. de Gubernatis, *Zoological Mythology*, 1872, II. 320-2.

5. J. Stecher, *Œuvres de L. de Belges*, Louvain 1882-91, III. 1ff. (Skelton's use of this poem was suggested by Sidney Lee, *French Renaissance in Eng.*, OUP 1910, pp. 101-7: though the great scholar's knowledge of the English poet seems to have been rudimentary.)

6. Rastell, *Four Elements*, ed. Halliwell, 1848, p. 31; cf. Mandeville on the Euphrates: 'And that ryuere cometh . . . towardes ynde vnder erthe . . .' (ed. cit., p. 98). At this point, in order to insert a learned side-note, Skelton took out of Reuchlin a quot. from Lucan. Once more, however, his trusted lexicon had misled him, for the tag actually comes from Boethius. (See *Breuiloquus*, s. v. 'Euphrates' – borrowing, as usual, from the *Catholicon*.)

7. See *OED*, s. v. 'Vicar-general' and 'Provincial.'

8. Ll. 57-70.

9. See resp. *Magnificence* 1040; *Ps.* xc. 6 (Vulg.); More, *Dial. of Comfort* II. xvii (A. V. Ps. xci. 6. has 'pestilence' for *negotium*). For the calf see Ps. cv. 19 (A. V. cvi), Exod. xxxii; for Melchisadec, Gen. xiv. 18-20; Heb. vii. 2; and cf. *Against the Scots* 115.

10. For Ur see Nelson, p. 176. For the children of Lot, Ps. lxxxii. 8 (A. V. lxxxiii); Gen. xix. 37-8. For Jerubbesheth, 2 Reg. xi. 21 in the 1519 Venice Bible (A. V. Samuel); and cf. Judic. viii. 28-31: see my note in *PMLA* LIII (1938), p. 617n. Nelson, *ibid.*, p. 622, and LI (1936), p. 76, prefers the modern trans., but does not explain where Skelton could have found it.

11. See *C. Landini Flor. in P. Vergilii interp. prohemium*, Florence 1487, *ad loc.*: 'DO: byrsa: quod et lingua greca . . . et punica . . . corium significat.' For complete text see the Teubner Donatus, Leipsig 1905-6, *ad loc.* The criticism of Skelton is by R. L. Dunbabin, *MLR* XII (1917), pp. 129-37.

12. For *burse* see *OED*, s. v. For the proverb, Skeat, *Early Eng. Proverbs*, OUP 1910, no. 86. For Wolsey's wealth, Brewer, I. 199.

13. *Court of Love* 1059-60; *Cant. Tales* 3877-9.

14. Ll. 215-28.

15. Gordon, p. 161. Cf. Nelson, p. 183: '[Parrot] must be none other than the laureate poet, John Skelton.'

16. 'Anima certe, quia spiritus est, in sicco habitare non potest.' (Pseudo-Augustine, *Quaest. Vet. et Nov. Test. CXXVII*, Leipsig 1908, qu. 23, pp. 49-51.) Cf. Rabelais, *Gargantua* 5: 'En sec jamais l'âme ne habite.'

17. Ll. 237-8.

18. J. de Morawski, *Pamphile et Galatée par J. Bras-de-Fer*, Paris 1917.

19. Ll. 239-66.

20. Chorus only, with music, in MS. Addit. 5665, fol. 143ᵛ; full

text, from a private MS., pr. Rimbault, *Little Bk. of Songs and Ballads*, 1851, pp. 71ff. I have preserved the spelling *Besse*, since the Elizabethans modernised the name to *Bessy* (see Rimbault), while all three parts of the music for l. 5, 'and besse ys mankynd,' contain six notes. But just preceding it in the MS. (5665) is another song which begins: 'In wyldernes / there found y besse / secret alone.' Here it is unquestionably *Bess*. To my ear Skelton's ditty also reads infinitely better with *Bess*. For the Shakespeare ref. see *Lear* 3. 6. 27.

21. See Gordon, *TLS*, 1 February 1934; Nelson, *PMLA* LI, pp. 59-82, and his subsequent discussion with me, *ibid*. LIII, pp. 601-22. The facts there collected amply discredit Professor Berdan's dating of the poem in 1517-18 (*MLN* XXX (1915), pp. 140-4), repeated in Henderson's ed. of the works.

22. *Laud and Praise* ('21'), *Chronique de Rains* ('24'), *Why Come Ye Not* ('34') and possibly *Against Venomous Tongues*: see above, Chap. IX, n. 20.

23. Brewer, I. 418.

24. Ll. 282-6.

25. Nelson, pp. 168-9.

26. Ll. 311-15. See resp. Hall, I. 227; Pace in *SP Hen. VIII*, I. pp. 70-1 (first noted by Nelson); Hall, I. 232.

27. Ll. 410-14, 433-5.

28. For a standard biography see J. Wegg, *Richard Pace*, 1932.

29. For mole-catching see *OED*, s. v. 'mole,' 8*b*. That the *pendugim* was a bird we know from l. 209. If Dyce is right, Skelton was referring not to the penguin proper, which was still unknown, but to the great auk (cf. *OED*, s. v. 'penguin').

30. See Wegg, *op. cit.*, pp. 178-82; *LP* III(ii). 1890, 1918, 1981; Pollard, *Wolsey*, pp. 126-7. The name Clerk is distractingly common; there were at least two and possibly three *John* Clerks in Rome during during our period: see Index to Wegg; *DNB*, *sub nom.*; A. Wood, *Ath. Ox.*, ed. Bliss, 1813, I. cols. 204-5.

31. For Lycaon see l. 293 (as *Lyacon*, a contemp. variant also used by Rabelais). For 'wolf's-head' meaning outlaw, see *OED*, s. v. For 'the garland' used of the papal crown see John Clerk's letter to Wolsey, 14 September 1523: '. . . it is hard to gyve jugement where the garland shall light' (qu. C. H. Williams, *Eng. under the Early Tudors*, 1925, p. 110).

32. R. W. Chambers, *Thomas More*, p. 242.

33. Nelson, p. 240, no. 40.

34. J. O. Halliwell, *Song of Lady Bessy*, Percy Repr., 1847; Rimbault, *loc. cit.*

35. Ll. 445-6.

CHAPTER TWELVE

1. For the Howards see *DNB*; G. Brenan and E. P. Statham, *The House of Howard*, 1907, vol. I; Edmond Bapst, *Deux gentilshommes poètes de la cour de Henry VIII*, Paris 1891. (The last is unusually well documented.)

2. *LP* XII(ii). 976.

3. For Buckingham see *DNB* and Brewer, I Chap. XIII.

4. *LP*, *loc cit*. Brenan and Statham make her born in 1494, while *DNB* says she was little more than fifteen. But she herself did not claim to be more than twenty years younger than her husband (*LP* XII(ii). 143).

5. Ramsay, *Magnyfycence*, p. cxxiv, argues that he opposed Wolsey throughout. But see Brewer, I. 258; Pollard, *Wolsey*, p. 113, n. 1; *DNB*. It looks as though Polydore was either inventing Norfolk's retirement or momentarily confusing him with Surrey.

6. Brewer, I. 257, 382n.

7. *LP* II. 3973, 4057; III. 1.

8. *LP* II. 2987; Brewer, I. 376.

9. Bapst, pp. 155-6.

10. Qu. *ibid.*, pp. 197ff.

11. For the date of Surrey's arrival I follow Brenan and Statham; *DNB* has July. Cf. also *LP* III(i). 669-70. For the rest see *LP* III(i). 940; XII (ii). 143. I do not understand how Miss Stearns reaches her conclusion that the Countess was in Ireland from 1519 to April 1522 (*MLN*, 1928, pp. 314-16; cf. Nelson, *PMLA*, 1936, p. 385n.).

12. Ll. 1220-3. For the Duchess's conventual tastes see Brenan and Statham, I. 269-70.

13. Bapst, p. 200, n. 1; *LP* XII(ii). 143; Mary A. E. Wood, *Letters of Royal and Illustrious Ladies*, 1846, II. 218-19.

14. Pollard, *Wolsey*, p. 316.

15. 'Malo me Galathea petit, lasciua puella' (Vergil, *Ecl.* 3. 64) is quoted opposite a stanza of the Besse ditty.

16. *LP* III(ii). 1888.

17. For Thynne see *DNB*; *LP* IV(i). g. 137(11); (ii). g. 2599(24), 4687(20); (iii). g. 6038(8).

18. Kingsley and Furnivall, *Francis Thynne's Animadversions*, EETS 1894, p. 7.

19. J. M. Berdan, *Early Tudor Poetry*, p. 118. For the Erith house see *DNB*.

20. Stow, *Survey*, p. 119. It may be added that (as Mr. L. E. Tanner kindly informs me) the very full Abbey muniments contain no record that Thynne rented a house in *Westminster*.

21. *Colin Clout* 287-90.
22. Ll. 162-9, 193-4.
23. Pollard, *Wolsey*, pp. 306-7; Brewer, I. 379.
24. Ll. 266-9, 303-22.
25. Qu. Herbert, p. 141.
26. Ll. 469-87.
27. Nelson's detailed proof (*PMLA*, 1936, pp. 381ff.) that *Colin Clout* was written 'in the spring or summer of 1522' and not, as Berdan suggested, in two versions, extending up to 1525, is ignored in Gordon's examination of the problem (pp. 151-6). While Gordon agrees in finding Berdan's evidence inadequate, he thinks that the poem preceded *Speak Parrot* and dates it 1519-20. The only arguments adduced are (i) 'a very strong tradition that *Colin Clout* is Skelton's first attack on the Cardinal,' and (ii) the 1518 bull by which Wolsey was empowered to visit monasteries. Of (i) I was ignorant; but in any case 'tradition' cannot stand before factual evidence to the contrary. And Skelton, in ll. 419-20, clearly refers to an actual suppression, while the water-mill (as Nelson observes) points unmistakably to Bromhall, suppressed on 5 December 1521. As for (ii), there were in fact no suppressions in 1519-20.
28. Ll. 491-6, 574-5.
29. Ll. 585-90.
30. Ll. 945-52.
31. Nelson, *PMLA*, 1936, p. 383.
32. E. Law, *Short Hist. of Hampton Court*, 1906, p. 28.
33. Ll. 991-6, 1043-51, 1237-42.
34. Cavendish, *Life of Wolsey*, p. 89n. (Dr. Barnes' description of his interview.) In 1523 More also saw the Cardinal 'in his gallery at Whitehall,' i.e. York Place: see Roper.
35. Ll. 1254-60.
36. Hall, I. 258, 264-6, 274; Pollard, *Wolsey*, p. 132.
37. Pollard, *Wolsey*, p. 142.
38. Ll. 226-9, 392-4.
39. The arguments brought by Gordon (pp. 161-2) for dating it October 1522–March 1523 ignore the vital figure '.xxxiiii.' at the close of the poem. For his other points, (1) l. 638 actually says it is *within* this sixteen year that Wolsey was Nanfan's chaplain; thus dating the reference *before*, not *about*, January 1523. (6) Although papal confirmation of St. Alban's did not arrive till 8 November 1522, Henry had given it to Wolsey a whole year before this, and writs for its temporalities were already issued by 7 December 1521 (*LP* III(ii). 1759, 1843). (8) The official date of the patent (15 March 1523) appointing a

successor to the King's French secretary, Meautis, who Skelton hints was executed for treason, has little relevance to the latter event. Tuke was no doubt at work long before his patent was confirmed. Of the other datable events the latest is (2), the appointment of goldsmith Mundy Mayor of London on 28 October 1522. And this occurs well toward the end of the poem (l. 904). In a word, Gordon has produced nothing to contravene Nelson's dating (pp. 161-3), i.e. shortly before 17 November 1522.

40. Ll. 442-7.

41. *Encyc. Brit.*, s. v. 'Wolsey.'

42. Ll. 457-66. Dyce was misled by the *cēcitate* of l. 471 to read 'a caeciam' for the *Acisiam* (*sic*) of all the prints.

43. Pollard, *Wolsey*, p. 328.

44. *Decastichon* ending *Why Come*, and *L'autre envoi* to *Garland*.

45. This was first demonstrated by Nelson, *PMLA*, 1936, p. 398; cf. his book, pp. 205-7.

46. J. Dover Wilson, *Fortunes of Falstaff*, CUP 1944, p. 119.

47. J. Gairdner, *Henry VII*, pp. 153-4.

48. Ll. 377–82.

49. Dyce, I. lxxii (tale xiv).

50. For North see *DNB*; Pollard, *Wolsey*, p. 226n.; and for his poems, MS. Harl. 2252, fols. 33ᵛff.

CHAPTER THIRTEEN

1. See resp. J. Leland, *Itinerary*, ed. Hearne, 2nd ed., Oxford 1744, I. 66-7; Dyce, II. 330; *LP* III(ii). 2412.

2. *Garland* 22-7.

3. Kindly calculated for me by Mr. J. Thorburn, University Coll., Cardiff.

4. Ll. 1516-19. Gordon (pp. 56-7) rejects January on the grounds (i) that Miss Stearns dated the retrogradation in April; (ii) that the calculations made for Nelson and me 'differ among themselves'; (iii) that Surrey did not become general in the north until February. *Re* (i), April marked the *end*, not the beginning of retrogradation in 1523. Miss Stearns was forced to choose this arbitrary interpretation for other reasons, which have been adequately dealt with by Nelson (*PMLA*, 1936, p. 385n.). For (ii), our calculations differ only within a few days and not, as Gordon implies, months; both make retrogradation begin in January. Argument (iii) works rather the opposite way. There is not the slightest mention of the Earl's presence at Sheriff Hutton: a fair presumption that he had not yet come north. Actually, no despatches from Surrey appear in *LP* between 4 October 1522 (when he was still

in France) and 10 April 1523, when he was at Newcastle (*LP* III(ii). 2592, 2937). Cf. my identification of Mars with Surrey, his sword now idle because of the winter. Finally, Gordon ignores the vital evidence of the full moon on 2 January and the mention of Janus at the end.

5. Ll. 665-75.

6. Nelson, pp. 197-201.

7. *Ibid.*, p. 210.

8. Mary Wood, *Letters of Royal and Illust. Ladies*, II. 358-9, 360-2; I. 336-8. The last is dated 4 November 1524 (?). On 19 September of that year the Duke had written to beg Wolsey for his recall. If not, he would like some other place than Newcastle to lie in, that he might send for his wife and put his affairs in order (*LP* IV(i). 672). For the clothier Darnell mentioned by the Countess, see *LP* IV(ii). 2375.

9. L. 777.

10. Ll. 1595-1603. For the authenticity of the dedication, which has been questioned, see Nelson, p. 202.

11. Froude, *Life and Letters of Erasmus*, p. 32.

12. Ll. 926-32.

13. Dyce, II. 324-5.

14. Pishey Thompson, *Hist. and Antiq. of Boston, Lincs.*, 1856, pp. 373-4. She is there described as 'd. of —— Brewse of Wenham, Suffolk'; but it seems most reasonable to take her as a sister of Thomas Brews, Esq. As Sir Philip married again, he does not mention Margaret in his will.

15. Ll. 1038-42.

16. Ll. 735-6, 740, 761-2. Dyce first noted the refs. to Persius, *Sat.* 5. 76 and Vergil, *Ecl.* 7. 26.

17. First deciphered by H. Bradley, *Academy*, 1 August 1896.

18. See App. I(J.2).

19. Ll. 1046-53.

20. *LP* XII(ii). 35: 5 June 1537.

21. For the later history of the Howards see their letters in *SP Hen. VIII* (in the original spelling) and in Mary Wood (modernised); *LP* XII summarises the most important of them. Bapst, *Deux gentilshommes poètes*, gives a generously documented account from the point of view least favourable to Elizabeth (he suggests, e.g., that she was tied up to prevent her smashing everything in her fury!). For Norfolk's later career see Merriman, *Life and Letters of Thomas Cromwell*.

CHAPTER FOURTEEN

1. Hall, ed. Whibley, I. 287; Pollard, *Wolsey*, pp. 187-91.

2. For the historical facts see Brewer, I, Chap. XVIII.

3. *Doughty Duke of Albany* 524-33. It is noteworthy that Skelton's suspicions are corroborated by Cromwell, who also condemned Wolsey for his 'many words without deeds' (Pollard, *Wolsey*, p. 226).

4. I quote from the MS. Genealogy at Arundel Castle, fols. 181ff., endorsed: 'The Coppy of the magnificent funerall of the most high and mighty prince Thomas Duke of Norff solemnized in Anno Dni 1524 . . . ' (1618). The account in Guthrie's *Peerage*, 1763, I. 37ff., is inaccurate.

5. App. II(3). I use the trans. of Professor Bryn Davies.

6. Herbert, p. 460; Brewer, II. 446; Pollard, *Henry VIII*, p. 426; *LP* IV(iii). 5743. A marginal note in the last indicates that this story was also attributed to Patch, the fool.

7. *DNB, sub nom.*

8. See Gordon, *TLS*, 20 September 1934, with my reply, 27 September. I have failed to trace the attribution to Erasmus earlier than Bailey's trans. of the *Colloquies*, 1725, pp. 11-12. Froude, *Erasmus*, p. 115, terms it 'a Chelsea tradition.'

9. *DNB*, s. v. 'Bilney'; J. Foxe, *Acts and Monuments of the Church*, ed. 1838, pp. 508-13.

10 *Replication* 71-2. The identification was first made by Mullinger, *Hist. Univ. Camb.*, I. 607-8.

11. *Replication* 389-98.

12. Wolsey was elected Cardinal on the title of St. Caecilia trans. Tiberim.

13. I do not find Nelson's attempt (pp. 217-19) to prove a last gibe at Wolsey in this poem very convincing.

14. Ll. 180-4. This was remarked by Nelson, pp. 213-15.

15. Qu. Foxe, *op. cit.*, p. 512.

16. See App. I(K); and cf. my refs. in *PMLA*, 1938, pp. 610-11.

17. For much of what follows I am indebted to 'Chivalry and the Idea of a Gentleman' by Professor A. W. Reed, in the volume *Chivalry*, ed. E. Prestage, 1928.

18. *Elizabethan England*, ed. L. Withington, n.d., pp. 7-8.

CHAPTER FIFTEEN

1. Hall, II. 153.

2. For du Bellay on the sweat see Brewer, II. 271. For Wolsey in 1529 see the abstract in *LP* IV. 5754 and E. Law's explanation in his *Short Hist. of Hampton Court*, p. 52. The sweat was certainly raging in early August (*LP* IV. 5825); and Skelton's administration significantly lacks any such phrase as 'et exhibuit eius testamentum': see App. I(L.2).

3. See App. II(1): *Skeltonus* is either a slip for *Skeltonis*, or the epitaph is not by Skelton. I do not understand why Nelson (p. 219) includes the words that follow as part of the inscription. Even if the date were given, it is hardly conceivable that Skelton's illegitimate offspring should have been advertised on his tomb. Surely the epitaph ended with 'hic situs est.'

4. Not eight, as Dyce has it, I. xlvi, n. 2.

5. See App. I(L.1). For the gild see esp. H. F. Westlake, *St. Margaret's, Westminster*, pp. 44ff. The facts quoted are drawn from the fragmentary accounts of the gild from 1475 to 1522, now at Caxton Hall, Westminster.

6. See App. I(L.2). For Mote (as he himself spelt the name) see R. Newcourt, *Repert. paroch. Londin.*, I. 351, 316; II. 290, 282; and Churchwardens' Accounts of St. Margaret's, 1526-8 – which also record the gift by him of 'an Imnall prentid.' Nelson (p. 220) refers to him as the 'curate' of St. Margaret's; but we have already noted that the term now bears quite a different meaning. For the final point see G. Lyndwood, *Provinciale*, Oxford 1679, p. 166: 'Clericus nihil Concubinis Testamento relinquat,' etc. .

7. Cavendish, pp. 377-93.

8. *Ibid.*, pp. 394, 399.

APPENDIX I

RECORDS

A. SKELTON AND THE UNIVERSITIES

(1) *Degrees*

(1492-3. From *Grace Book B (Pt. I)* . . . *of the University of Cambridge*, ed. Bateson, CUP 1903, p. 54.)

Conceditur Johanni Skelton poete in partibus transmarinis atque oxonie laurea ornato ut apud nos eadem decoraretur

(1504-5. *From Grace Book* Γ . . . *of the University of Cambridge*, ed. Searle, CUP 1908, p. 37.)

De magistris arcium

Item conceditur Johanni Skelton poete laureato quod possit stare eodem gradu hic quo stetit Oxoniis et quod possit vti habitu sibi concesso a principe

(2) *Skelton and Suckling.*

(1496, after Pentecost. From *Grace Book B (I)*, p. 92.)

Item die Mercurii pro Jantaculo cum Magistro Skelton quia fuit cum episcopo Sarum v^d . . .
Item die saboti pro Jantaculo cum Magistro Skelton apud Symsons $iiij^d$

(1501, Hilary term (11 January – 24 March). From *ibid.*, pp. 148-9).

Item die Mercurii apud Westmonasterium in iantaculo nostro ij^d
Item eodem die pro cena nostra et Magistri skelton vj^d . . .
Item eodem die [Martis] pro cena nostra et magistro skelton vj^d . . .
Item eodem die [Marcurii] pro cena cum Magistro skelton in hospicio vj^d . . .
Item [die Jouis] in camero pro focali et potu cum Magistro skelton ij^d

(3) *Louvain*

(Title of *Opusculum Roberti Whittintoni*, Wynkyn de Worde: 22 April 1519. The poem is too long and uninformative to quote in full: for a modern reprint see Dyce, I. xvi-ix).

APPENDIX I: RECORDS

IN CLARISSIMI SCHELTONIS LOUANIENSIS POETÆ LAUDES EPIGRAMMA

B. HOLY ORDERS

(1498. From Register 'Hill' (1489-1505) of dioc. of London, re-printed Dyce, I. xx-xxi.)

(1) *Subdeacon*

[In ecclesia conuentuali domus siue hospitalis sancti Thome martiris de Acon ciuitatis London. per Thomam Rothlucensem episcopum vltimo die mensis Marcii]

M. Johannes Skelton London. dioc. ad titulum Mon. beate Marie de Graciis iuxta Turrim London.

(2) *Deacon*

[In cathedra sancti Pauli London. apud summum altare eiusdem per Thomam permissione diuina London. episcopum in sabbato sancto viz. xiiii die mensis Aprilis]

Johannes Skelton poete [sic] laureatus London. dioc. ad titulum Mon. de Graciis juxta turrim London.

(3) *Priest*

[In ecclesia conuentuali hospitalis beate Marie de Elsyng per Thomam Rothlucensem episcopum ix die mensis Iunii]

M. Johannes Skelton poeta lureatus [sic] London. dioc. ad titulum Mon. de Graciis iuxta turrim London.

C. SKELTON AT COURT

(1) *The Lady Margaret's Poet*

(1497, 3-4 December. From P.R.O. MS. E101. 414-16: account-book of John Heron, H.M. Treasurer of the Chamber, 13-15 Hen. VII, unpaginated.)

iij° iiij° & v° diebus   Sunday Monday & Tewesday
Decembris [xiij^{mo} Regis
h vij^{mo}] [4] Item to my lady the kinges moder poete lxvj s viijd

(2) *Skelton's Mass*

(1498, 11 November. From *ibid.*)

[Sun.-Fri., 11-16 November, 14 Hen. VII.]
Item for offring opon Sonday   vj s viij d
Item for offring at master Skelton masse   xx s

(3) *The Tutor's Parting Gift*

(1502. From P.R.O. MS. E101. 415-3: account-book for 15-18 Hen. VII.)

[Sat.-Fri., week ending 29 April, 17 Hen. VII]

[13] Item to the duc of york Scolemaster   xl s

[Sun.-Sat., week ending 25 June, 17 Hen. VII.]

[Last but one] Item to my lorde prince Scolemaster   iiij li

D. ERASMUS'S PRAISE OF SKELTON

(1) *The Poem*
(1499. From the autograph MS. Egerton 1651, fol. 6ᵛ.)

Carmen Extemporale

Quid tibi facundum nostra in preconia fontem
Soluere collibuit
Aeterna vates Skelton[1] dignissime lauro
Casthalidumque decus
Nos neque pieridum celebramus antra sororum
Fonte nec aonio
Ebibimus vatum dicantes ora liquores
At tibi appollo chelim
Auratam dedit: & vocalia plectra sorores
Inque tuis labijs
Dulcior hybleo residet suadela liquore
Se tibi Calliope
Infudit totam: tu carmine vincis olorem
Cedit et ipse tibi
Vltro porrecta cithara Rhodopeius orpheus
Tu modolante [*sic*] lyra
Et mulcere feras et duras ducere quercus
Tu potes et rapidos
Flexanimis fidibus: fluuiorum sistere cursus
Flectere saxapotes [*sic*]
Grecia meonio quantum debebat Homero
Mantua virgilio
Tantum Skeltoni iam se debere fatetur
Terra britanna suo
Primus In hanc Latio deduxit ab orbe Camenas
Primus hic edocuit
Exculte pureque loquere: Te principe Skelton
Anglia nil metuat
Vel cum Romanis uersu certare poetis
Viue valeque diu

[1] Preceded by *stelkon* struck through.

APPENDIX I: RECORDS

(On fol. 10 – the last in the volume – Erasmus repeated the first lines thus:

Ad Skeltoni carmen extempo.

Quid tibi facundum nostra In preconia fontem
Soluere collibuit?
Aeterna vates Skelton dignissime lauro ut habetur.)

(2) *The Dedication to Prince Henry*
(From *ibid.*, fol. 1.)

. . . & domi haberes Stelkonum [sic] vnum britannicarum[1] litterarum lumen ac decus: qui studia tua possit non solum accendere verum eciam Iuuare[2] Bene uale

E. COURT OF REQUESTS
(1) *Ottey v. Skelton*
(1501, 14 May. From P.R.O. Court of Req. Misc. Bks. II, fol. 133.)

Eodem die

In causa petri Ottey contra Iohannem skelton respectuatur usque in crastinum ad horam nouenam ante merediem sub spe concordie et datus est terminus eidem Iohanni skelton sub pena xl li ad comparendum coram Reuerendo in xpo patre Ricardo Dunelmensis Episcopo & alijs de consilio domini Regis apud london' eadem hora nouena si interim concordia nunc factus[3] fuerit in eadem causa inter partes predictas.

(2) *Bray v. Prior of St. Bartholomew's*
(1502, 10 June. From *ibid.*, fol. 3.)

Iohannes Skelton comparet coram consilio domini Regis virtute obligacionis in qua prior sancti bartholomei et alij tenentur Reginaldo Bray et alijs in ducentis libris et committitur carceribus genitoris domini regis quousque priuilegia dicti prioris coram dicto consilio edoceantur et aliter super visu huiusmodi statuantur Et ideo decretum quod obligacio remanens in custodia maioris ciuitatis london' deliberatur dicto priori aut cassetur &c

F. SKELTON AT DISS
(As the originals are not now available I follow, with one exception, the transcripts kindly supplied me by Dr. William Nelson.)

---

[1] *lumen* struck out.   [2] eds.: consummare.
[3] Nelson plausibly emends to *non facta*.

APPENDIX I: RECORDS

(1) *Wills*
    (a) 1504, 10 April. Will proved of Margery Cowper of Diss. From Norwich Consist. Court Register 'Rix' (1504-7), fol. 112.

. . . Theise beyng witnesse Master Iohn Skelton laureat parson of disse and Sir Iohn Clarke sowle preest of the same towne

    (b) 1506, 14 April. Will proved of John Clarke of Diss. *Ibid.*, fols. 460-1. (Text from Blomefield, ed. 1805, I. 27.)

[Clarke leaves money] to a pylgrym, a priest, to be in prayer and pilgrimage at *Rome* the whole Lent, there to pray and syng for me and myn children, my fader and moder, *Robert* and *Cate*, *John Kew* and *Maut*, *Steven Brightled*, and *John Payne*, the which I am in dett to.

[His executor is Sir John Clarke, the soul priest cited in (a).]

(2) *The Episcopal Court*
    (a) *Skelton v. Pickerell*
    (1509-10. From Consist. Court Act Book, Norwich Cathedral.)

[Before John Huchons: 3 December 1509.]
Eisdem die mensi anno & loco Iohannes Chapman certificauit coram iudice se vigore mandati siue citationis per eum exhibiti perempter citasse Thomam pykerell de dys ad comparendum istis die & loco ad respondendum certis articlis siue interrogatorijs concernendis anime sue salute ad promocionem magistri Iohannis Skelton rectoris ibidem eidem obijciendi Et quia non comparuit ideo dominus pronunciauit eum contumacem postea absolutus est dictus Thomas iiij die Ianuarij per dominum officialem et habet ad comparendum die lune post festum hillarij.

[14 January 1510.]
In Skelton contra pykerell preconisatum non comparuisse dominus igitur ad peticionem pronunciauit eum contumacem.

[4 February 1510.]
In Skelton contra pykerell pykerell suspensus.

    (b) *Bishop Nick v. Rev. William Dale*
    (1511. From Institution Book XIV (Norwich Cathedral), fols. 60 k-k^v, l^v, o.)
[On 6 Nov. Dale, Rector of Redgrave, appears and denies the charges brought against him by Thomas Revet. These are even-

tually reduced to one, and the parties promise to abide the decision of the court. On 11 Nov. the case continues.]

Magistri Simonis Dryuer decretorum doctoris & magistri Iohannis Skelton' Rectoris de Disse / arbitratorum &c / inter partes predictas indifferent[er] electorum &c / de et sup[er] omnibus & singulis causis.

[In case of non-agreement within 8 days the case is to come before the bishop on the Monday after the Feast of St. Edmund's. They are successful, for within a week Dale appears with a satisfactory letter of correction.]

(3) *Skelton's Substitutes at Diss*
(a) 6 May 1515. Will of Margaret Bache of Diss. From Norf. Archdeac. Register, 1515-20, 1523, fol. 220.

[Witnessed by] Sir William Beget parish prest.

(b) November 1517. Will of Roger Foleser the Elder of Diss. *Ibid.*, fols. 209-10.

[Witnessed by] Sir William Bekett paresshe preste of disse.

(c) 5 February 1522. Will of Richard Lynd of Diss. From Norwich Consist. Court Register 'Harman' (1522-3), fols. 7-8.

[Witnessed by] sir William Brakes my curate.

(d) 1529. Will of John Smyth of Diss. From Norf. Archdeac. Register, 1524-31, fol. 177.

[Witnessed by] sir wylliam gallyott prest.

G. JANE SCROPE
(1) *Her Father's Will*
(1485: made 4 April, pr. 28 June. From *Test. Ebor.*, III. 297-9, which see for complete text.)

In Dei nomine, amen. I Richard Scrop [a younger son of Henry, 4th lord Scrope, of Bolton, by Elizabeth, daughter of John, lord Scrope, of Masham. His patrimony included, among other things, the estate of Bentley near Doncaster, Langley castle near Durham, and Weighton in Yorks. He married Eleanor, daughter of Norman Washburn, esq., a Worcestershire lady. The marriage licence is dated on Nov. 25, 1467. They were to be united in the chapel of the earl of Warwick and Salisbury, within Sheriffhutton castle (Reg. Geo. Neville, i. 57b.)], beyng in ffwll mynde, and holle witte, and in charite w^t all ye worlde, the iiij day off Aprill, the yere off owr Lorde Godde M.CCCC.iiij^{xx}v, make my wille and testyment in thys wysse. . . . and my body to be beryd in the chyrche off the Frere Prechowrys in London. . . . Item I will my wyffe haffe, yff schoo lewe sole, all my lands and gudds, meweabill and vnmewabill, exepte soche as I beeqweth to other folke; And soche as mwste be bestowyd for my sowle bee the descrescion off myn exectorrys. And yff itt for(tune) my sayde wyffe to bee weddyd, I will than that sche haffe Wyghton and Langeley, the terme off her lyffe. Also to haffe xx li. in platte, and xx li. in monay, and all her jwellis, and all that bee longys to her chamber w^t all her arayment. Item, yff thys childe that my wyffe is w^t bee a son, I will that itt bee maryd bee the descrescion off myn exsecturis; and, yff itt be a dowghter, and my wyffe happyn to be marryd, than I will that Bentelay bee sowllyd on to the beehaffe off my childer, yff myn exsecturs thynke itt to be don. . . . Item to my lady Northtfolke [Margaret, duchess of Norfolk, died 1490]. . . . Franse boke. Item the remander off Franse bokes to my lorde my broder. . . . It' a couercop off syluer w^t drappis off golde I will that dame Anne my dowghter haffe, wen scho comys to ye age off xxiiij yerrs. . . .

(2) *Her Mother's Will.*
  (1505: made 11 December, pr. January 1506. From P.C.C.: 1 Adeane.)

Test' Alianore In the name of god Amen The xjth day of the
Wyndam Moneth of Decembre In the xxjth yere of the Reigne of king harry the vijth. And in the yere of our lorde god M^l v^C and fyve. I. Elianore Wyndam widowe late the wyfe of sir Iohn Wyndam knyght hole of mynde and in good remembraunce being god be lawded at Carowe by norwiche make my testament and last will in this wise. ffirst I commende my soule to god almighty our blissed lady saint Mary the virgyn And to all the holy company of hevyn And my body to be buried in the Quere of the Austen ffreres in Norwiche besides the high Awter there / to whos high Awter of the same ffreres I bequeth a peir Chaleys siluer and gilt to the entent that the ffreres there shall pray for the soules of me the said Alianore and sir Iohn wyndam late my husbonde / Item to the same hous of ffreres I bequeth xxs. Item to the priour of the same hous the day of my burying xxd and to eche

ffrere there beyng A preest viijd And to eche Novice of the same place iiijd. Item I will haue a ffrere preest to syng and pray for my soule wᵗin the said place by the space of an hole yere. Item I will that ffrere be assigned by the said Priour there and he to haue for his salary or stypende liijs iiijd. Item I bequeth to the white ffreres of Norwiche xxs. to be devided amonge the pouer ffreres there. Item to the blak ffreres in Norwiche xiijs iiijd to be devided amongest them Item to the Grey ffreres in Norwiche xiijs iiijd to be devided amongest them. Item to the Abbesse. of Berkyng xxs. And to Dame Margaret Shuldham vjs viijd And to euery lady there xxd to the entent to pray for me. Item to euery preest there iiijd and to euery Clerk there ijd. Item I bequeth to the prioresse of Carrowe xxd and to eche Nonne there xijd. Item to the preest there viijd. And to the Clerk there iiijd to thentent to pray for me as is aforsaid Item I bequeth to the high Awter of the parisshe Churche of Carrowe vjs viijd Item I bequeth to the pouer Susters and half Susters of Normannes hospitall in Norwiche iijs iiijd equally to be devided amongest them Item I will there be dispoased for me the day of my burying in Almes vli and besides that I will that at my burying day my vijᵗʰ day moneth day and yere day there be disposed for me xl li aftre the discrecion of myn executours Item I woll that my housholde be susteyned and kept at Carrowe aforsaid well and honestly by the space of a moneth next aftre my deceas. Item I will haue an honest preest to syng for me in the vniuersite of Cambrigge by the space of ij yeres And I will that preest haue either of the same ij yeres for his stypende viij mark. Item I will haue xxx Trigintall to be songe for me as shortly as they may conueniently be doon aftre my decesse And to be paid for eche trigintall xs. the summe xvli. Item I bequeth to the Churche of ffelbryg vjs viijd And to the parisshens there amonges them vjs viijd to pray for my soule Item to the pouer prisoners within the Castell of Norwiche iijs iiijd by the discrecion of myn executours Item I bequeth to my lorde of Oxenforde A Crosse of golde wᵗ diamondes. and to my lady his wyfe A Ryng wᵗ a Rubye Item I bequeth to my lady Beamonte my doughter A purfle of Sabylles / my best ffetherbedde wᵗ the bolster to the same bilonging A peir of ffustyans ij peir of my fynest Shetes and ij pylowes of downe and a Canape of grene Sarsenet my best table Clothe / of diaper. Item I bequeth to Thomas Wyndam my son in lawe A vestment A Masse boke a peir of Chales iij hanginges vj cusshens of verdour and all the stuff of my kechyn Item to my doughter Alianore wyndam wyf of the said Thomas A gowne of blak velvet furred wᵗ Marters A gowne of blak Cloth purfled with Tawny velwet. A Counterpoynt wrought w^t the iij kinges of Coleyn And A Sparver of grene Sarsenett / Item I bequeth to dame Anne Scrope my doughter x li And to my doughter Mary Scrope I bequeth a blak gown purfled w^t Shankes. A kirtell cloth of blak worsted Item I bequeth to my doughter Iane Scrope a gowne of blak velwet lyned w^t Crymsyn velwet / A gowne of blak Cloth ffurred w^t Shankes and a kyrtill of tawny velwet / Item I bequeth to my doughter kateryn Scrope A gowne of blak Saten ffurred w^t white / and a blak gowne furred with Mynkes and A kirtyll of Damask. Item to my doughter ffraunceis Wyndam l li to be paid by Thomas Wyndam my sonne as appereth by byll made and wretyn w^t his owne hande at suche daies as appereth in the same bill Item I bequeth to the same ffraunceys A gowne of blak Chamlet w^t a purfle of grey. A kyrtill of blak worsted. A ffetherbedde / A bolster. A peir blankettes ij peir Shetes A Couerlight and A Sparver / Item I bequeth to George Wyndam xxs. Item I bequeth to Elizabeth Wyndam A brode gyrdell harnysed w^t siluer and gilt Item to Margaret Wyndam a nother brode girdell the harnes siluer and gilt Item to Elyanore Wyndam a nother brode girdell harnesed w^t siluer and gilt Item I bequeth to Edmunde Wyndam A ffetherbedde. A bolster / A peir blankettes ij peir Shetes a Couerlight and A Sparver. / | Item I bequeth to Iohn Wyndam A Crosse of golde. Item I bequeth to my doughters vnmaried which I had by my first husbonde Richard Scrope all the residue of myn araye and my housholde stuffe before not bequethed. Item I bequeth to sir Iames my preest xxs. Item to Edwarde Iervice my seruant vjs. viijd Item to Thomas Nicholson my seruant vs. Item to Thomas Wyndore my seruant iijs iiijd Item to Iuliane my seruant vs. A gowne and a kirtill Item I bequeth to Anne Blundell my seruant iijs iiijd The residue of all my goodes before not bequethed I committe to the good disposicion of myn executours to dispose them for my soule and for all good cristen soules as shall seme them best to please god and to profite my soule. And of this my present testament and last will I make constitute and ordeyn myn executours Sir Thomas Tirrell knyght Iohn Tey Esquier and Richard Wode gentilman And I geve to the said sir Thomas Tirrell taking charge of this my said testament v li. And to either of the said Iohn Tey and Richard Wode so they take charge to approve this my said testament v mark And fynally I constitute Elizabeth the lady Beamonte to be Supervisour of the same my testament and last will To the confirmacion and witnes wherof I haue sett my Seall to thes presentes yoven day and yere abouesaid.

APPENDIX I: RECORDS

(3) *Her Husband's Will*

(1514: made 5 November, pr. 5 February 1515. From P.C.C.: 4 Holder.)

T Thome   In the name of god Amen The vth daye of Nouember in
Brewys   the yere of oure Lord god M^l v^C xiiij I Thomas Brews
Esquyer of the Countie of Suff' of the Dioces of Norwiche / beyng in
good mynd and hole memory make and ordeyn this my testament /
and last will in maner and forme herafter folowyng / ffyrst I bequeth
my soule to Almyghti god / And to his moter oure Lady seynt mary
And to all the holy company of hevyn / And my body to be buried
in the Chauncell of Wenham / Item I charge myn Executors to
performe my fathers will to the vttermoste Item I will that Iane
my welbeloved wyff have my Lordshipp of Topcrofte w^t all the
advauntage And my seid wyff to paye to my mother duryng her
Lyff a yerly pencyon of ffourty poundes oute of the same Maner at
ij termes in the yere Item I will that my seid [wyff] have Barton
myll duryng the noneage of Iohn myn Eldest sonne and heire /
Item I wyll that my seid wyff have my lordship of hawkers payng
the pencion owte of it whiche is x li payd at ij termes in the yere /
Item I will that my mother have wenham vause Germyns And all
the proffites therof duryng the lyff of my Lady Debenham payng the
pencion / And after her deth to remayne to my seid wyff with all
the proffites / And my mother then to have the seid Lordship her
dwellyng duryng her lyff Item I will that Iohn myn Eldest sone have
my fathers Chayne and all the plate that was my grandams when
he comyth to the age of xxj yeris / Item I will that my brother have
my Scarlet gaberdyn with all that is in myn other wyll / Item I
will that my seid wyff have all my moveables as wel those that be
at Wyuenhoo as those that be at Wenham / And also all the
Revenues of my landes due at Mighelmas last past Item I woll that
Richard Apleton gentylman have my Russet gowne ffurred with
ffoxe Item I will that Sir Thomas Gardyner have xx^s and sir
william Reve vj^s viij d Item I will that Benett my parker have
yerly duryng his lyff xxvj^s viij d he doyng suche service as my
mother shall commaunde hym / Item I orden and make myn
Executors Kateryn brews my mother and Ioane my wyff /

(4) *Her Inheritance*

(1522, 28 April. Codicil to will of her brother-in-law, Sir Thomas
Wyndham, made 22 October 1521, pr. 4 March 1523. From P.C.C.:
3 Bodfelde.)

And also I haue paid to Mary Iane. and Kateryn Scrope my first wyfes susters / a Mᴵ li in redy money the which was owyng for the purcheas of Bentley and Hamethwayte in Yorkshire purchased by my fader sir Iohn Wyndam

(5) *Pedigrees*

(*a*) *Scrope*

(Based on Sir N. H. Nicolas, *Scrope and Grosvenor Controversy*, II. 60-1, with corrections.)

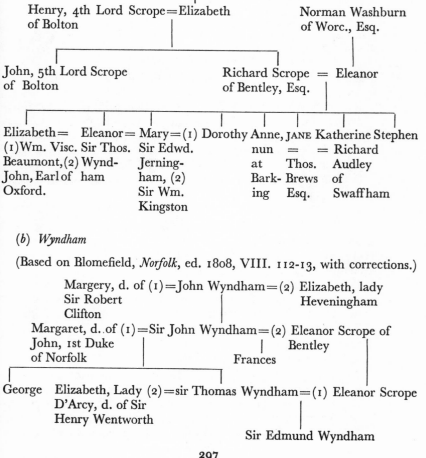

(*b*) *Wyndham*

(Based on Blomefield, *Norfolk*, ed. 1808, VIII. 112-13, with corrections.)

APPENDIX I: RECORDS

(c) Brews
(Based on *ibid.*, X, 186, with corrections.)

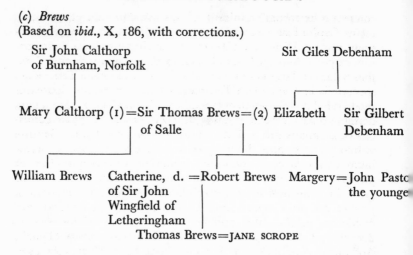

H. SKELTON'S PARDON
(1509, 21 October. From P.R.O. Supp. Patent Rolls, C.67/57, m. 31.)

Iohannes Skelton nuper de london' clericus alias dictus Iohannes Skelton nuper de london' clericus poeta laureatus alias dictus Iohannes Skelton nuper de Disse in Com' Norff' clericus alias dictus Iohannes Skelton nuper de Disse in Com' Norff' clericus ac poeta laureatus alias dictus Iohannes Skelton nuper de Dysse in Com' Norff' seu quocumque &c Teste R apud Westm' xxj die Octobris per ipsum Regem

I. SKELTON AT WESTMINSTER
(1) *Dinner with the Prior*
   (1511, Saturday 5 July. From W. A. M. 33,325, fol. 17ᵛ.)

Item ij playce	vij d	
Item ij copull soliz	vj d	this day at dyner wᵗ youʳ
Item ij Congger snekes	xiiij d	Maisterchp the soffrecan and
Item a syd saltffishe	ij d	Skeltun the poet wᵗ othere
Item ij disches buter	ij d	

(2) *Skelton's House*
   (1518, 8 August. From W. A. M., Register II, fols. 146-7.)

Indentura alicie   Hec Indentura facta inter Iohannem permissione
Newebery   diuina Abbatem monasterii beati petri Westmon-
asterii priorem et eiusdem loci conuentum ex vna parte et Aliciam
Newebery ex altera parte Testatur quod predicti abbas prior et

conuentus ex eorum vnanimi [sic] assensu concensu et voluntate
tocius Capituli sui concesserunt tradiderunt et ad firmam dimis-
erunt prefate Alicie vnum Tenementum situatum infra Sanctuar-
ium ex parte Australi Magni le Belfrey dicti monasterii cum domibus Solariis celariis et omnibus suis pertinenciis eidem Tenemento
spectantiis in quoquidem Tenemento Iohannes Skelton laureatus
modo inhabitat Habendo et tenendo predictum Tenementum cum
domibus solariis celariis et suis pertinenciis prefate Alicie executori-
bus et assignatis suis a ffesto Natiuitatis sancti Iohannis Baptiste
vltimo preterito ante datam presencem vsque ad finem et term-
inum quatuordecem annorum extunc proxime sequencium et
plenarie complendorum Reddendo inde annuatim prefati abbati
priori et conuentui et successoribus suis vel Sacriste monasterii
predicti qui pro tempore fuerit aut eius in hac parte deputato pro
duodecem primis annis quolibet anno Septem Solidos et octo
denarios ad quatuor anni terminos Viz ad ffesta sancti Michelis
Archangeli Natalis domini Annunciacionis beate Marie virginis et
Natiuitatis sancti Iohannis Baptiste per equales porciones ac
reddendo pro duobus vltimis annis Triginta vnum solidos et
octo denarios ad ffesta predicta per equales porciones
[Here follow the conditions of tenure.]
Data in domo Capitulari predictorum Abbatis Prioris et Conuentus
apud Westmonasterium predictum octauo die Augusti Anno
domini Millesimo quingentesimo decimo octauo Et Anno regni
Regis henrici Octaui Decimo

(3) *William Bedell*
(a) *His Will*
(1518, pr. 11 July. From P.C.C.: 8 Aylotte.)

Testm̄ Willm̄i   In the name of god amen I William Bedell hole of
Bedell   body and parfite of mynde thanked be our lorde
make this my last will and testament in maner and foʳme
hereafter folowynge / ffirst I bequeth my soule to god almighty the
fader the sonne and the holy goost / and to the most and pure
virgyn mary mother vnto our savyour crist Ihesu and to all the
holy saintes of hevyn / and my most synfull and wreched body to
be buried at the lower ende in my ladies Chapell at Westm' called
Scala Celi / yf I dye at london or Chestount / And if it be my fortune to dye elleswhere then to be buried as it shall please myn
executours if it shuld be to chargeable the same to be brought to
Westm' / Also I will that Immediatly after my decesse to haue an
honest preest to synge for my soule there that my said wreched
body shalbe buried by the space of a hole yere / And the said prest

to be bounde to sey euery day duringe the said yere / placebo and dirige w^t deprofundis clamaui / for my soule and for all those soules that I am most bounde to pray for / Also I woll that Immediatly after my decesse to haue an honest preest to synge in my ladies Chapell at westm' called Scali Celi for my soule and for the soules of my lady Margaret Countesse of Richemounte / my fader and moder my wyfes and all those soules that I am most specially bounde to pray for and for all xpen soules by the space of vij yeres / and the same preist to sey iij daies in the weke placebo and dirige for my soule and theirs / and to haue for his stipende euery yere duringe the said terme of vij yeres vj li xiij s iiij d Also I woll that a Cupp of golde weyinge lij ounces / and also my two great chaynes of gold weyinge by estymaçion xxxvij ounces be solde Immediatly after my decesse by myn executours / And the money of the same to be distribute and gevyn discretely vnto pouer people and in other charitable almes dedes most requysite for the soule of my most singuler good lady Margarete Countes of Richemount by whom I had all that I haue / Also I will that my lande in ffob-bynge in the Countie of Essex. remayn vnto my wife duringe her lyfe / and afterward to be solde by myn Executours. And the money therof to be disposead for my soule and my frendes soules aboue specified ALSO I woll that all suche londes and tenementes in Watlyngton that I recouered of Iohn Roys and his wife / | by fyne / remayn to my said wife and she to dispoase it at her pleasure / Also I will that all suche my feoffees as be enfeoffeed in all suche landes and tenementes w^t thappurtenances in Chestount Waltham Crosse and Wormeley in the countie of hertforde whiche landes and tenementes my wife dud [sic] geve vnto me and to myn heires / doo make release agayn of all the same landes and euery parcell therof vnto my said wife / and she to dispoase the same as it shall please her in as large and ample wise as euer she dud geve it me w^{t}out any lett of myn heires or of any other parsone or persones / the said gyfte to her before gevyn to me notw^{t}standynge / Also I wille that the horne and all other londes and tenementes that I haue purchaced in Chestount and Waltham Crosse remayne vnto my wife for terme of her lyfe / And after her decesse to be solde by myn executours / and the money to be disposead as aforsaid / Also I geve vnto Cicell my wyfe in plate of the best to the value of xl li / Item I geve to her of my best wethers fyve hundred Item viij oxen and xij bestes / Item I geve to her all my stuffe of housholde / Item to Iohn Hungate in plate to the valure of x ounces. Item I geve to the iiij orders of ffreres in London to euery of the places xxs to synge for me iiij trentalles to be doon Immediatly after my decesse / Item I woll that almaner of pouer people that shall resorte vnto my buriall haue euery of them to pray for my synfull soule j d. / The residue of all my goodes whatsoeuer they be / my dettes paide and my legacies deliuered I leve to Cecill my wife whom I make soole myn executrice / to dispose the same goodes to the most profite of my synfull soule as truely and lovyngly as she wolde I shulde doo for her. yf she were in caase like whom I trust aboue all creatures / Also I will that Raufe Bapthorp haue my standynge Cup of siluer and gilt wᵗ the Couer of our lady and saint xpofer in the topp / Also I will that Iane haue in money and plate to the value of xxˡⁱ towardes her mariage yf she be ordered / and ruled by my said wyfe orelles not / In witnesse herof I haue writen this forsaid wille & testament wᵗ myn owne hande and sette my Seall. / the iiijᵗʰ day of Septembre. Anno regni henrici octaui / quinto / . Also I make maister Robert Shorton ouerseer of this my said testament and last will / Item I will that the Commaundre of Stanford whiche I haue of my lorde of saint Iohnes vnder Chapter Seall for yeres [sic] remayn vnto my forsaid wife duringe all my said yeres. Item the tenement in writell which my susters dwell in that my moder dud geve vnto me after the decesse of Iohn Browne my father in lawe / I will that it Remayn vnto my brother Richard secunde sonne / And for faute of him vnto the thirde sonne And soo from one to another and for lak of suche heires to be solde by myn executoʳs / Item I geve vnto my suster Anne one hundred Shepe to be deliuered her by myn executours. . / .

Probatum fuit testamentum supradicti defuncti habentis &c Coram domino apud Lamehith xjᵒ die mensis Iulij Anno Domini Millesimo quingentesimo xviijᵒ Iuramento Cecilie Relicte & executrici in huiusmodi testamento nominata. ac approbatum & insinuatum Et commissa fuit administracio omnium bonorum & debitorum dicti defuncti prefate executrici De bene & fideliter administrando Ac de pleno & fideli Inuentario citra festum sancti Bartholomei Apostoli proxime futurum exhibendo necnon de plano & vero compoto reddendo Ad sancta dei euangelia Iurato

(b) *Bedell and St. Margaret's.*
(i) In his will Bedell leaves to John Hungate ten ounces of gold plate. In the year 1511-12 he appears in the Churchwardens' Accounts of St. Margaret's, Westminster, observing the anniversary of Mrs. Hungate's death (16 May 1510–27 May 1512: 2nd year, 23rd week.)

Item received of maister william bedil for theres mynd of maistres hungate for iiij tapers   xvjd

(ii) His funeral is recorded in *ibid.* for 20 May 1518–24 May 1520, 7th week (i.e. 1st week in July) of 1st year:

> Item for licence of torches & tapers at the Buryall of M William Bedill   vjs viijd

His month's mind is also recorded:

> Item at the monyth mynde of M William Bedill for iiij tapers xvjd

J. THE LADIES OF THE *GARLAND*

(1) *A Tilney Pedigree*

(Adapted from Pishey Thompson, *Hist. and Antiqs. of Boston*, 1856, pp. 373-4.)

Sir Philip Tilney=Isabel de Thorpe of Boston

— Sir Hugh Tilney

— Sir Frederick Tilney=Elizabeth Cheyney of Ashwell Thorpe

Sir Philip=*Margaret,* Tilney of *d. of* —— Shelley, *Brewse of* Suffolk *Wenham*

Agnes(2)=Thomas Howard=(1)Elizabeth=Sir Hum phrey Bourchi(2nd Duke of Norfolk

Elizabeth Howard (3rd *daughter*)

Elizabeth Stafford(2)=Thomas (*Skelton's Countess*) Howard, 3rd Duke of Norfolk.

Lady Anne Dacres of the South

(2) *The Stathams.*

(From MS. Addit. 6667, fol. 227).

Roger Stathum   =   Gertrude dr. of John & 22ᵈ July   sister of [heir *interlined*] 22 E: 4.   Anthony Ansty of Stoke Quy in Cambrige shire

Roger Stathum of —— in the County of —— married Gertrude sister of Anthony Ansty the Elder of Stoke Quy in Cambrige shire esqr who made his will dated the 22ᵈ of July in the 22ᵈ year of King Edward the 4ᵗʰ and gave to the said Roger & Gertrude all the maner lands &c. that John Ansty his father by his will gave to him and his heirs willing his feoffees to make estates to them thereof accordingly proved 20 of may the said y^r. William Stathum Henry Odmasely [?] & Robert Chapman witnesses Registr' Cokke in the bishop of Londons office

[Extensive search has failed to reveal any further information about the pair. The name Roger certainly existed in the important Statham family of Morley, Derbyshire, which descended from Ralph de Statham, Lord of Morley (died 1380). A Roger occurs among those remembered in the wills of both Sir Thomas and his brother Nicolas Statham (1470, 1472: P. C. C.: 1, 7 Wattys). A Roger Statham, gentleman, with Derbyshire connexions, died in 1509: his will is in Comm. Court West.: 52 Wyks. For the will of John Ansty, Senior, see P. C. C.: 21 Stokton.]

K. BOWGAS'S ABJURATION

(From Strype, *Ecclesiastical Memorials*, 1822, I(ii). p. 58.)

Quarto die mensis Maii, anno Dni.mill^o quingenti^{mo} xxviii^o in capella infra manerium reverendi Patris Norwicen. Epi. juxta Charyng Crosse, London. . . .

[The summary in *LP* IV(ii). 4242 follows:

Abjuration by Thomas Bowgas, of the parish of St Leonard's, Colchester, fuller, before Cuthbert bishop of London, of the following heresies, viz., that a man need not go on pilgrimage to St Thomas of Canterbury, or to our Lady of Grace; that there is no other church of God but man's conscience; that he had as leve be buried in his own house as in the church; "that I would Our Lady of Grace were in my bakehouse"; . . . that if he had the crucifix, the image of our Lady and other Saints, and crosses, in a ship, he would drown them all in the sea. Desires a penance.

On the 4 May Bowgas appeared . . .; and on reading the above abjuration received absolution, the bishop enjoining him, on pain of relapse, to go in procession on Sunday, 10th May following, at the parish of St. Leonard at Hithe, near Colchester, bearing a faggot on his shoulder, and afterwards hear mass on bended knees on the steps of the choir. Says he is willing to undergo the penance. . . .]

Presentibus tunc ibid., venerabili viro Mro. Galfrido Wharton Cancellario, Willo. Layton Regrario principali, Dno. Thoma Chambre Capellano; necnon Mag. Skelton, Marmaduco Tunstall, Generosis; et Georgio Bedyll, Thoma Pilkyngton, Thoma Dowman, Antonio Tunstal, Nicho. Tunstal, Willo. Westwray, et Humfrido Odyngsalis, Literatis, testibus et cet.

APPENDIX I: RECORDS

(1) *The St. Margaret's Records.*
(From Churchwardens' Accounts, biennial, 1512-30 (vol. E.2, unpaginated, at Caxton Hall), *sub fin.* account for 27 May 1528–2 June 1530.)

Receiptis by the sayde Wardens Receyuyd in the second yere of this ther accompte for buryalles obittes and lyghtis as perticuler[l]y folowyth

Item of Master skelton for iiij tapers	ij^s viij^d
Item of hym for iiij torches	iiij^s

Receptys of the belles for knylles and peales This second yere

Item of M Iohn skelton for knyll and peales	vj^s viij^d

Paymentes leide oute by the saide accomptantes this seconde yere ffor Ryngyng off knylles ande pealles.

Item paid to o^r lady brotherhed for M skelton	xx^d
Item paid for Ringyng of his knyll and peales	xij^d

(2) *The Administration*
(From Comm. Ct. Westm. (Somerset House): 6 Bracy.)

Mag͞r Ioh͠nes
Skelton poeta
laureatus
decessit xvi^{to} nouembris anno domini predicto in domo registrarii coram Magistro Roberto bennett Archidiacono comparuit Magister Willielmus Mott curatus sancte Margarete westm' et pecijt administracionem bonorum infra Iurisdictionem existentem sibi committi cui in forma Iuris Iurato dominus commisit administracionem huiusmodi saluo Iure &c deinde exhibuit Inuentarium eorundem bonorum &c

EARLY LIVES

(I) HORMAN'S AND BRAYNEWODE'S

(Collected by Bale and edited from his notebook by Lane Poole under the title: Ioannes Baleus, *Index Britanniae Scriptorum*, OUP 1902, pp. 252-3.)

Ioannes Skelton, pastor ecclesie de Dysse in Nordouolgia, Oxonij poeta laureatus, vates ac pręceptor regius erat. De quo Erasmus in quadam epistola ad Henricum octauum regem. Skeltonum Britannicarum literarum lumen ac decus, qui tua studia possit non solum accendere, sed etiam consummare, hunc domi habes, &c. Hic scripsit,

Carmen inuectiuum in Guilhelmum Lilium poetam laureatum, li. I. 'Vrgeor impulsus tibi Lille retundere dentes.' Versus sunt, lxiiij.

Ex Guilhelmo Horman

Ioannes Skeltonus, poeta laureatus, ac theologię professor, parochus de Dysse in Nordouolgie comitatu, habebatur. Facetijs in quotidiana inuentione deditus multum erat, non tamen omisit sub persona ridentis (vt habet Horatius Flaccus) veritatem fateri, tam aperte ac mordaciter, vt alter videretur Lucianus vel Democritus, vt ex operibus liquet. Neque in scripturis absque omni iudicio erat, quamuis illud egregie dissimularet. In clero plęraque videbat mala, quę nonnunquam viuis carpebat coloribus, atque scommatibus non obscoenis. Cum quibusdam me[n]dicantium fratrum blateronibus, pręcipue Dominicanis, continuum gerebat bellum. Sub pseudoepiscopo Nordouicensi Ricardo, mulierem quam secreto desponsauerat, vt Antichristi vitaret obprobria, sub concubinę titulo custodiebat, quam tamen in mortis articulo confitebatur se pro legitima semper tenuisse coniuge. Ob literas in Cardinalem Wolsium inuectiuas, ad Westmonasteriense asylum confugere pro vita seruanda coactus fuit, vbi tamen sub Islepo abbate fauorem inuenit. Mortuus tandem, in D. Margarete templo ante summum altare conditus est, cum hac scriptione alabastrica. Ioannes Skeltonus vates pierius hic situs est. Animam egit xxj. die Iunij, A.D. 1529. . . .

(Lists of his works follow, which are obviously drawn chiefly from the catalogue in the *Garland*.)

Ex collectionibus Edwardi Braynewode.

APPENDIX II: EARLY LIVES

(2) BALE'S

(An expansion of the above information, published in his *Scriptorum illustrium maioris Brytanniæ . . . catalogus*, Basle 1557-9, pp. 651-2.)

Ioannes Skeltonus

Ioannes Skeltonus, poeta laureatus, ac theologiæ professor, parochus de Dyssa in Nordouolgiæ comitatu, clarus & facundus in utroque scribendi genere, prosa atque metro, habebatur. facetijs in quotidiana inuentione plurimum deditus fuit: non tamen omisit sub persona ridentis, ut in Horatio Flacco, ueritatem fateri. Ţam aptè, amoenè, ac salse, mordaciter tamen, quorundam facta inamoena carpere nouit, ut alter videretur Lucianus aut Democritus, ut ex opusculis liquet. Sed neque in scripturis sacris absque omni iudicio erat, quamuis illud egregiè dissimulauit. In clero non ferenda mala uidebat, & magna & multa: quae nonnunquam uiuis perstrinxit coloribus, ac scommatibus non obscoenis. Cum quibusdam blateronibus fraterculis, praecipuè Dominicanis, bellum gerebat continuum. Sub pseudopontifice Nordouicensi Ricardo Nixo, mulierem illam, quam sibi secretò ob Antichristi metum desponsauerat, sub concubinae titulo custodiebat. In ultimo tamen uitae articulo super ea re interrogatus, respondit, se nusquam illam in conscientia coram Deo, nisi pro uxore legitima tenuisse. Ob literas quasdam in Cardinalem Vuolsium inuectiuas, ad Vuestmonasteriense tandem asylum confugere, pro uita seruanda coactus fuit: ubi nihilominus sub abbate Islepo fauorem inuenit. De illo Erasmus in quadam epistola, ad Henricum octauum regem, sic scribit: Skeltonum, Brytannicarum literarum lumen ac decus, qui tua studia possit non solum accendere, sed etiam consummare: hunc domi habes, &c. Iste uerò edidit, partim Anglicè, partim Latinè, . . .

[A list of Skelton's works follows.]

Vuestmonasterij tandem, captiuitatis suae tempore, mortuus est: & in D. Margaritæ sacello sepultus, cum hac inscriptione alabastrica: Ioannes Skeltonus, uates Pierius, hic situs est. Animam egit 21 die Iunij, anno Domini 1529, relictis liberis. De morte Cardinalis uaticinium edidit: & eius ueritatem euentus declarauit.

(3) *Elis Gruffydd's*

(*c*. 1560. From MS. Mostyn (Nat. Lib. Wales) 158, fols. 471-2.)

Ac oherwydd I gam arweddiad ef ar preladiaid or dyrnas i gwnaeth poieth yr hwn a elwid ysgelttwn lawriett lyvyr mewn

mydyr dogrel yr hwn yn saessneg a elwir kolun klowtt ynn y man
I gall dyn weled ynn eglur gwbwl o vuched y gwyr eglwysig o
boob graadd val I gilid yr hyn a oedd ddigon gwrtthun i vynnegi
neithyr nidoedd arnaunt twy gywilidd ynn y byd ynn i wneuthud
ef yn yr amser Ir ydoedd breladiaid y dyrnnas ynn yni ddyrchyvu
oll mewn balchedd Ac yn pashio dynnion ynn y byd o chwant i
daa bydol ynn yr amser ir ydoedd y ddwy raadd boob un ynn
erbyn i gillidd Ac ynn wir y bai mwyaf a vwrid ar benneathiaid
yr eglwys yr hrain ollo a oedd ynn kroppio o ddydd bigillid i lys
y brenin Ac oddiynno drwy orawag dduwiolaeth o nerth ariann
I gyrheuddud kappan fforchog pan vai yr un gwedi digwyddo
hevaid ynn y kyvamser yma Ir ydoedd y kardnal o loegyr gwedi
gosod serttein o gwyr kelvydda ar a vedrid I dewis o vewn holl
gred ynn y grefft i wethio prees a main mynnor or hrain Ir ydoedd
ef gwedi ymkannu gwneuth medrod ne vedd mawr weithiog i
osod i gorwgl i bydru pan vai ef varw A megis ac ir ydoedd y
kardnal ynn marchogaeth oi blaas i vannachlog westmynystyr
yvo a ddigwyddodd Iddo eff gyvarvod ac ysgeltwn y poiett yr
hwn ai dilynnodd ef ir vanachlog ac ir man lle ir ydoedd y gwyr a
dreithir ynn y blaenn ynn gweithio ac ynn ol ir kardnal vwrw I
olwg ar y gwaith o gornel bigilidd Ac iddo ef ganvod y poiett yvo
a ddyvod ynn y modd hwn Wele sr sgelttwn beth a ddywedi di
am hyn o lavur a gwaith yr hynn a ganmoles y prydydd ner
poiett yn vawr megis ac i gellid Neithyr ynn ol hir ymddivan yvo a
ovynnodd ir kardnal ar vedyr pwy ir ydoedd ef ynn ymkanu gwneu-
thud y gost honno ar vedrod ir hynn ir attebodd y kardnal ac a
ddyvod mae ar vedyr i gorf i hun ir geiriau Ir attebodd y poiet
dan gellwair drwy ddywedud pe gwneich i vynghyngor i chwi a
gymerych veddiant oi vewn ef ynn ych bowyd ac ynn ych Iechyd
hrag ovynn na wnelo ych suckuttorion gymaint o lavur ach dodi
chwi i mewn pan darffo Ir ennaid ar korff ymado bob un ai
gilidd y geirriau a gymerth y kardnal megis ynn soredig ac ar
wartwar neithyr yntwy a ddoethant ynn wir

LATIN PASSAGES TRANSLATED IN THE TEXT

p. 22. (1)   . . . Doctrinae tibi dum parare famam

Et doctus fieri studes poeta,
Doctrinam nec habes, nec es poeta.
(Cf. Dyce, I. xxxviii.)

(2) *Philip Sparrow* 830:

Per me laurigerum Britonum Skeltonida vatem

(3) *Ware the Hawk* 239-40:

Sic, velut est Arabum phęnix auis vnica tantum,
Terra Britanna suum genuit Skeltonida vatem.

(4) *Colin Clout* (Latin) 6-7:

Vndique cantabor tamen et celebrabor vbique
Inclita dum maneat gens Anglica. . . .

(5) *Why Come Ye Not* 27-8 (and tail-piece):

Hęc vates ille
De quo loquuntur mille.

p. 44. Carmeliano's *Carmen Responsum* 21-2:

Angle, petis pacem frustra: nil amplius instes:
Bella geras! pacem Gallia victa dabit.

(See my text in *MLR* XXXII (1937), p. 432.)

p. 74. *Speculum principis* (MS. Addit. 26,787, fol. 6):

Principes igitur mea sentencia attenciori animo immercessibili
virtutis gloria quam vana diuiciarum superbia suam vitam com-
ponerent.

p. 75. (fols. 16-17^v):

Quisquis es, genus nullum, ordinem nullam, sexum nullum excipio,
princeps licet magnificentissimus, forte ratus iure me oportere

APPENDIX III

tibi minus gratum meum compescere labellum, auorum et proauo-
rum reuerenciam et fastum tuę generacionis me contra obiciens
claraque familiam splendore, gloria, luxa, fama regalibusque
titulis illustratam, vnde tibi promittis securitatem; et quia occas-
ionem tui notandi forte accipio meritissimam, eapropter Lucilio
ciuica mordacitate auctori non penitendo cupio me relegabis. Sed
pace tua sine, quęso, tibi prius respondeam, succincte et sub com-
pendio, quia hac nostra, vt ita dicam, procellosissima tempestate
fulmine verborum opus est (Iuuenale teste, difficile est saturam non
scribere, &c). Sed nunc accinctus ad respondendum venio:
aduerte, obsecro, diligenter.

p. 93. *Trental* 5-19:

> Ioannis *Clerc,* hominis
> Cuiusdam multinominis,
> Ioannis *Iayberd* qui vocatur,
> *Clerc* cleribus nuncupatur.
> Obiit sanctus iste pater
> Anno Domini MD. sexto.
> In parochio de Dis
> Non erat sibi similis:
> In malicia vir insignis,
> Duplex corde et bilinguis,
> Senio confectus,
> Omnibus suspectus,
> Nemini dilectus,
> Sepultus est *among the wedes,*
> *God forgive him his misdedes!*

p. 94. *Adam's Epitaph* 10-13:

Dis, tibi baccatus	baliuus prędominatus,
Hic fuit ingratus	porcus velut insaciatus,
Pinguis, crassatus:	velut Agag sit reprobatus,
Crudelisque Cacus	baratro, peto, sit tumulatus.

p. 123. *Garland* 1365-7:

> Inferias, Philippe, tuas Scroupe pulchra Iohanna
> Instanter peciit: cur nostri carminis illam
> Nunc pudet?
>   – Est sero: minor est infamia vero.

p. 129:

> Tribuat michi Iuppiter Feretrius ne teram tempus apud Eurotam,
> &c.

p. 130. (1) *Skeltonis laureatus didasculus quondam regius, &c., tacitus secum in soliloquio ceu vir totus obliuioni datus aut tanquam mortuus a corde, &c.*

Proh deum atque hominum fidem! vnde hoc mihi, quod ego seorsum ab aliis tanto tamque singulari sim fato, cui nec regalis munificentia nec fortunę benignitas adhuc opulentius dignatur aspirare? O cęlum! o maria! cui imputabo illud? Ah, imponam-ne illud diis iratis forsan mihi? Insaniam tantam non committam. Sed-ne imponam ego tanto tamque munifico regi remissę largitatis notabilem labem? Auertat hoc Deus optimus maximus, qui omnia ponderat cum ęquabilissima lance in statera amplissimę largitatis suę quique dat omnibus affluenter et non improperat, &c.

(2) Regere, non regi. Audi Samuelem. Lege Danielem. Tolle Ismaelem.

.tolle. .tolle.

(MS. Addit. 26,787, fols. 26ᵛ, 28ᵛ, 29-30ᵛ, 30ᵛ.)

pp. 131-32:

hic puer est natus
Nunc est ad sceptra vocatus
Rex modo castra struit

(MS. C. C. C. Camb. 432, fols. 4, 7, 13ᵛ.)

Obstrue Galle tuum (loqueris in vana) labellum

(*Ibid.*, fol. 16.)

Vltor celestis da. cur ruit iste scelestus?
Quod petis instanter. Thome loca sacra loquantur.

(*Ibid.*, fol. 7.)

I, liber, et propera, regem tu pronus adora,
Me sibi commendes humilem Skeltonida vatem.
Ante suam maiestatem per cetera passim
Inclita bella refer, gessit quę maximus heros
Anglorum, primus nostra de gente Ricardus. . . .

(*Ibid.*, dedication 6-10.)

p. 136. *Eulogy* 35-6:

> Si tibi fata fauent (faueant precor atque precabor)
> Anglia, tunc plaude; sin minus, ipsa vale!

p. 145. *Epitaph for Henry VII* 27-8:

> Quem Leo candidior rubeum necat ense Leonem
> Et iacet vsque modo non tumulatus humo.

p. 157. *Epitaph on Bedel:*

M.D. XVIII.

In Bedell quondam Belial incarnatum deuotum epitaphium

> Ismael, ecce, Bedel, non mel sed fel sibi des, El,
> Perfidus Achitophel luridus atque lorel!
> Nunc olet iste Iabel nebulo, Nabal ecce ribaldus,
> Omnibus exosus atque perosus erat,
> In plateaque cadens animam spirauit oleto;
> Presbyteros odiens sic sine mente ruit.

p. 164. *Against Venomous Tongues* 16 gloss:

Hic notat purpuraria arte intextas literas Romanas in amictibus post-ambulonum ante et retro.

p. 237. *Garland* 742-51:

Interpolata, que industriosum postulat interpretem,
satiri in vatis aduersarium

> Tressis agasonis species prior, altera Daui.
> Aucupium culicis, limis dum torquet ocellum,
> Concipit, aligeras rapit, appetit, aspice, muscas!
> Maia quęque fouet, fouet aut quę Iuppiter aut quę
> Frigida Saturnus, Sol, Mars, Venus, algida Luna,
> Si tibi contingat verbo aut committere scripto,
> Quam sibi mox tacita sudant pręcordia culpa!
> Hinc ruit in flammas, stimulans hunc vrget et illum,
> Inuocat ad rixas, vanos tamen excitat ignes,
> Labra mouens tacitus, rumpantur vt ilia Codro.

17.4.7.2.17.5.18.
18.19.1.19.8.5.12.

APPENDIX III

p. 244. MS Egerton 2642, fol. 130ᵛ:

> Non meministi
> Quod mihi scripsisti
> De corpore Christi
> [Crede quod edas et edis]
> Sic tibi rescribo
> De tuo palfrido
> Crede quod habe[a]s et habes

p. 247. *Replication*, dedication:

Honorificatissimo, amplissimo longeque reuerendissimo in Christo patri ac domino, domino THOME, &c., tituli sanctę Cecilię sacrosanctę Romanę ecclesię presbytero, cardinali meritissimo et apostolicę sedis legato a latereque legato superillustri, &c., Skeltonis laureatus, ora. reg., humillimum dicit obsequium cum omni debita reuerentia tanto tamque magnifico digna principe sacerdotum totiusque iustitię ęquabilissimo moderatore necnon pręsentis opusculi fautore excellentissimo, &c., ad cuius auspicatissimam contemplationem sub memorabili prelo gloriosę inmortalitatis pręsens pagella felicitatur, &c.

INDEX

INDEX

INDEX

Carthage, 188
Carver, P. L., 263-4
Cassian, 58
Catherine of Aragon, 72-3, 75-7, 82, 113, 127, 136, 141-5, 206, 252-3
Catholicon, 279
Cato, 74
—, Petty, 75
—, Dionysius, 254
Cattawade (Catywade, Catwade), 152, 274
Catullus, 23, 107
Cavendish, George, 161, 165-6, 256, 275-6, 282, 286
Caxton, 85
Caxton, William, 34, 36-7, 46, 61, 106-7, 254, 260
Cayre, 152, 274
Cefas (Cephas), 194
Chamberlen, 179
Chambers, R. W., 280
Chambre, John a', 41
—, Thomas, 303
Champion, P., 262
Chanteclere, 107
Chapel Royal, 47-8, 80-1, 98, 137, 139, 155, 254, 262, 266
Chapman, John, 291
—, Robert, 303
Chapuys, 207
Charing Cross, 224, 249
Charles, Archduke. See Charles V.
— V, Emperor, 137, 148, 171, 178, 188, 194, 196-7, 255
— VIII (of France), 43-6
Chartier, Alain, 61
Chaucer, 16, 26-8, 31, 35, 53, 62, 88, 100, 105, 111, 116-17, 120, 189, 208-9, 227-8
Chelsea, 285
Cherry Hinton, 32
Cheshunt, 156, 299-300
Chesten, Sir, 153
Chestount. See Cheshunt.
Cheyney, Elizabeth, 302
Cheyney Gates, 128
Chieregati, 277
Childe-Pemberton, W. S., 264
Chillingham, 141
Christ's College, Cambridge, 86
Churchyard, Thomas, 73, 265
Cicero, 21, 34, 40
Cicero's *Letters*, 34-5, 54
— *Offices*, 35, 54
— *Paradoxes*, 54
Cincinnatus, 74
Circumspection, 174
Clarence, Duke of, 70
Clarke, John, 87, 92-3, 100, 268, 291
—, Sir John, 85, 92, 268, 291

Claudian, 21
Clement VII, 252-3, 255
Clerk, John, 197, 280
—, Thomas, 197
Clerke, William, 268
Cleros, 196-7
Clifton, Margery, 297
—, Sir Robert, 297
Cliftons, 32
Clio, 42
Cloaked Collusion, 173
Clout, Colin, 99-100, 210-15, 255
Cocklodge, 41
Coggeshall. See Paycock.
Cokayne's *Peerage*, 269, 271
Colchester, 249, 303
Coldharbour, 53, 60
Colet, John, 17, 20, 67, 163, 263
Collier, J. P., 271
Collingbourne, 223
Colloquies, 84, 285
Collyweston, 55
Commendations, 109-11
Constable, Marmaduke, 32
Constantinople, 15
Cooper, C. H., 263, 265, 267
Coper, Dr., 269
Copinger, W. P., 270, 274
Coppe, 107
'Cornish War,' 60, 264
Cornish, William, 47-8, 81, 86, 168, 222, 262, 267
Cornwall, 60
Corpus Christi College, Cambridge, 33
Corinna, 107
Corunna, 73
Coulton, G. G., 260
Counterfeit Countenance, 173
Court of Love, 27, 189
Courtly Abusion, 173, 176
Coward, Noel, 47
Cowley, 156
Cowper, Margery, 85, 291
Crafty Conveyance, 173
Creighton, Bishop, 275
Crema, Francesco de, 46, 262
Crisp, F. A., 271
Cromwell, Thomas, 17, 95, 138, 207, 231, 239-40, 285
Culley, M. T., 260
Curial, The, 61
Cushing, Mr., 267

Dacres, Lady Anne, of the South, 302
—, Lord, 219
Dale, William, 101, 131, 291-2
Daniel, 130
Dante, 42, 182, 278
D'Arcy, Elizabeth, Lady, 297
Darnell, 284

INDEX

Dartmouth, Earl of, 254
Dathan, 221
Daubeney, 60
David, 183
Davies, Bryn, 13, 276, 285
Day, J., 143
Deane, Archbishop, 80, 159
Debenham, Elizabeth, 298
—, Sir Gilbert, 113, 274, 298
—, Sir Giles, 298
—, Lady, 296
Deguileville, 206-7
Deimling, H., 268
Democritus, 305
Denny Abbey, 113
Description of Britain, 67
Deucalion, 183, 190
Dialogue against Heresies, 249
Diccon, 87
Dictamen, 158
Dido, 189
Diodorus Siculus, 24, 34, 54
Dionysos, 183
Disdain, 62, 64
Diss, 31, 64, 73, 78, 80, 82-7, 90-101,
    106, 110, 114, 122, 126, 128-9,
    131, 139-45, 156, 205, 241-3,
    266-7, 275, 290-2, 298, 305-6
— Choir, 139-43
— Church, 90
— Mere, 84
— Moor, 84
— Rectory, 99
Dissimulation, 62
Docwra, Sir Thomas, 148
Donatus, 188, 279
Doncaster, 292
Donne, 58
Dorset, Marquess of, 134, 159, 170
Dover, 136, 143, 162
Dowman, Thomas, 303
Dread, 62, 78
Driver, Simon, 101, 292
Dublin, 203, 206
Dudley, Edmund, 81, 127
Duessa, 198
Duff, E. Gordon, 264
Dugdale, Sir William, 269
Dunbabin, R. L., 279
Dunbar, William, 150
Dunmow, 83
Duque, 59
Durham, 292
Durham, Bishop of. See Ruthal.
Dyce, Alexander, 20, 29, 79, 98, 109,
    143, 148, 196, 234, 238, 259, 262
    264-70, 272-6, 280, 286-8

Eagle Tavern, 50, 115
East Harling, 271

East Wretham, 91-2
Eclogues (Barclay's), 61, 275
— (Vergil's), 198
Ecton, J., 267
Edmund, Prince, 56, 67
Edward IV, 70, 200
— VI, 56, 144
Edwards, H. L. R., 258-60, 262, 272,
    274-5, 279-80, 283, 285
Elias, 182
Eliot, T. S., 88
Elizabeth, Queen, 16, 40, 50, 95, 115,
    198
— of York, 60, 80, 198
Ellis, H., 269
Eltham, 55, 59-61, 64-5, 66-9, 72-3, 264
Ely, Bishop of. See Fox.
Elyot, Thomas, 276
Empoli, 138
Empson, Sir Richard, 81, 86, 127, 161,
    222, 254
Eneydos, 34
Enoch, 182
Envious Rancour, 237
Epistres de l'amant verd, 184
Erasmus, 15, 20-1, 33, 46, 66-9, 74, 77,
    84, 126, 137, 233, 245, 264, 266,
    272, 274, 285, 289-90, 305-6
Erith, 209, 281
Escalles. See Scales.
Etaples, Treaty of, 45
Eumenides, 169
Euphrates, 182, 279
Eurotas, 129-30
Eusebius, 54
Ewes, Giles d', 40

Fabricius, 74
Falstaff, 222
Fame, Queen of, 227-9
—, Palace of, 229-30
Fancy, 172-3, 186
Faral, E., 258
Farlyon, John, 262
Favell, 62, 64
Fawkes, Richard, 142, 217
Fazio, 150
Felbrigg, 102, 104, 112, 294
Felbrigg, Sir John, 16
Felicity, 173
Fendrayton, 33
Ferdinand of Spain, 134, 137, 148, 160,
    171
Feylde, Thomas, 234, 238
Fiddes, R., 276
Field of Cloth of Gold, 48, 114, 155, 271
Filelfo, 150
Fisher, John, 18, 30, 33, 35, 56, 71, 80,
    85-6, 138, 260, 263, 267
—, Robert, 66

316

INDEX

INDEX

INDEX

INDEX

321

INDEX

INDEX